Cyril Dodd

Private Bill Procedure

A guide to the Procedure upon Private Bills

Cyril Dodd

Private Bill Procedure
A guide to the Procedure upon Private Bills

ISBN/EAN: 9783337158897

Printed in Europe, USA, Canada, Australia, Japan

Cover: Foto ©Suzi / pixelio.de

More available books at **www.hansebooks.com**

PRIVATE BILL PROCEDURE.

A GUIDE

TO THE

PROCEDURE UPON PRIVATE BILLS:

TOGETHER WITH

FORMS,

STANDING ORDERS OF THE HOUSE OF COMMONS,
CONDENSED STANDING ORDERS OF THE HOUSE OF LORDS,
TABLES OF FEES, RULES, &c.

BY

CYRIL DODD, Q.C.
(*Formerly Member of Parliament for the Maldon Division of Essex*),

AND

H. W. W. WILBERFORCE
(*Of the Inner Temple, Barrister-at-Law*).

London:

EYRE & SPOTTISWOODE,
Government, Legal, and General Publishers,
EAST HARDING STREET, FLEET STREET, E.C.
1898.

Price 7s. 6d.

PREFACE.

In preparing the present work for publication it has been the aim of the authors to provide for the practitioner, within the limits of a book of moderate size, such information as is ordinarily required in the conduct of the business of private bill legislation, and to furnish him with sufficient examples of the petitions, notices of objection to *locus standi*, and other documents ordinarily required to enable him to frame the documents which he needs for the particular bill he may be engaged in promoting or opposing.

The general scheme of the book is, that chapters dealing with the distinction between private and public bills, the classification of bills, the procedure to introduce bills into Parliament, and the mode in which private bills are passed through committee, and through Parliament come first, and then comes a chapter dealing in some detail with questions of *locus standi*, followed by short chapters on Provisional Orders, Costs, Parliamentary Agents, and on the drafting of Bills, and at the conclusion of this part of the book the

Standing Orders of the two Houses (those of the Commons at full length with its index), Resolutions and Rules for Practice, &c., are placed, with occasional notes and with references to the earlier portion of the book, in an Appendix, in which also the forms of the various documents commonly required in Parliamentary practice will be found, supplemented by like notes and references.

The authors have to acknowledge with gratitude the assistance they have derived from Sir Erskine May's most accurate work on Parliamentary Practice, which contains a valuable account of the system of Private Legislation in Parliament, and of the practice of the two Houses both in relation to public and to private business. They would likewise refer to Mr. Smethhurst's little treatise on *locus standi*, of which they have to some extent availed themselves, and which in any difficult question of *locus standi* the practitioner would do well to consult, notwithstanding the fact that many alterations have been made in the Standing Orders and many fresh cases have been reported since the last edition of it was written. The thanks of the authors are specially due to the Right Honourable the Speaker of the House of Commons, to the Right Honourable Sir John Mowbray, M.P., to Mr. Ferguson-Davie and other officials of Parliament, to Messrs. Sherwood & Co., Messrs. Grahames,

Currey & Spens, and Messrs. Lock & Co., all of Great George Street, Westminster, parliamentary agents; to Messrs. Martin & Leslie, of Abingdon Street, Westminster, and to Messrs. Dyson & Co., of Parliament Street, Westminster, parliamentary agents.

It is beyond the scope of the present work to consider the suggestions which have at various times been made, whether for simplifying the procedure in regard to private bills, or for entrusting some portion of the work of private legislation so far as relates to Scotland or to Ireland to local commissions, or other bodies, in lieu of the present Parliamentary Committees, or to discuss the propriety of giving to the Examiners of Standing Orders or to the Court of Referees further powers enabling them to amend mistakes or errors at the cost of the party in fault, or to consider the desirability of lessening the number of instances in which a bill keenly fought before a Committee of one House is again fought before a similar Committee of the other House, by providing that opponents in whichever may be the second of the two Houses should be liable to pay the costs of the promoters in the second House, unless their continued opposition should be justified by a success of a complete, or at least of a substantial character. The present book deals with none of these questions, but is confined to a consideration of the procedure as it now exists.

It is intended for the practical use of those engaged in private bill legislation, and is submitted to them by the authors with a full appreciation of the magnitude, value, and importance of the work done by the Committees of both Houses of Parliament.

C. D.

H. W. W. W.

2, Harcourt Buildings, Temple,
    January 1898.

CONTENTS.

APPENDIX.

CHAPTER I.

Private Bills—Their Subject Matter.

It will be convenient, in the first instance, to indicate the distinctions between those schemes which are considered by Parliament proper to be promoted by public bill, and those for which a private bill is the appropriate method of procedure. The keynote of the distinction between the subject matter proper for a private bill and that for a public bill is to be found in the Resolution of the House of Commons of June 4th, 1751, which is as follows :—

"Every bill for the particular interest or benefit of any person or persons, whether the same be brought in upon petition, or motion, or report from a committee, or brought from the Lords, has been and ought to be deemed a private bill within the meaning of the Table of Fees."

This distinction of the private bill as one "for the particular interest or benefit of any person or persons," as contrasted with the public bill intended for the general or public benefit, or dealing with a general or public interest, is to be regarded as the principal criterion.

Estate Bills, Divorce Bills, Naturalization and Name Bills are, in all cases, necessarily private bills, being "for the particular interest or benefit" of certain persons.

In the Standing Orders of the House of Lords, Estate, Divorce, Naturalization and Name Bills are all

classed as, or termed "Personal Bills": and it may be
observed that all "Personal Bills," within the meaning
of that expression as used in those Orders, must be
private bills.([1])

The difficulty which occasionally arises in determining
whether a scheme should be proposed as a private bill,
or whether it must be made the subject of legislation by
public bill, arises in relation to those matters which, if
dealt with by private bill, would be embodied in a bill of
the character denominated in the Standing Orders of the
House of Lords as a "Local Bill," a term which includes
all private bills other than "Personal Bills" ([2]).

"Local Bills" frequently affect the general or public
interests of particular localities: and in some cases, from
the extent to which such interests are affected, measures
proposed as private bills have been declared unfit for
private legislation, and the parties have been required to
proceed by public bill.

A bill incorporating or giving powers to a particular
company would in general be required to be a private
bill; so would a bill authorising the making of a particular
railway, or a particular bridge, or street; whilst a bill
amending the law applicable to railways in general, or
giving to all towns in a particular district or of a particular size additional powers of police or other local
regulation, would be required to be promoted as a public
bill.

Bills relating to the management or government of
particular provincial cities or boroughs, promoted by the
Corporations of such cities or boroughs, are treated in
general as private bills: and this rule is usually applied
to bills dealing with the City of London when promoted
by the City Corporation, but it is not applied to bills
promoted by the London County Council affecting the

([1]) S. O. 1, 149, H. L.   ([2]) S. O. 1. H. L.

whole of the metropolitan area other than those bills specially mentioned in the Standing Orders, 194 to 194 D (¹).

Thus, upon the City of London (Inclusion of Southwark) Bill, Mr. Speaker Gully, on March 22nd, 1897, declined to rule that the bill, which was promoted by the City Corporation, was improperly brought in as a private bill, its main object being to extend the boundaries of a borough, a subject matter considered proper in general to be dealt with by private bill. (²) Whilst upon the debate in the House of Commons of February 14th, 1895, upon the London Valuation Assessment Bill—a bill introduced as a private bill, promoted by the London County Council—Mr. Speaker Peel gave his reasons to the House for holding that it was a bill which ought to be introduced as a public bill, pointing out that the magnitude of its scope, the area touched upon, and the extent of the interests implicated were such that full publicity ought to be given to the bill, and that it ought to go through all the stages of a public bill, and when placed upon the Statute Book it ought to be placed among the Public Acts so as to be accessible to all, and not placed amongst those which were merely Local and Personal Acts. He further said that though it did not quite follow from all the precedents that a bill affecting the entire Metropolis must necessarily be introduced as a public bill, still he thought that a review of the precedents established the conclusion that bills affecting the whole Metropolis should, as a rule, be introduced as public bills. He referred to a Thames Navigation Bill, which in 1857 was introduced as a private bill, and to a Weighing of Corn Bill in 1864 which was introduced—and in his opinion properly so—as a public bill; and also to the Coal

---

(¹) *See* S. O. 194—194 D, *post*, p. 153.
(²) Parl. Deb., 4th Series, Vol. 47, p. 1078.

Duties Bill, which in the year 1889 was similarly dealt with as a public bill, as precedents in support of his views. ([1])

Upon the second reading of the Weighing of Corn Bill in 1864, Mr. Speaker Denison stated to the House that the policy of late years had been to introduce bills relating to the Metropolis as public bills on account of the great extent and the general interests involved, though if those bills had related to other towns they would have been regarded as proper to be dealt with by private bill legislation. ([2])

Bills involving questions of general policy, though limited in their application to particular areas, are in general to be introduced as public bills. Thus, bills relating to the sale of liquors in Cornwall, in Durham, in Yorkshire, &c., have been introduced as public bills ([3]): and upon a private bill brought in, in 1865, to alter the licensing system in Liverpool, the House of Commons, upon the second reading, carried an amendment to the motion for the reading, that the granting of licenses was a subject which ought not, at the then present time, to be dealt with by private bill. ([4])

In the House of Lords, upon objection being taken, on May 14th, 1897, during the progress of the Dublin Corporation Bill, that some of its clauses dealt with a question of general policy, by giving a municipal franchise to women in Dublin, and that such a question was not proper to be dealt with by a private bill, the clauses giving rise to the objection were struck out by the House. ([5])

In cases where it is doubtful whether the bill should be public or private, the doubt is often to be solved by

---

([1]) Parl. Deb., 4th Series, Vol. 30, p. 707.

([2]) Parl. Deb., 3rd Series, Vol. 176, p. 171.

([3]) May, p. 640.

([4]) May, p. 640 ; 120 C. J. 92 ; Parl. Deb., 3rd Series, Vol. 177, p. 642.

([5]) Parl. Deb., 4th Series, Vol. 49, p. 454.

a consideration of the extent to which the bill affects general public matters or interests.

When the Belfast Corporation Bill (a private bill) was before the House of Commons, March 6th, 1896, Mr. Speaker Gully said of that bill: "The clauses relating to public matters are not so great in number or importance as to make it necessary to introduce it as a public bill. It is always a question of degree whether the quantity of matter bearing on Public Acts is such as to make it necessary to bring in the bill as a public bill." [1]

Where a public bill is found to affect private rights it is what is termed a "hybrid" bill, and the House, upon sending it to a Committee after the second reading, may empower the Committee to hear evidence, and permit the attendance of counsel in the same way as if it had been brought in originally as a private bill; and then, when reported from that Committee to the House, it is recommitted to a Committee of the whole House, thus passing through the two Committees—the one as though a private bill, and the other as though an ordinary public bill— before becoming what is virtually a Public Act.

[1] Parl. Deb., 4th Series, Vol. 38, p. 335.

CHAPTER II.

Classification of Private Bills.

THE Standing Orders of the House of Lords conveniently divide private bills into two kinds, " Personal Bills " and " Local Bills," and then sub-divide " Local Bills " into two distinct classes. (¹)

In the Standing Orders of the House of Commons, the expressions " Personal Bills " and " Local Bills " are not used, but private bills are therein divided into two classes, which correspond almost exactly with the two divisions into which " Local Bills " are sub-divided in the Standing Orders of the House of Lords : whilst the difficulty which might otherwise arise from the absence of any mention of " Personal Bills " in the Standing Orders of the House of Commons is removed by special provision being made, so far as is necessary, for bills not falling within the two classes into which that House thus divides bills.

Divorce, Estate, Naturalization and Name Bills are not within either of the two classes into which private bills are divided by the Standing Orders of the House of Commons, but provision is made for them, so far as is necessary, by subsequent Orders of that House. (²) These bills are in the Standing Orders of the House of Lords, termed " Personal Bills," and they are required by the practice of Parliament to be brought in, in the first instance,

(¹) S. O. 1, H. L.
(²) S. O. 1, *post*, p. 65 ; S. O. 188b—192, 208, 211. *post*, pp. 152, 158, 159.

in the House of Lords.(¹) This practice doubtless furnishes
the explanation of the somewhat curious fact that the
Standing Orders of the House of Commons in dividing
private bills, as above stated, into two classes, place bills of
the kind termed in the House of Lords "Personal Bills"
in neither class. The object of the division into two classes
thus made by the Standing Orders of the House of Commons
would seem to be to enable each class to be more readily
referred to in subsequent Standing Orders than if on each
occasion a particular description of the bills intended to be
dealt with had to be given.(²) Class 2 appears to be confined to bills which authorize the making, maintaining or
varying, railways, tramways, or works of an engineering or
structural character, whilst in Class 1 bills not partaking
of that character are placed, though there are placed with
them many bills which involve the construction of works,
such as gas bills, market bills, and drainage of land bills.(³)

To the practitioner this division is of importance,
because the Standing Orders prescribe various steps to be
taken by reference to the Class in which the bill is, and
because, with the petition for the bill to the Lower House,
a declaration signed by the agent for the bill has to be
deposited in the Private Bill Office, stating to which of the
two the bill, in the judgment of the agent, belongs.(⁴)

Estate, Divorce, Naturalization and Name, and all
other private bills, not specified in Order 1 of the Standing
Orders of the House of Lords as "Local Bills," are, in the
Standing Orders of that House, termed "Personal Bills."(⁵)

(¹) S. O. 1, 149, H. L.; and see *post*, p. 9.
(²) See S. O. 1, 4, 11, 21, &c., *post*, pp. 85, 87, 91, 95.
(³) S. O. 1. *post*, p. 85, which sets out the classes *in extenso*.
(⁴) S. O. 32, *post*, p. 98.
(⁵) S. O. 149, H. L.

CHAPTER III

Introduction into Parliament.

PRIVATE bills falling within either of the two classes into which private bills are divided by the Standing Orders of the House of Commons,([1]) or, which is practically the same thing, within the description of "Local Bills" as used in the Standing Orders of the House of Lords,([2]) may, it would seem, be lawfully brought in, in the first instance, in either House of Parliament, but the practice is to commence them by the presentation of a petition to the House of Commons for leave to bring in the bill, and afterwards, when the session commences, the Chairman of the Committee of Ways and Means, on behalf of the Lower House, and the Chairman of Committees of the House of Lords, on behalf of that House, meet and arrange in which House each of such bills should be first considered, thus securing a proper distribution of the business of private legislation between the two Houses.([3])

Estate, Divorce, Naturalization, and Name Bills, and any other bills not falling within the description of "Local Bills" as used in the Standing Orders of the House of Lords are "Personal Bills," and are in the first instance brought into the House of Lords.([4]) They are not within either of the classes into which the Standing Orders of the House of Commons divide bills,([5]) and are commenced by petition to the Lords for leave to bring in the bill([6])

([1]) S. O. 1, *post*, p. 85; and see *ante*, p. 6.

([2]) S. O. 1, H. L.

([3]) S. O. 79, *post*, p. 121.

([4]) See S. O. 1, 149, H. L.

([5]) S. O. 1, *post*, p. 85, and see *ante*, p. 6.

([6]) S. O. 150, H. L.

The petition required by the Standing Orders of the House of Commons for leave to bring in a bill to that House, must be signed by the parties, or some of them, who are "suitors for the bill."(¹) A printed copy of the bill is annexed, and these documents are accompanied by a declaration, signed by the agent, stating to which of the two classes into which the Standing Orders of the House of Commons divides private bills, the bill proposed, in his judgment belongs,(²) and if the proposed bill gives power to effect any of certain objects specified in Standing Order 32 (*post*, p. 98), the declaration must state which of such powers are given, and further expressly state that the bill gives no power to effect any of the named objects other than those thus stated.(³)

If the proposed bill contains no power to effect any of the named objects, the declaration must so state. The declaration must in any case contain a statement that the bill does not give any powers other than those in the notices for the bill.(⁴)

Forms of petition and declaration will be found *post*, pp., 246, 248.

The petition must be written, not printed or lithographed. It must contain a prayer, and be signed, as before stated, by at least one person, or sealed, on the skin or sheet on which the prayer is written. No erasures or interlineations may be made in the petition. It is to be addressed "To the Honourable the Commons of the United Kingdom of Great Britain and Ireland, in Parliament assembled."(⁵) Except as above, no particular formalities are prescribed or required. "Personal Bills" are originated in the House of Lords by petition, to which a printed copy

(¹) S. O. 193, *post*, p. 153.
(²) S. O. 32, 193, *post*, pp. 98, 153.
(³) S. O. 32, *post*, p. 98.
(⁴) S. O. 32, *post*, p. 98 ; as to notices see *post*, pp. 87—91.
(⁵) See Rules as to Petitions against Private Bills, House of Commons, *post*, p. 321, and see Form, *post*, p. 246.

of the bill is annexed. That House requires that the petition should be signed by one or more "of the parties principally concerned in the consequences of the bill."(¹) No declaration of objects, it will be observed, is required by the House of Lords, either in the case of Personal or other bills; and in the case of "Local Bills," no petition for leave to bring in the bill is presented to that House if a petition has been presented to the Commons for leave to bring it in to the Lower House.(²)

Where the legislation is initiated in the House of Lords, as is the case with "Personal Bills," as has been already stated, the petition, which is then to the House of Lords, is, with the bill annexed, deposited at the offices of that House; and where, as is ordinarily the case with all bills other than "Personal Bills," it is initiated in the Commons, the petition, which is then one to the Commons, is deposited, with the bill annexed, and with the declaration, in the Private Bill Office at Westminster.(³)

A register is kept at the Private Bill Office upon which the petition is, upon payment of the required fees, entered, and a general list of petitions is afterwards made out in that office and printed.(⁴)

The Standing Orders of both Houses contain a number of requirements as to notices, advertisements, deposits, &c., which have to be complied with before bills of the two classes dealt with by the Standing Orders of the Commons, or "Local Bills," as the House of Lords terms them, can be introduced into those Houses(⁵); and in order to ascertain whether such requirements, and the similar requirements which may arise at later stages, have or have not been complied with, officials, termed Examiners, have been

(¹) S. O. 150, 151, H. L.
(²) See S. O. 86, H. L.
(³) S. O. 32, 193, *post*, pp. 98, 153.
(⁴) S. O. 227, 229, *post*, p. 162; Table of Fees, *post*, p. 290; Regulations for the Deposit of Petitions, *post*, p. 322.
(⁵) See S. O. 3 – 59, *post*, pp. 87—109; S. O. 3—59, H. L.

appointed by both Houses, whose duty it is to inquire into compliance with the Standing Orders, and report to the Houses the result arrived at.(¹)

The same Examiners act for both Houses. Their sittings are fixed by the Standing Orders. Under the present Orders they commence Jan. 18th.(²) Their procedure is regulated by the Standing Orders and by the Speaker's Regulations.(³)

It is at this stage of the proceedings, when compliance with Standing Orders has to be proved, that the first opportunity for opposition to the bill arises Promoters, whether opposed or not, have to prove compliance with Standing Orders. Opponents of a bill desiring to oppose at this stage, do so by depositing at the Private Bill Office a " Memorial " complaining of non-compliance with such of the Standing Orders of either House as they allege have not been complied with.

Under the present Standing Orders the depositing of Memorials is as follows : if they relate to bills numbered in the general list of petitions published by the Private Bill Office—

From   1—100   ⎞ They must be depo- ⎰ Jan. 9th
        101—200   ⎬   sited before two ⎱   „   16th
        201 and upwards ⎠   o'clock on   „   23rd

These memorials are the notices of objection taken by the opponents of the proposed legislation on the ground of non-compliance with Standing Orders. A Memorial, where there is one, is addressed to the Examiner. It must state specifically what the non-compliance with the Standing Orders is which is complained of.(⁴) As soon as the time for depositing Memorials has expired, the petition is marked

---

(¹) S. O. 2, 71, *post*, pp. 86, 119 ; S. O. 2, 76, H. L.

(²) S. 69, *post*, p. 119 ; S. O. 70, H. L.

(³) S. O. 69—78, *post*, pp. 119—121 ; S. O. 70—79 H. L. ; Notice, &c., *post*, p. 323.

(⁴) S. O. 74, *post*, p. 120 ; S. O. 230, *post*, p. 162 ; S. O. 73, H. L. See for a Form of Memorial, *post*, p. 249.

in the general list "*opposed*" or "*unopposed*," as the case
may be, and it is heard in its order as it stands in the list,
precedence being given, when necessary, to unopposed petitions.([1])   Daily lists are made out in the Private Bill Office
shewing the order in which the petitions will be taken.([1])

The promoters, whether their petition is opposed or
unopposed, must appear at the time appointed for the
hearing, otherwise their petition will be struck out of the
list: and there is a special provision in the Standing Orders
of the House of Commons, that the Examiner shall not
re-insert it except by order of that House.([2])   Upon the
hearing, the agent supporting the petition—that is to
say, the agent in favour of the bill—brings before the
Examiner a "Statement of Proofs," shewing that the
Standing Orders have been complied with, and giving the
name of each witness opposite each proof, who is to prove
each of the matters therein stated.([3])   The witnesses thus
named will, where the Examiner does not admit of proof
by affidavit, be examined *rivâ voce* by the agent in the
order in which they appear in the Statement of Proofs;
and where the Examiner does admit of proof by affidavit,
the affidavit of such witnesses will in like order be handed
in.   By the Standing Orders of both Houses, the examiners
are empowered to admit affidavits in proof of compliance
with Standing Orders, or to require further evidence, as
they may think most desirable.([4])   Where the petition is
unopposed, the examiner will, in general, be satisfied by
proof by affidavit: but where there appears likely to be a
serious conflict upon any material matter of fact, the witnesses will usually be examined *rivâ voce*.

By the Standing Orders any parties are entitled to
appear and be heard, by themselves, their agents and wit-

([1]) See Notice as to the Hearing of Petitions, *post*, p. 323.

([2]) S. O. 70, *post*, p. 119.

([3]) May, 685.   For form of Statement of Proof see *post*, p. 259.

([4]) S. O. 76, *post*, p. 120; S. O. 77, H. L.; see form of affidavit, *post*, p. 263.

nesses, upon a Memorial addressed to the examiner, complaining of a non-compliance with the Standing Orders, provided the matter complained of be specifically stated in such Memorial, and the party (if any) specially affected by the non-compliance have signed such Memorial, and not withdrawn his signature thereto, and such memorial have been duly deposited in the Private Bill Office.(¹)

Where the petition is opposed by the deposit of a Memorial, and the agent opposing has entered his appearance as agent upon the appearance paper at the Private Bill Office, the examiner, after taking the formal statement of proofs from the promoters of the bill, or their agent, will hear the matters specifically complained of in the Memorial.

Though the Standing Orders of both Houses make provision permitting Examiners to receive proof by affidavit of compliance with Standing Orders, no such provision is made as to proof of non-compliance.(²)

If it is necessary to resort to compulsion to bring any particular witness or documents before the Examiner, it would seem that this must be done by an order of the House, and that in general such an order will be made when the Examiner reports to the House that such a course is necessary.(³)

If any preliminary objection exists to the right of the memorialists to be heard, as, for example, that the Memorial has not been signed duly, or the like, such objection should be taken before the memorialists or their agent commence their case. The preliminary points, if any, having been disposed of, the complaints specified in the Memorial will be dealt with *seriatim,* and finally the Examiner will decide whether he should certify that the Standing Orders have

(¹) S. O. 74, *post,* p. 120; S O 73. H L ; Rules as to proof of compliance, *post,* p. 321.
(²) S. O. 76, *post,* p. 120; S. O. 77, H. L.
(³) May, 687 ; Wandle Water Works Bill, 1853, 108 C. J. 257 ; 121 *ib.* 114, 127.

been complied with or not, or whether, instead of deciding that matter himself, he should make a special report to the House.([1])

If the Examiner decides that the Standing Orders have been complied with, he endorses the petition with his certificate to that effect, and it is then returned to the Private Bill Office, from which the agent will obtain it, and arrange for its presentation to the House of Commons by a member, upon which being done the bill is ordered to be brought in ;([2]) whilst, if the bill is one to be first considered in the House of Lords, the petition remains in the Private Bill Office, no petition to the House of Lords being necessary in the case of a " Local Bill " for which a petition has been presented to the Commons.([3])

If he finds that the Standing Orders have not been complied with, he so endorses the petition, and reports the facts to the House and any special circumstances there may be.([4]). If he makes the special report above mentioned, instead of himself deciding definitely one way or the other, he reports the facts to the House and endorses the petition accordingly.([5])

Where he decides that the Standing Orders have not been complied with, or makes a special report without coming to a definite decision himself, the report is referred to " The Select Committee on Standing Orders," who, after the petition has been presented to the Commons, consider whether the Bill, or any portion of it, should be proceeded with, and then report to the House the opinion they have arrived at, and whether the Standing Orders ought or ought not to be dispensed with.([6]) Where the Examiner has definitely found that any Standing Order has not been

([1]) S. O. 71, 77, 78, post, p. 119—121 ; S. O. 76, 78, H. L.
([2]) S. O. 195, 196, post, p. 156.
([3]) S. O. 86, H. L.
([4]) S, O. 71, post, p. 119 ; S. O. 76, H. L.
([5]) S. O. 78, post, p. 121 ; S. O. 78, H. L.
([6]) S.O.91—95, post, p.123; S.O.80--85, H. L. ; S.O.199, 200, post, p. 157.

complied with, or has found definitely any matter of fact, the Select Committee will not question his finding. But where he has not decided whether the particular Standing Order, as to which question arose, was complied with or not, but has made a special report, they will themselves deal with the matter and report the result to the House of Commons, and that even in the case of bills originating in the Lords.([1]) There is a similar committee in the House of Lords to deal with the cases where the Examiner has not certified compliance with their Standing Orders.([2])

Where the parties opposing the bill desire to contend before the Select Committee on Standing Orders of the Commons upon a Special Report referred to them that the facts therein stated show that the Standing Orders have been complied with, they must prepare a written or printed statement of their argument strictly confined to that question for the use of the committee, and deliver copies of it to the chairman and members of the committee, at their residences, twenty-four hours before the meeting of the committee.([3])

The promoters desiring to raise the opposite contention should prepare a similar statement of their argument, and similarly deliver it to the chairman and members.

If the committee comes to the conclusion that there has not been a compliance with the Standing Orders, the further consideration of the case is adjourned in order to give time for the promoters and opponents to prepare and deliver similar statements upon the question of a dispensation with the Standing Orders being granted.([4])

Upon these statements the committee may hear arguments, but they only hear one counsel on each side.([5]) The procedure before the Standing Orders Committee of

---

([1]) S. O. 92, 93, *post*, p. 123; and see Resolutions, *post*, p. 324.
([2]) S. O. 80—85, H. L.
([3]) Resolutions, *post*, p. 324.
([4]) Resolutions, *post*, p. 324.
([5]) Resolutions, *post*, p. 325.

the House of Lords is practically the same as that before
the Select Committee on Standing Orders of the House of
Commons, except that before the Lords' Committee the
statements must in all opposed cases be printed.([1])

Upon questions of dispensation with Standing Orders, it
is open to either side to present a petition to the House
by depositing it with the Private Bill Office, and paying
the required fees, in favour of or against a dispensation.([2])
Every such petition, when deposited, stands referred to the
Committee on Standing Orders.([3]) Copies of such petitions
must be delivered to the members of the committee and at
the Committee Office.([4])

The petitions must set forth the grounds on which
dispensation is prayed, and should contain in fact the
statement of the case relied on, since, where there is a
petition, no statement in addition to the case set forth in
the petition is received.([4])

The decisions of the committee are, when arrived at,
reported to the House in the form of a resolution, which is
read. In the House of Commons, if the resolution is
favourable to the bill, it is read a second time, agreed to,
and the bill ordered to be brought in ; if it is unfavourable
the report is ordered to lie on the table. In the House of
Lords the practice is to agree with the resolution in either
case. The shape of the resolution depends upon the way
the matter has come before the committee. If it is upon a
report (or certificate, as it is called in the House of Lords)
of the Examiner that the Standing Orders have not been
complied with, the resolution runs that the Standing Orders
ought not to be dispensed with, or that they ought to be
dispensed with and the parties be permitted to proceed
with their bill either unconditionally or with some condition to be fulfilled by them. If there has been a special

[1] S. O. 85, H. L.
[2] S.O. 200, post, p. 157; Resolutions, post, p. 325; Table of Fees, post, p. 290.
[3] S. O. 200, post, p. 157.
[4] Resolutions, post, p. 325.

report by the Examiner the resolution first states whether or not the Standing Orders have been complied with.

Where the resolution is unfavourable to the bill and has been ordered to lie upon the table, it is still open to the promoters to procure a motion that the report be referred back to the committee for reconsideration, and this has occasionally been done. For instance, in the case of the Felixstowe Ipswich and Midlands Railway Bill the report of the Examiner that the Standing Orders had not been complied with was referred to the Standing Orders Committee. They resolved that the Standing Orders ought not to be dispensed with, and their report was ordered to lie upon the table.(¹)

Subsequently it was moved that the report be referred back to the committee to inquire whether special circumstances existed which rendered it just and expedient that the Standing Orders should be dispensed with.(²) In the debate upon this motion it was urged that great distress existed in Essex, owing to want of employment, which would be materially alleviated by the works proposed in the bill, and that fresh plans had been prepared, which could be substituted for those deposited which conflicted with the Standing Orders.(³) The motion was carried, and ultimately the committee resolved that the Standing Orders ought to be dispensed with, and the parties ought to be permitted to proceed with the bill, provided that proof was given before the Examiner that amended plans and sections had been deposited. This resolution was agreed to by the House, and leave was given to bring in the bill.(⁴)

It may be here stated that the sanction of the Chairman of Ways and Means is required to every notice of motion for dispensing with any Sessional or Standing Order of the House of Commons.

(¹) 141 C. J. 36, 52.

(²) 141 C. J. 196.

(³) Parl. Deb., 3rd series, vol. 305, p. 722.

(⁴) 141 C. J. 205. Ultimately the committee on the bill reported that the preamble was not proved. *Ib.* 279.

CHAPTER IV.

Progress of Bill through the Commons, up to and including the Committee Stage.

WHEN a private bill has been ordered to be brought into the House of Commons, as above described, it must be presented to the House by depositing it in the Private Bill Office ([1]) not later than one clear day after the presentation to the House of the petition for the bill, unless there has been a reference to the Standing Orders Committee, in which case the deposit must be not later than one clear day after the House has given leave to proceed.([2]) It must be printed on paper of a size to be determined by the Speaker (at present it is folio), with a cover of parchment attached to it, upon which the title is to be written.([3]) The names of the members who are bringing in the bill (who must not be less than two nor more than six in number) should appear on the back of it. If the clauses of the bill contain any charges in any way affecting the public revenue, such charges must be printed in italics.([4]) Printed copies of the bill are to be delivered to the Vote Office for the use of members.([5])

When everything is thus in order, one of the clerks of the Private Bill Office takes the bill from that office and lays it on the table of the House for the first reading, which is a matter of course. The bill is at the time of first reading ordered to be read a second time, and the next

([1]) S. O. 196, *post*, p. 156.
([2]) S. O. 197, *post*, p. 156.
([3]) S. O. 201, *post*, p. 157.

([4]) S. O. 202, *post*, p. 157.
([5]) S. O. 203, *post*, p. 157.

stage of the bill, except in the cases of company bills, bills brought from the Lords, or other bills specially directed by the Standing Orders to be referred to the Examiners after having been read a first time, is the second reading.

The Standing Orders 62–68 and 72 specify the cases in which the bill has after the first reading to be brought before the Examiner, in order that he may see that the Standing Orders not already shewn to have been complied with have in fact been complied with. It will be seen that it is at this stage that he examines into the consents of shareholders or proprietors of companies where their consents are required.([1])

The second reading, where there is no reference needed to the Examiner, takes place not less than three clear days nor more than seven after the first reading.([2])

Where there has to be a reference to the Examiner under Standing Orders 62–68 or 72 the second reading takes place not later than seven clear days after the Examiner or the Select Committee on Standing Orders, as the case may be, has reported on it.([3])

It is the duty of the clerks of the Private Bill Office between the first and second reading of all private bills to themselves examine whether they are in conformity with the rules and orders of the House.([4])   The bill is in the custody of the clerks of the Private Bill Office until laid upon the table for the second reading.([5])   The agent for the bill must give three clear days' notice in writing to the clerks in the Private Bill Office of the day proposed for the second reading.   He may not give such notice until the day after the order for the second reading.([6])   If there is no opposition the bill is read a second time on the day fixed,

---

([1]) S. O. 62–68, *post*, pp. 111–118; S. O. 72, *post*, p. 119.
([2]) S. O. 204, *post*, p. 157.
([3]) S. O. 204, *post*, p. 157.

([4]) S. O. 234, *post*, p. 163.
([5]) S. O. 233, *post*, p. 163.
([6]) S. O. 235, *post*, p. 163.

but if it is then opposed the second reading is adjourned to the day on which the House next sits.([1])

The House does not profess to decide upon the second reading as to the truth or otherwise of the allegations of fact upon which a proposed bill is based, and in conceding a second reading to a private bill the House is regarded as merely giving its sanction to its general principle on the hypothesis that the committee to which it afterwards is referred finds those allegations proved. It is usual, therefore, to allow a second reading, except where the bill enunciates some principle which the House is not prepared to affirm.([2])

A recent instance of the rejection by the House of a private bill upon the second reading is to be found in the case of the Petersham and Ham Lands and Footpaths Bill, 1896, where an amendment to the proposal for a second reading was carried to the effect that the House was not prepared to entertain a bill for the enclosure of metropolitan common lands.([3])

Where the principle of the bill is one of novelty which appears to any considerable body of members objectionable a division is usually taken against the second reading, or some instruction is moved to modify the portion of the bill objected to. If the bill is read a second time it is, as a matter of course, ordered to be committed, and then stands referred to a committee. Where an instruction has been carried it stands so referred with the instruction to guide the committee.([4]) After the interval required by Standing Order 211 from the second reading the bill is taken before the committee.([5])

In the case of opposed bills important questions often arise at this stage as to the *locus standi* of parties desiring to oppose before the committee on the bill, those only being

---

([1]) S. O. 207, *post*, p. 158.
([2]) Parl. Deb., 4th series, vol. 37, p. 1053.
([3]) Parl. Deb., 4th series, vol. 38, p. 729, *et seq.*
([4]) See " *Instructions*," *post*, p. 32.
([5]) S. O. 211, *post*, p. 159.

allowed to be heard, in general, who have taken the proper steps for that purpose, and who have not been objected to upon the ground of having no such interest as entitles them to a *locus standi*, or who have, notwithstanding objection, established their *locus standi*.([1]) It is before the committee to which the bill is referred that the opponents of the bill, if they have taken the proper steps and are persons entitled to be heard, have the opportunity of contesting the proposed legislation by submitting evidence and attacking that produced in favour of the bill.

Whether the bill is opposed or unopposed it will have been examined by the chairman of the Committee of Ways and Means, for the purpose of calling the attention of the House or the chairman of the committee to which, as above stated, it is referred, to any point which may seem to him to require it : and in order to enable him, with the assistance of the Speaker's counsel, to fulfil this duty, the agent for the bill is required, at an earlier stage, namely, the day after the Examiner of Petitions has endorsed the petition for the bill at the latest, and again two clear days before the committee meets, to lay copies of the bill before the chairman of the Committee of Ways and Means, and also before the Speaker's counsel.([2])

Opposed bills are bills against which a petition has been presented, not later than ten clear days after the first reading, containing a prayer to be heard, and bills which the Chairman of Ways and Means has reported as proper, to be treated as opposed.([3]) The composition of the committees appointed to deal with opposed bills is prescribed by the Standing Orders,([4]) as is also that for dealing with unopposed bills.([5]) For the purpose of dealing with

---

([1]) As to *Locus Standi*, see *post*, pp. 34—63.

([2]) S. O. 80, 82, *post*, p. 121.

([3]) S. O. 107, *post*, p. 126.

([4]) S. O. 108, 110, 116, 117, *post*, pp. 126, 127.

([5]) S. O. 104, 109, 110, *post*, pp. 125, 126.

railway and canal bills a committee called "The General Committee on Railway and Canal Bills" is appointed at the commencement of every Session by the Committee of Selection. Their principal functions are to appoint from among themselves the chairmen to preside over the committees dealing with such bills, and to refer such bills when not opposed, if they think fit, to the Chairman of Ways and Means together with two other members not locally interested, or to him with one such member and a referee to be nominated by the Committee of Selection.([1])

The parties desirous of opposing the bill in committee must present a petition against it. This is done by depositing it in the Private Bill Office not later, in general than ten clear days after the first reading, except in the case of bills to confirm a provisional order or certificate where the time is by the Standing Orders to be not later than seven clear days after the Examiner has given notice of the day on which such bill for confirmation will be examined.([2]) The petition against the bill is not to be heard before the committee on the bill unless it has been prepared and signed in strict conformity with the Rules and Orders of the House and duly presented within the proper time,([3]) and if any contest as to the *locus standi* of the petitioners is raised by the promoters before the Court of Referees, the body appointed to deal with objections to *locus standi*,([4]) that body deals with the rights of the petitioners only which are stated on or sufficiently appear from the petition itself.([5]) It is, therefore, of the utmost importance to see that the petition is in all respects in conformity with the requirements of the House.

([1]) S.O. 99, 101, 104, *post*, p. 125; see further S. O. 208, 208A, *post*, p. 158.

([2]) S. O. 107, 129, 210, *post*, pp. 126, 129, 159. See as to Provisional Orders, *post*, pp. 71—76.

([3]) S. O. 128, 129, *post*, p. 129.

([4]) S. O. 87, *post*, p. 123; and see as to *Locus Standi*, *post*, p. 34.

([5]) See *post*, pp. 26, 46.

There must be endorsed on the petition the name or short title of the bill, and a statement that the petition is against the bill, together with the name of the member, party, or agent thus depositing it.([1]) It may be withdrawn on a requisition to that effect being deposited in the Private Bill Office, signed by the petitioner or the agent who deposited it.([2]) If the promoters of the bill intend to object to the right of the petitioners to be heard against the bill, they must give notice of their intention and of the grounds of their objection to the clerk to the Referees and to the petitioner's agents not later than the eighth day after the day on which the petition was deposited in the Private Bill Office: this time may, however, be extended by the Referees. The notice must be endorsed with the name of the petitioner's agents.([3]) Notice of objection may be withdrawn by giving notice of withdrawal to the same persons.([4]) In the absence of such withdrawal the objection will be heard before the above-mentioned Court of Referees.

When the bill is committed it is taken charge of by the committee clerk, and remains in his custody until reported.([5]) Provision is made by the Standing Orders for notice to be given of the first meeting of the committee, or of any postponement by the committee clerk to the clerks in the Private Bill Office,([6]) and for a filled-up bill as proposed to be submitted to the committee, signed by the agent for the bill, to be deposited in the Private Bill Office two clear days before the meeting of the committee, and for copies of proposed amendments to be supplied to opponents applying therefor.([7]) The agent for the bill must also

([1]) S. O. 205, *post*, p. 158. As to the contents of the petition see *Locus Standi*, *post*, p. 46, and for a form *post*, p. 265.

([2]) S. O. 206, *post*, p. 158.

([3]) R. 1 of Rules for Referees, *post*, p. 326.

([4]) R. 3. *ib*.

([5]) S. O. 233, *post*, p. 163.

([6]) See S. O. 126, 236, 238, *post*, pp. 128, 163, 164.

([7]) S. O. 237, *post*, p. 164.

lay signed copies of the bill as proposed to be submitted
to the committee two clear days at least before the day appointed for the hearing in committee before the Chairman
of Ways and Means, and before the Speaker's Counsel.(¹)

If a Referee is a member of the committee a similar
copy must be similarly deposited at the Referee's Office.(²)
The reason for requiring the deposit of these copies would
seem to be found in the fact that promoters not un-
frequently find it expedient to alter in some particular the
clauses of the bill as originally deposited before placing it
before the committee on the bill. It may, however, be
noticed that alterations cannot be permitted which go
beyond, or are at variance with, the order giving leave to
introduce the bill, or which contravene Standing Orders, or
which are excessive in extent (³)

The agents opposing the bill must, in order that their
petitions in opposition may be heard before the committee,
enter their appearances at the Private Bill Office,(⁴) and
those promoting must likewise enter similar appearances.(⁴) Petitioners in favour of bills are not heard on
their petitions, though where they have any evidence to
give they may, of course, be called as witnesses by the
promoters in whose charge the conduct of the case for the
bill before the committee is.(⁵)   The petitioners against
the bill supply the committee with printed copies of their
petitions, and the promoters supply the committee with
signed copies of the bill as proposed to be submitted to
them.(⁶)

A list is prepared daily in the Private Bill Office of all
private bills in the House of Commons upon which any
committee is appointed to sit; specifying the room in

(¹) S. O. 82 ; see ante, p. 21.
(²) Rules for Referees, No. 9, post, p. 327.
(³) May, p. 723.
(⁴) S. O. 126, post, p. 128 ; Regulations for Agents, No. 8, post, p. 329.
(⁵) May, 731 ; S. O. 205, post, p. 158.
(⁶) 120 C. J. 69 : S. O. 138, post, p. 132.

which and the hour at which it is to sit, and is hung up in the lobby of the House.(¹)

The committee to which the bill is referred hear the petitioners by themselves, their agents or counsel, in accordance with the prayer of the petition, and also the promoters by their counsel.(²)   Evidence is given before them *vivâ voce*, the witnesses being examined by the party producing them or their agents or counsel, and cross-examined by the opposite party or their counsel, and re-examined as in ordinary courts of justice.   The petitioners are heard only upon the grounds of objection specified in their petition.(³)

The committee upon the hearing would seem, in strict-ness, not bound by the rules of evidence applicable to courts of justice, but in general they will be guided by the principles of those rules in the conduct of the business before them, except perhaps where they consider that injustice might be done or needless expense caused by a too rigid application of those principles.   In regard to the cross-examination of witnesses, counsel are, it would seem, allowed less latitude in putting questions which are irrelevant to the matters before the committee, and which are intended merely to discredit the particular witness, than in cases of trials in the law courts.

The attendance of counsel being by permission rather than as of right, the committee would appear to have a greater power to check questions which may seem to them improper than is permitted to the courts of justice.   All matters, whether arising in the course of the proceedings or upon the final decision or report, are determined by the vote of the majority of the committee, the chairman, in case of equality, having a second or casting vote.(⁴)

The opposition to the bill may be either to the preamble or to the clauses of the bill, or to both.   The second reading

---

(¹) S. O. 248, *post*, p. 165.   (³) S. O. 128. *post*. p. 129.
(²) S. O. 210, *post*, p. 159.   (⁴) S. O. 125, *post*, p. 128.

is supposed to have been assented to by the House upon the assumption that the preamble is true, and it is open to the opponents, if by their petition they have distinctly raised that ground of objection,([1]) to contend, and to produce evidence to show, that the preamble is in fact untrue, and they may, even if they fail to induce the committee to find the preamble not proved, similarly attack such clauses of the bill as by their petition they have placed themselves in a position to attack. Whether the opposition is to the preamble or to the clauses, it cannot go beyond the petition, the petition is practically that which has to be tried by the committee.([1])

The conduct of the business before the committee is regulated as the committee may think most convenient, but the ordinary course is, for the counsel in support of the bill to explain the proposed measure, and then produce his evidence in its support, and for the counsel for the opponents afterwards to open their grounds of objection, and then bring forward their evidence, each side testing by cross-examination those of his opponent's witnesses whose evidence he desires to minimise or discredit, and for the counsel producing the witness to re-examine upon such cross-examination. Committees have on various occasions laid it down as their rule that no counsel not present during the examination of a witness should be permitted to cross-examine that witness. It is believed that it is not the usual practice of committees to enforce this rule, except where, from the lengthy nature of the evidence or from the complication of the matter dealt with, it appears expedient to do so ; though, of course, it is within the power of any committee, at any time, to lay down and rigidly enforce the above, or any similar rule for their own procedure.

Where the opposition is both to the preamble and to clauses, that to the preamble is naturally first dealt with.

([1]) S. O. 128, *post*, p. 129.

It would seem to be open to any member of the committee to ask of the witnesses any question he may think fit, or make any inquiry of the counsel engaged, but it is usual in practice for such questions or inquiries to be put or made through the chairman, or with his permission. The chairman, unless his ruling is challenged by some other member of the committee, decides as to whether evidence offered by the one side and objected to by the other should be received by the committee. If it is so challenged the committee, if the challenge is persisted in, have to vote upon the matter.([1])

When the committee have completed their inquiry it is the duty of their chairman in all cases, to report the bill to the House.([2])

([1]) See S. O. 125, *post*, p. 128.   ([2]) S. O. 149, *post*, p. 134.

CHAPTER V.

Report – Third Reading Sending Bill to Lords.

It would be beyond the scope of this work to discuss in detail the form of the report on the various matters with which it may deal, in accordance with the Standing Orders and the practice of the House. It is sufficient to say that the committee may report to the House that the preamble of the bill has not been proved, or they may report the bill without amendment, or they may report it with amendments, either in the preamble or the clauses, or in both. In the first case the result usually is that the bill is dropped, although instances exist of the bill having been re-committed, owing to the withdrawal of opposition, or the acceptance of amendments by the promoters.

If the bill has passed through committee unamended, and is not a railway or a tramway bill, it is immediately ordered to be read a third time.([1]) One clear day's notice in writing must be given by the agent of the bill to the clerks in the Private Bill Office of the day proposed for the third reading, and the notice cannot be given until the day after the bill has been ordered to be read a third time.([2]) Upon the third reading only verbal amendments can be made,([3]) and in addition the Chairman of Ways and Means must have informed the House or signified in writing to the Speaker whether the amendment ought

---

([1]) S. O. 213, *post*, p. 159. ([2]) S. O. 243, *post*, p. 164.
([3]) S. O. 219, *post*, p. 160.

or ought not to be entertained by the House without being referred to the Committee on Standing Orders.([1]) One clear day's notice of any such amendment must be given in the Private Bill Office.([2]) The agent must submit the amendment on the same day to the Chairman of Ways and Means and the Speaker's Counsel, and it must be printed, S. O. 217.([3]) After the third reading the bill is printed fair at the promoters' expense,([4]) and before it is sent to the Lords is examined by the clerks in the Private Bill Office with the bill as read a third time, and endorsed with a certificate of such examination.([5])

If, however, the bill was amended in committee, or is a railway or tramway bill, instead of being immediately upon report ordered to be read a third time, it is ordered to lie upon the table, with a view to the bill being subsequently considered.([6])

Copies of the bill as amended in committee, printed at the expense of the promoters, must be delivered at the Vote Office for the use of members three clear days before the consideration of the bill.([7]) This print is examined by the clerks in the Private Bill Office with a print of the bill which the committee clerk delivers at the office after the report is made out.([8])

Three clear days must elapse between the report and the consideration of a bill, and before the consideration takes place the Chairman of Ways and Means must have announced whether the bill contains the provisions required by the Standing Orders.([9]) One clear day's notice must be given by the agent for the bill to the clerks in the Private Bill Office of the day proposed for the consideration of the bill.([10]) Three clear days before the consideration takes

---

([1]) S. O. 216, *post*, p. 160.
([2]) S. O. 242, *post*, p. 164.
([3]) S. O. 85, *post*, p. 122.
([4]) S. O. 221, *post*, p. 161.
([5]) S. O. 245, *post*, p. 165.

([6]) S. O. 213, *post*, p. 159.
([7]) S. O. 214, *post*, p. 159.
([8]) S. O. 240, 241, *post*, p. 164.
([9]) S. O. 215, *post*, p. 159.
([10]) S. O. 239, *post*, p. 164.

place, a copy of the bill must be laid by the agent before the Chairman of Ways and Means and the Speaker's Counsel, and other copies deposited as provided by Standing Order 84. The provisions as to clauses or amendments which it is desired to propose on the consideration of the bill are similar to those with regard to verbal amendments on the third reading above-mentioned.([1])

When the consideration of the bill takes place, if no amendments or new clauses are offered, or if offered are not opposed, the bill is usually ordered to be read a third time ; but instances have occurred where the bill in its passage through committee has been altered to such an extent that the House has ordered a reference to the examiners to inquire " whether the amendments involve any infraction of the Standing Orders."([2])

The formalities governing the third reading stage of bills not amended in committee apply also to bills amended in committee and to railway and tramway bills.

The third reading affords to opponents a final opportunity of asking the House to reject the bill, though at this stage they are met with the further difficulty that they have to make out such a case as to satisfy the House that it is right to sterilise the labours of the committee and reverse the conclusion come to on the second reading apparently by the House. A recent example of an unsuccessful attempt to do this will be found in the Cambridge Corporation Bill.([3]) When a bill has been read a third time and passed, if it is a Commons' bill, it is sent up to the Lords by the clerk, and the concurrence of the Lords desired. If it is a Lords' bill, a message is sent to the Lords stating that the bill has been passed with, or without amendment, and if with amendments, desiring the

([1]) See S. O. 216, 217, 242, *post*, pp. 160, 164.

([2]) May 787.

([3]) Parl. Deb., 4th series, vol. 24, pp. 579, 750.

Lords' concurrence thereto.　Similarly in the Lords after the third reading of a bill messages to the same effect are sent to the Commons.　Where amendments have been made by the Lords in a Commons' bill, the day (or any subsequent day) after the bill has been returned from the Lords one clear day's notice must be given in the Private Bill Office that the amendments are to be taken into consideration, and the same notice given of any amendments it is intended to propose to such amendments, and a copy deposited at the same time.([1])　The agent for the bill must also lay a copy of the Lords' amendments and of the proposed amendments to them, if any, before the Chairman of Ways and Means and the Speaker's Counsel before two o'clock in the day before their consideration by the House.([2])　Both sets of amendments must be printed and circulated in accordance with Standing Order 220.　When the amendments by either House have been ultimately agreed to by the other, the bill is then ready to receive the Royal assent.

([1]) S. O. 246, post. p. 165.　　　　([2]) S. O. 86, post. p. 122.

CHAPTER VI.

Instructions.

WHEN a bill has been read a second time an instruction may be given by the House of Commons either to the Committee of Selection or to the committee on the bill. An instruction to the Committee of Selection may prescribe the particular committee by whom the bill is to be considered, or the constitution of the committee, or the date at which it is to sit, or that the bill is to be considered in a group with certain other bills or other similar matters of procedure.

Instructions to the committee on the bill are of two distinct kinds : in the one case the committee are peremptorily directed to take a particular course—such instructions are termed mandatory—and in the other case the committee are simply empowered to inquire into and report upon (and sometimes to make provision in the bill for) matters, which, though relevant to the bill, they might otherwise not have considered.

An example of a mandatory instruction is afforded by that moved, although not carried, in the case of the Glasgow Corporation and Police Bill, 1895, by which the committee were directed to leave out parts of the bill, on the ground that they contained provisions of a public character which ought not to appear in a private bill.[1] A permissive instruction was given to the committee on the

[1] Parl. Deb., 4th series, vol. 30, p. 1450.

Birmingham Corporation Water Bill, 1892, "that they have power to inquire and report whether it is necessary to extinguish the rights of the commoners" over the district covered by the bill.([1])

Instructions, whether mandatory or permissive, must not go beyond the scope of the bill. For instance, on a bill enabling a town to take compulsory powers to acquire land for waterworks, an instruction proposing to extend the municipal franchise is, out of order,([2]) although where there was no opposition to the principle of the instruction the rule has not been so rigidly applied.([3]) On the other hand, where, as in the Dublin Corporation Bill, 1897, a bill alters the register by enabling persons to get on the register on different terms from before, an instruction to extend the franchise would not be out of order.([4]) Another rule of some importance is, that an instruction may not seek to alter the general law in a particular case. Thus, in the London and North-Western Railway Bill an instruction to the committee to insert provisions compelling the company to run third-class carriages in its mail trains was ruled out of order.([5])

A permissive instruction that a power should be conferred upon a committee which they already possess is out of order, as is also an instruction of the same kind which goes into matters of detail which are the proper subject of amendments in committee; but neither of these rules apply to mandatory instructions.([6])

([1]) Parl. Deb., 4th series, vol. 2, p. 614.
([2]) Parl. Deb., 4th series, vol. 46, p. 1571; and for other instances, see Parl. Deb., 4th series. p. 625; ib. p. 1154.
([3]) Parl. Deb., 4th series, vol. 12, p. 1306.
([4]) Parl. Deb., 4th series. vol. 46, p. 151.
([5]) Parl. Deb, 4th series, vol. 39, p. 1707.
([6]) Parl. Deb., 3rd series, vol. 287, p. 875; ib., 4th series, vol. 46, p. 623; and see as to permissive instructions, Parl. Deb., 4th series, vol. 2, pp. 622, 626; Voluntary Schools Bill, 1897, Parl. Deb., 4th series, vol. 46, p. 1154.

CHAPTER VII.

Locus Standi, Inquiry before the Court of Referees as to Locus Standi.

THE Court of Referees was established to secure uniformity in the decisions upon *locus standi*, or the right to be heard in opposition to bills before Committees, and to relieve opponents of bills from the necessity of having to be prepared with their evidence for the committee, although it might, upon the hearing before committee, be rejected upon a preliminary objection that they had no *locus standi* to oppose.

The committees on the bills no longer deal with questions of *locus standi*, except so far as they may happen to arise incidentally in the course of the proceedings before them.([1])

The Court of Referees now deals with the questions of *locus standi* in all cases of private bills before the the hearing takes place by the committee on the bill. It is governed by the Standing Orders, the rules framed for their guidance by the Chairman of Ways and Means, and the practice of Parliament.([2])

The duty of the Court of Referees is limited to deciding upon questions as to the *locus standi* of opponents of private bills to be heard by the committees thereon upon their petitions against such bills.([3])

([1]) S. O. 89, *post*, p. 123.
([2]) S. O. 87—89; Rules for Referees, *post*, pp. 326, 327; S. O. 128—135, *post*, pp. 129—131.
([3]) S. O. 89, *post*, p. 123.

The rules framed as above stated require promoters objecting to the *locus standi* of petitioners to give notice of their intention to object, and of the grounds of their objection, to the clerks of the Referees and to the agents for the petitioners not later than the eighth day after the day on which the petition has been deposited in the Private Bill Office ; but the referees have power, under special circumstances, to allow such notices to be given, although the time thus limited may have expired.([1]) The notices must be endorsed with the names of the agents for the petitioners.([1])

The petition must be deposited not later than ten days after the first reading of the bill, and must distinctly specify the grounds of objection.([2])

A list of the cases and of the order in which they will be heard by the Court of Referees is kept in the Referees' Office.([3])

When the bill is called on before the court, the agent supporting the petition against the bill must produce a certificate of appearance from the Private Bill Office, in which the names of the petitioners, their counsel and agents, are stated.([4])

In the absence of a special authorisation by the court, one counsel only may appear on each side.([5])

The court has, by statute, power to examine witnesses upon oath([6]), it has in cases as to *locus standi* no power to award costs.

The right of an opponent who has duly petitioned against a bill to be heard before the committee on the bill

---

([1]) Rule 1 of Rules for Referees, *post*, p. 326 ; see for a form of notice of objection, *post*, p. 283.

([2]) See *ante*, p. 22 ; and S. O. 107, 128, 129, 210, *post*, pp. 126, 129, 159.

([3]) Rule 4 of Rules for Referees, *post*, p. 326.

([4]) Rule 5 of Rules for Referees, *post*, p. 326.

([5]) S. O. 88, *post*, p. 123.

([6]) 30 and 31 Vict. c. 136, ss. 1, 2.

upon his petition depends, if his *locus standi* is objected to,
upon whether he has, in the opinion of the Court of
Referees, shewn such an interest in opposing the bill, or
some portion of it, as is, by the practice of the court,
deemed a sufficient interest to give him a *locus standi* to
oppose, or upon whether he can bring his case within one of
those Standing Orders which in certain specified cases give
an absolute right to oppose, and in certain other specified
cases a right dependent upon the discretion of the Court.

There are certain interests which are always considered
sufficient to give a *locus standi*, as, for example, the interest
of a landowner, part of whose land it is proposed by the
bill to take compulsorily. There is no Standing Order
giving to landowners this right in express terms, but it is,
and has long been, the settled practice of Parliament to
give a *locus standi* in such cases.

There are other cases, which will be hereafter specified,
where a *locus standi* is given expressly by various Standing
Orders, or where power is given by them to the Referees to
allow a *locus standi*, if in their discretion they think fit
to do so.

The practice of the court, in cases where the matter is
not expressly dealt with by Standing Orders, is to a considerable extent settled by a long series of reported decisions; and it will be found that the question to be considered in those cases usually is, whether the facts of the
particular case bring it more properly within the principle
of one, or other, of the reported decisions.

The right to a *locus standi* is founded on the existence
of some power in the bill which would affect the petitioner
(see *Southampton Docks Bill*, 1871, 2 C. & S. 161). It
is not because petitioners have, or think they have, a
grievance under existing legislation that they are to be
heard, for the foundation of all *locus standi* is, that the
future legislation proposed by the bill in some way
affects the interests of the parties claiming a *locus standi*

injuriously (*Gloucester and Berkeley Canal Bill*, 1874, 1 C. & R. 76, 77), or, to adopt the expression made use of by one of the Referees (Mr. Rickards), there must be something in the bill which tends to injure the petitioners (*South Staffordshire Water Bill*, 1875, 1 C. & R. 187, 189). A landowner is not, as a matter of course, allowed a *locus standi* in relation to bills which are merely for the extension of time for the completion of works authorised by a previous bill, or for the abandonment of a scheme, or part of a scheme, sanctioned by a previous bill; such bills are regarded differently from bills authorising the compulsory taking of an owner's land.

Owners, lessees, and occupiers of land which is proposed to be compulsorily taken by a bill are, by the practice of Parliament, entitled to a *locus standi* against the whole of the bill, and are not restricted to those portions which relate to the taking of their property (*London and North Western Railway Bill*, 1868, 1 C. & S. 62: *Bute Docks Bill*, 1890, R. & S. 14, 15: *Cork and Fermoy Railway Bill*, 1890, R. & S. 19, 20: *Great Western Railway Bill*, 1891, R. & S. 117, 120; *Cardiff Corporation Bill*, 1894, R. & S. 328, 330).

Thus, in the case first cited of *London and North Western Railway Bill*, 1868, 1 C. & S, 62, a case commonly known as the " post" case, when the counsel for the promoters asked, " Am I to understand that your decision goes to this extent: if a landowner has a post in a field at Preston and we take it, that he can be heard against all parts of an *omnibus* bill, one of which may be for stopping up a footway at Willesden ? "—the chairman, Mr. Dodson, M.P., replied, " If he is a landowner, we have no power to limit him," and one of the Referees (Mr. Rickards) added, " The landowner's post is his castle, and it admits to the whole extent of his petition and no further."

This case is usually regarded as the leading case upon the rights of landowners to be heard upon all parts of a

D

bill which proposes to take lands of theirs. These rights
are subject, of course, to the petition being so framed as to
shew the extent of the intended opposition, for the opposition may not travel out of the petition (*Thames Deep
Water Docks Bill*, 1882, 3 C. & R. 233).

The case of the *Rhymney Railway Bill*, 1890, R. & S.,
64, 67, affords an illustration of the extent of the right of
general opposition permitted to landowners. The bill was
one for the construction of certain separate short lines of
railway, one of which crossed a small plot of land belonging
to the petitioner; it was held that the petitioner was, as
owner, entitled to a general *locus standi* against the whole
bill. This right of general opposition by landowners whose
land it is proposed to take extends to lessees of all kinds,
and even to tenants at will liable to be ejected upon a
month's or other similar notice (*Caledonian Railway Bill*,
1870, 2 C & S. 37).

A railway company whose land it is proposed by a bill
to take compulsorily has the same right in regard to *locus
standi* as a private owner of land (*London and North
Western Railway Bill*, 1868, 1 C. & S. 62, known as "the
post case:" *Caledonian Railway Bill*, 1872, 2 C. & S. 256 ;
Ryde and Newport Railway Bill, 1872, 2 C. & S. 297, 298 ;
London and Eastbourne Railway Bill, 1883, 3 C. & R.
301, 302).

An owner of minerals proposed to be taken compulsorily
is an owner within the above rule (*Great Western Railway
Bill*, 1876, 1 C. & R. 221). A commoner having rights of
common is regarded as an owner. The general *locus standi*
allowed to owners is given, not only to the freeholder, but
to any person having a vested interest in the land proposed
to be taken (*Cardiff Corporation Bill*, 1894, R. & S. 328, 329).

Upon the petition of the magistrates, &c., of the Burgh
of Newton-upon-Ayr, it was held that a right in the petitioners to take gravel from fore-shore proposed by the bill
to be taken compulsorily entitled them to a *locus standi*

to oppose the bill (*Glasgow and South Western Railway Bill*, 1895, 1 S. & A. 15).

An owner of the subsoil of a public street is an owner within the above rule. Thus, where by a bill it was proposed to make a railway in a tunnel under certain streets in Glasgow, which by the Glasgow Police Act, 1866, were vested in the corporation, the owners of the subsoil were allowed a *locus* as owners against the bill, and were not limited to those portions of it specially affecting their rights to the subsoil (*Glasgow City and District Railway Bill*, 1882, 3 C. & R. 156).

Wherever the property of an owner or occupier is interfered with by the bill, the general rule is that he is entitled to oppose, and this applies to cases of substantial interference with rights of light, and even to such rights as those of a Telephone Company who have by the consent of the owners of lands or buildings placed their wires upon such lands or buildings (*Edinburgh Improvement Bill*, 1893, R. &. S. 259, 261; *South Eastern Railway Bill*, 1876, 1 C. & R. 258; *Midland Railway Bill*, 1890, R. & S. 213, 214). It must, however, be noted, that a mere injurious affection of land, where the land itself is not interfered with, and where the easements, such as the right to light, are not injured, does not in general give a right to oppose. Thus, nuisance from trains passing near the land of an owner, none of whose land is taken, or the loss of mere amenity, such as loss of view, gives no right to a *locus standi* (*London and North Western Railway Bill*, 1889, R. & M. 263; *Crystal Palace, &c., Railway Bill*, 1869, 1 C. & S. 45; *Metropolitan District Railway Bill*, 1881, 3 C. & R. 86). No right to a *locus standi* is given by the fact that the proposed works would depreciate the value of an owner's land (*West Highland Railway Bill*, 1889, R. & M. 309, 314).

Temporary occupation of lands by promoters for the purposes of their undertaking, under a bill incorporating

the Railways Clauses Acts which give compensation for
such occupation, does not afford to the landowner a ground
for a *locus standi* (*Dundee Harbour Bill*, 1869, 1 C. & S.
45, 46).

It is the general rule applicable to all classes of cases
before the Referees, that it is no answer to a petition to say
that the clause or portion of the bill objected to will be
struck out, and a landowner cannot be deprived of his
general *locus standi* by the promoter undertaking to strike
out of the bill the clauses affecting such landowner (*Neath
and Brecon Railway Bill*, 1867, 1 C. & S. 109; *Great
Eastern Railway Bill*, 1895, 1 S. & A. 19).

In the case of an extension of time bill, the original
bill has become an Act of Parliament, the propriety of the
compulsory taking of the land has become *res judicata*, and
the landowner, if he has received notice to treat in regard
to his land or has agreed to sell it, has become a creditor of
the company having a lien on the land until receipt of the
purchase money, and is no longer to be regarded, for the
purpose of *locus standi*, as an owner (*Uxbridge and Rick-
mansworth Railway Bill*, 1886, R. & M. 133; *St. Helens
District and Tramways Bill*, 1881, 3 C. & R. 94; *London
Riverside Fish Market Bill*, 1885, R. & M. 43). It would
seem correct to say that upon a mere extension of time bill
a *locus standi* is only given where there are special
grounds shown, and that neither owners whose land has
been taken or who have had notice to treat, nor persons
who, from proximity or otherwise, are affected by the proposed scheme are entitled to oppose where the bill is a mere
extension of time bill and there are no special circumstances (*Brymbo Water Bill*, 1896, 1 S. & A. 1, 3; *City and
South London Railway Bill*, 1896, 1 S. & A. 71; *London
Riverside Fish Market Bill*, 1885, R. & M. 43; *St. Helens
and District Tramways Bill*, 1881, 3 C. & R. 94).

Abandonment Bills are, in regard to *locus standi*,
treated upon similar lines with Extension of Time Bills. The

mere loss of the advantages that a landowner or other person would have derived if the purposes of the original Act had been carried through does not suffice to give a right to a *locus standi* (*Manchester, Sheffield and Lincolnshire Railway Bill*, 1881, 3 C. & R. 78; *Great Northern Railway Bill*, 1884, 3 C. and R. 399).

An instance of what has been considered as a special circumstance sufficient to entitle a landowner to a *locus standi* against a bill for extension of time is afforded by the *Brynno Water Bill*, 1896, 1 S. & A. 1, 5. In that case the landowner petitioning had agreed to certain terms of compensation on the footing of the works being completed within the time originally fixed, and it was not clear that under the bill he could claim any additional compensation for injury caused by the extension of time. In another case, where by a previous Act the promoters had power to make a weir across the Clyde and to maintain it until the completion of their waterworks, and they proposed by the bill, *inter alia*, to extend the time for completion of their waterworks and for the removal of the weir a *locus standi* was allowed to owners and occupiers of wharves, &c., on the banks above the weir, who alleged that the weir was a nuisance and an obstruction to the navigation and detrimental to their interests as such owners and occupiers, whilst at the same time a *locus standi* was not allowed to owners of factories to be supplied with water under the Act, because to these latter it was a mere extension of time bill (*Glasgow Corporation Water Bill*, 1873, 1 C. & R. 24, 25).

Upon an Abandonment Bill a landowner has been given a *locus standi* whose land had been taken and paid for under the powers of the Act where the Abandonment Bill contained a clause permitting the sale of such land without giving the landowner a right of pre-emption similar to that given on the sale by a railway company of its superfluous land (*West Lancashire Railway Bill*, 1879, 2 C. & R. 231.

Whilst on a bill to sanction the abandonment of a proposed line of railway the *locus standi* of an owner, some of whose land had been taken and paid for under the Act, was disallowed, although he complained that the leaving the land taken with partly finished works upon it would be an injury to the rest of his estate, the principle being, that the company, having bought and paid for the land taken, were, in the absence of special agreement with the landowner, under no legal liability to him to complete their works (*London, Brighton, and South Coast Railway Bill*, 1868, 1 C. & S. 18).

Where there has been a special agreement with the landowner he will be allowed a *locus standi* to oppose so far as may be necessary for the purpose of saving any legal rights he is entitled to under such agreement (*Great Northern Railway Bill*, 1884, 3 C. & R. 399).

Landowners whose land may be thereafter taken under an Act, and who have neither received notice to treat nor been settled with, have in many instances been allowed a *locus standi* to oppose bills for extension of time for compulsory purchase (*North Metropolitan Railway Bill*, 1870, 2 C. & S. 24 ; *Pontypridd, &c., Railway Bill*, 1885, R. & M. 59 ; *South Eastern Railway Bill*, 1885, R. & M. 67 ; *East and West Yorkshire Railway Bill*, 1886, R. & M. 98 ; *Drayton Junction Railway Bill*, 1867, 1 C. & S. 28). It would seem that the practice is to give them a general *locus standi* limited only by their petition (see *East and West Yorkshire Railway Bill*, *supra* ; *Great Western Railway Bill*, 1891, R. & S. 117).

Where proximity to works proposed by a bill is not in itself a ground for obtaining a *locus standi*, an owner or occupier of land in such proximity, none of whose land is proposed to be compulsorily taken, if he is given a *locus standi*, is given only a *limited locus standi*, as opposed to the *general locus standi* to which one whose land is proposed to be taken compulsorily would be entitled. It is limited, in general, to such portion of the bill (if any) as affects some special interest of his which appears entitled to be protected.

Diminution in value, for instance, that will be caused to an estate, none of which is taken, by the making of a railway near it, gives no right of *locus standi* to the owner or occupier (see *ante*, p. 39), but the obstruction or partial destruction of a right of access to business or other premises, where it is a serious and substantial injury to the premises, has been considered a sufficient ground for allowing a *locus standi* to the owners and occupiers of such premises against the portion of the bill relating thereto (*Lancashire and Yorkshire Railway Bill*, 1876, 1 C. & R. 235; *London and North-Western Railway Bill*, 1878, 2 C. & R. 119; *Hull, Barnsley and West Riding Junction Railway Bill*, 1880, 2 C. & R. 249; *Greenwich Dock and Railway Bill*, 1881, 3 C. & R. 60; *Lancashire and Yorkshire Railway Bill*, 1881, 3 C. & R. 70; *Manchester, Sheffield and Lincolnshire Railway Bill*, 1892, R. & S. 212). It is in these cases a question of degree, and if the injury is but slight, as, for instance, where one road only, out of several, to a school, was proposed to be interfered with by the bill, the *locus standi* was not allowed (*London, Tilbury and Southend Railway Bill*, 1882, 3 C. & R. 185, *Liverpool Corporation Bill*, 1886, R. & M. 112).

The injury in these cases must also be special, that is to say, it must be one affecting the interests of the petitioner in some way other and beyond the inconvenience which the public in general will suffer (*Stockton Curvs Railway Bill*, 1884, 3 C. & R. 466). Thus the *locus standi* of occupiers of a manufactory was disallowed where the obstruction would merely compel their workmen, like the rest of the public, to go by a longer route (*ib.*).

Trustees or owners of public hospitals in close proximity to proposed railways have been disallowed a

locus standi where they sought it upon the ground that
the working of the railways would seriously diminish the
utility of the hospital and injure the patients (*North
British Railway Bill*, 1877, 2 C. & R. 54; *London and
North-Western Railway Bill*, 1889, R. &. M. 263). In the
latter case, however, the Metropolitan Asylums District
Board, the petitioners, obtained a *locus standi* in the
House of Lords, and secured a clause containing provisions for their protection.

In another case, where it was proposed to take certain
land in a street in order to make therein shafts to ventilate
an underground railway which had been constructed under
statutory powers, a *locus standi* was conceded to the
road authority, but not to the owners or trustees of public
baths and washhouses in the street who petitioned against
the bill, alleging that the steam and smoke coming through
the shafts would seriously affect their premises, and create a
probable nuisance. The Court upon the hearing disallowed
the *locus standi* of the owners or trustees, holding that
they would suffer no special injury not shared by the
general public (*Metropolitan District Railway Bill*, 1881,
3 C. & R. 86).

The owner or occupier of a well or stream has, if it is
proposed to take it compulsorily, a landowner's right to an
unlimited *locus standi*, but it is no ground for a *locus
standi* that the effect of works proposed will be to withdraw, from a well or stream, underground water not in a
defined channel, which would otherwise find its way to
such well or stream by percolation (*Birkenhead Improvement Commissioners Bill*, 1867, 1 C. & S. 11; *Southport
Water Bill*, 1867, 1 C. & S. 13; *Tilbury and Gravesend
Tunnel Railway Bill*, 1882, 3 C. & R. 239; *Cambridge
Water Bill*, 1886, R. & M. 95, 98; *Ince Water Bill*, 1871,
2 C. & S. 199).

In underground water running in a defined channel
there is the same right as in surface streams, and the pre-

venting the flow of such water coming to a proprietor entitled to have such flow may give him a *locus standi* (*Chasemore* v. *Richards*, 7 H. L. C. 349 ; *Cambridge Water Bill, supra*).

It is sufficient for the person entitled to allege in his petition that he is so entitled, and to give upon the hearing, if it is contested, *primâ facie* evidence of his title, and of the fact that the water runs in a defined channel underground (*London and South-Western Spring Water Bill*, 1882, 3 C. & R. 179 ; *Croydon Corporation Bill*, 1884, 3 C. & R. 385 ; *West Gloucestershire Water Bill*, 1884, 3 C. & R. 477).

The important questions of *locus standi* which arise where it is sought to take water for the benefit of one district from an area claimed by the authorities or inhabitants of another district as the natural proper gathering ground for their supply, depend to a considerable extent upon the provisions of the Standing Orders which are treated of hereafter.

Bills for the extension of municipal boundaries, or the boundaries of counties, or local government districts, may be opposed by any owner of land proposed to be included who will be injured by new or increased rates or charges that may be imposed upon his land in consequence of its inclusion within the proposed area (*Sunderland Corporation Bill*, 1885, R. & M. 73, 76, 78 ; *Edinburgh Extension Bill*, 1896, 1 S. & A. 78).

So, too, an individual owner of land whose property would by the proposed bill be made liable to fresh sanitary regulations and additional burdens has a *locus standi* to oppose upon all portions of the bill to which the grounds of his complaint, as embodied in his petition, relate (*Hove Improvement Bill*, 1873, 1 C. & R. 30 ; *Edinburgh Municipal and Police Bill*, 1878, 2 C. & R. 149).

It has been said that an owner whose land may be depreciated by new rates holds the same position as one

whose land is taken, but his *locus standi* has in some cases
been limited to that portion of the bill which deals with
or imposes the new burden (*Walsall Gas Bill*, 1876,
1 C. & R. 273 ; *Belfast Improvement Bill*, 1878, 2 C. & R.
67 ; *Sunderland Corporation Bill*, 1885, R. & M. 73, 76, 78).

Where a bill deprives an owner of a substantial legal
right, the general rule is, that he should be given a *locus
standi*, though it may be limited to that part of the bill
which affects him, if none of his land is taken compulsorily.

Thus, where by a bill it was proposed to stop up a public
footpath which gave convenient access to neighbouring
villages from the petitioner's land, which but for the bill
could not be stopped up without an order of Quarter
Sessions, the making of which the petitioners could have
opposed, it was held that the petitioner was entitled to a
locus standi (*Bristol United Gas Bill*, 1877, 2 C. & R. 2).

Where a landowner had sold off a portion of a building
estate, subjecting it to certain restrictive covenants as to the
houses to be built, &c., for the mutual benefit of the various
purchasers, and for the benefit of the estate as a building
estate, and a railway company proposed by a bill to take
the land thus sold off and use it for stations, cottages, and
railway purposes not in conformity with the covenants, it
was held that the landowner, though he had sold off the
land intended to be taken, was entitled to a *locus standi* to
object to the proposal (*London and South Western Railway
Bill*, 1882, 3 C. & R. 175).

The petition against the bill or against certain clauses of
it is treated as the formal complaint against it. It must
set forth the title of the petitioner to complain and the
grounds of his complaint distinctly (see S. O. 128, *post*,
p. 129). Where the petitioner claims a *locus standi* as
owner or occupier, the petition must state specifically or
show clearly that he is owner or occupier of the property
to be interfered with (*Thames Deep Water Dock Railway
Bill*, 1882, 3 C. & R. 233).

If the promoters intend to dispute an allegation in a petition, as, for instance, an allegation that the petitioner is owner of land proposed to be taken, they must in their objections specifically deny the allegation (*Furness Railway Bill*, 1876, 1 C. & R. 217). If the promoters desire to deny the title alleged, they must deny it specifically in their objections, and then the petitioner will have to give before the Referees *prima facie* evidence of it. It is not necessary that title deeds should be produced or that strict legal proof of title should be given. Where title is thus denied the court does not try title, but merely requires to know with some degree of precision the real nature of the interest of the party who claims a *locus standi* (*Ely and Clydach Valley Railway Bill*, 1873, 1 C. & R. 18 : *Glasgow Street Improvement Bill*, 1875, 1 C. & R. 158, 159 : *Belfast Improvement Bill*, 1878, 2 C. & R. 69, 70 : *Hundred of Hoo Railway Bill*, 1880, 2 C. & R. 258). The practice is the same as to all material allegations in petitions (*Woolwich and Plumstead Tramways Order Bill*, 1880, 2 C. & R. 321, 323).

A frequent ground of opposition is that of "competition." By S. O. 130 the Referees, if they think fit, may allow a *locus standi* upon this ground. Although it is in each case matter for the discretion of the Referees, the general principles upon which cases of this class are dealt with have become to a considerable extent fixed by the decisions which have been given.

Thus, a *locus standi* is not given upon the ground of competition where the competition anticipated is merely an improvement of competition already created by existing legislation (*Northwich Local Board Water Bill*, 1885, R. & M. 57 ; *Mersey Railway Bill*, 1886, R. & M. 118 ; *Manchester, Sheffield and Lincolnshire Railway Company (Steamboats) Bill*, 1889, R. & M. 270, 275 ; *East Stonehouse Water Bill*, 1893, R. & S. 246). But it may be given where it is competition of a new character. For instance, where there has been competition merely in goods traffic or local passenger traffic, a *locus standi* might be allowed against a bill which would create competition in through passenger traffic (*Bedford and Peterborough Railway Bill,* 1886, R. & M. 87).

A *locus standi* on the ground of competition has, amongst other cases, been allowed in the following :—

(1.) To steamboat proprietors against railway companies applying for special powers to own and work steamboats (*Clyde, &c., Railway Bill,* 1889, R. & M. 143, 144 ; *Cambrian Railway Bill,* 1889, R. & M. 243 ; *Glasgow Railway Bill,* 1891, R. & S. 115).

(2.) To omnibus companies or proprietors against Tramway Bills (*Woolwich and Plumstead Tramways Order Bill,* 1880, 2 C. & R, 321, 322).

(3.) To owners of ferries against bills for erecting bridges which would interfere with the ferries (*Cork and Fermoy Railway Bill,* 1890, R. & S., 23).

(4.) To gas companies against bills promoted by municipal corporations for electric lighting, and against new gas companies seeking to place mains in and supply gas to their districts (*Hull Lighting Bill,* 1880, 2 C. & R. 251 ; *Westgate, &c., Gas Bill,* 1879, 2 C. & R. 229).

(5.) To owners of slaughter houses against a bill by a municipal corporation to erect a slaughter house.

(6.) To water companies against a bill for supplying sea water within their districts for watering the streets and for other purposes (*London Sea Water Supply Bill,* 1881, 3 C. & R. 75).

(7.) To a steam tramway against a railway (see *Sutton and Willoughby Railway Bill,* 1884, 3 C. & R. 441).

(8.) To an ordinary railway company against a light railway (*Elham Valley Light Railway Bill,* 1880. 2 C. & R. 240).

(9) To canal companies against railway companies *Stourbridge Railway Bill*, 1885, R. & M. 72).

It has been refused in the following cases :—

(1.) To railway companies against street tramways (see *London Street Tramways Bill*, 1870, 2 C. & S. 85 : *Tramways Orders Confirmation (London Street Tramways) Bill*, 1871, 2 C. & S. 199 : *Glasgow Tramways Bill*, 1872, 2 C. & S. 282 : *Woolwich and Plumstead Orders Bill*, 1880, 2 C. & R. 321)

(2.) To the owners of a hotel against a bill by a railway company containing powers to enable the company to build and maintain a hotel in proximity to that of the petitioners (*Caledonian Railway Bill*, 1881, 3 C. & R. 23, 25).

(3.) To carriage and engine builders against a bill by a railway company to enable them to make their own carriages and engines (*North British Railway Bill*, 1877, 2 C. & R. 50).

(4.) To manufacturers of gas and water fittings against bills by gas or water companies to enable them to supply fittings (*Bolton Improvement Bill*, 1882, 3 C. & R. 131).

(5.) Cab proprietors against tramways (*Woolwich and Plumstead Tramways Orders Bill*, 1880, 2 C. & R. 321).

A *locus standi* is given, on the ground of competition, only where there appears to be a substantial competition, and in cases of this class the question is generally one as to the amount of competition (*Swindon, Marlborough and Andover Railway Bill*, 1883, 3 C. & R. 348).

The *locus standi*, if allowed, is not necessarily allowed against the whole bill, but may be limited to so much of the preamble and clauses as relates to the competition (see *Swindon, Marlborough, &c., Bill, supra ; Great Eastern Railway Bill*, 1872, 2 C. & S. 231).

Where competition is relied on, the petition must allege
the fact of competition, or else it must contain statements
from which it is clearly to be inferred that the petitioner
relies on competition, and must in the same way by distinct
averment or necessary implication show that the interests
of the petitioner are injuriously affected by the competition (see *King's Cross Subway Bill*, 1885, R. & M. 32:
Worcester and Broom Railway Bill, 1889, R. & M. 315,
316; *Harrow, &c., Railway Bill*, 1887, R. & M. 159).

S. O. 131, 132 (*post*, pp. 129, 130) deal with the cases in
which shareholders in incorporated companies are to be
allowed a *locus standi* against bills promoted by the companies in which they hold shares, and are not to be disallowed a *locus standi* by the application of the general
principle that corporations are bound by the action of their
corporation and should not be heard against the corporate
seal, a principle which practically means that the minority
are bound by the action of the majority.   By S. O. 131
shareholders are not be heard against bills promoted by
their companies unless their interests as affected are distinct
from the general interests of the company, and by S. O. 132
any shareholders who have dissented at a meeting of the
company (called as required by S. O. 62–66) are to be permitted to be heard.

Reading these two orders together, the result would
seem to be, that shareholders whose interests affected are
distinct from the general interests of the company, and who
have dissented at a meeting as required, have an absolute
right, if their petition is in proper form, to be heard upon
so much of the bill as affects such interests of theirs (see
Liverpool Tramway Bill, 1880, 2 C. & R., 273), that shareholders whose interests are thus distinct may, if the court
thinks fit, be allowed a *locus standi* even if they have not
dissented as required (see *Milford Docks Bill*, 1884, 3 C. &
R. 446), that shareholders whose interests are not thus distinct, but who have dissented at a meeting as required, are

probably entitled to a *locus* just as much as if their interests had been distinct from the general interests of their companies (see *Liverpool Tramway Bill*, 1880, 2 C. & R. 273, 275; *Electric Lighting Orders Bill*, 1890, R. & S. 26, 27, 28).

S. O. 131 expresses the general rule that a dissentient shareholder is not to be heard unless he has a distinct interest, and the S. O. 132 makes an exception in the case of companies within S. O. 62 and the Standing Orders immediately following (*Electric Lighting Orders Bill*, 1890, R. & S. 26, 27).

By S. O. 133 (*post*, p. 130) where a railway bill contains provisions for taking or using any part of the lands, &c., of another company, or for running upon or across the same, or for other facilities such company is to be heard upon their petition against such provisions or against the preamble and clauses of the bill.

This Standing Order would seem to permit the court in the cases within it to exercise its discretion as to whether the *locus standi* should be unlimited, or whether it should be limited to the provisions of the bill which fall within the words of the Order (*East and West Yorkshire Railways Bill*, 1882, 3 C. & R. 142; *Bridgewater Railway Bill*, 1886, R. & M. 89; *Great Western Railway Bill*, 1889, R. & M. 252; *Forfar and Brechin Railway Bill*, 1891, R. & S. 108, 110).

Where, by a railway bill, running powers or other similar facilities, or a right to cross over its lines are to be acquired compulsorily against another railway company, and there is no compulsory acquisition of the land of that other company, it would seem that in general the *locus standi* allowed will be a limited one (*Rotherham, &c., Railway Bill*, 1891, R. & S. 152; *Forfar and Brechin Railway Bill*, *supra*), but if land is to be permanently taken the company will, if its petition claims a *locus standi* as owner be granted an unlimited *locus* as landowner (see *ante*, p. 36; and *Devon and Cornwall Railway Bill*, 1882, 3 C. & R., 136 ; *Bridgewater Railway Bill*, 1886, R. & M. 89).

By S. O. 133A (*post*, p. 130) passed in 1883, the Referees, if they think fit, may allow a *locus standi* against the bill to Chambers of Commerce or Agriculture, or other similar body, sufficiently representing any trade or business in any district to which the bill relates, if in the petition it is alleged that such trade or business will be injuriously affected by the rates and fares proposed to be authorised by the bill, or is so affected by rates and fares already authorised by Acts relating to the railway undertaking, or against any portion of the bill, or against the rates and fares authorised by such Acts, or any of them, subject to the proviso that the Referees are not by this Order authorised to entertain any question within the jurisdiction of the Railway Commissioners.

This order appears to be intended to give protection in cases where, by the bill, rates and fares will be enforceable which will injuriously affect any trade or business in the district, and to require an allegation to that effect in the petition (see *Metropolitan District Railway Bill*, 1895, 1 S. & A. 123 : *Wrexham Railway Bill*, 1888, R. & M. 231 : *Great Western and Cornwall Railways Bill*, 1889, R. & M. 255, 258).

S. O. 133 B. (*post*, p. 130), passed in 1895, gives a further power of allowing a *locus standi* to Chambers of Commerce, &c., extending the right to bills injuriously affecting agriculture, trade, mining, or commerce in the district, but, following the previous Order, the body petitioning must sufficiently represent the agriculture, trade, mining, or commerce of the district, and there must be an allegation in the petition that such agriculture, trade, mining or commerce, will be injuriously affected by the provisions in the bill.

In 1889 the Chamber of Commerce of Hull, composed of shipowners of Hull and the neighbouring port of Goole,

instituted to look after the shipping trade and commercial
interests of Hull, were admitted to oppose a bill to
empower a railway company to own and run steamboats
between Grimsby and a number of ports in Sweden,
Norway and the Baltic, to which the shipowners traded
largely (*Manchester, Sheffield and Lincolnshire Railway
Company (Steamboats) Bill*, 1889, R. & M. 270; and see
S. O. 156, *post*, p. 135).

In 1892, where individual shipowners directly interested
were going to be heard the *locus standi* of two Associations, the Steamship Owners Association and the Irish
Steamship Association, composed largely of firms who had
no steamers trading between the ports named in the bill or
contiguous thereto, and no interest in the trade to be
accommodated under the bill was disallowed against a bill
to give a railway company power to provide and run
steamboats between certain named ports in England and
Ireland. The matter was one for the discretion of the
Referees, and they appear to have thought that the Associations were not sufficiently interested in the particular
trade which was fully represented by the individual owners
(*Lancashire and Yorkshire Railway (Steam Vessels) Bill*,
1892, R. & S. 199). This decision was founded a good
deal upon a former decision in the similar case of the
Glasgow and South-Western (Steam Vessels) Bill, 1891,
R. & S., 115, where owners directly interested were opposing, and the Steamship Owners Association represented
steam shipping in general rather than the particular trade
as required by S. O. 133A.

In 1892 an Association of South Yorkshire Coal Owners
were allowed a *locus standi* against bills to amalgamate
the Hull Docks Company with the North-Eastern Railway
Company's undertaking (*North-Eastern Railway (Hull
Docks) Bill, and North-Eastern Railway Bill*, 1892, R. & S.
217). It may, however, be observed that this Association
represented the particular coal trade, and also that on

E

Amalgamation Bills there is a practice of allowing, as far as practicable, all interested to be heard (see *post*, p. 61).

S. O. 134 (*post*, p. 130) permits a *locus standi* to be allowed, if the Referees think fit, to municipal or other local authorities having the management of the Metropolis or of any town, or to the inhabitants of any town or district alleged to be injuriously affected by a bill.

No definition of the meaning of "district" in the above S. O. is given, but it has been held that it is not restricted to local government districts, and may include any definite locality having tangible limits, and might, it would seem, be even satisfied by an area of definite extent in proximity to proposed works or to a proposed railway (see *Grand Junction Canal Bill*, 1879, 2 C. & R. 165; *Manchester, Sheffield and Lincolnshire Railway Bill*, 1891, R. & S. 133, 135; *London Tramways (Extension) Bill*, 1889, R. & M. 268).

The area of a Rural District Council may be a "district" within this Order or S. O. 134A (*Bilston Improvement Bill*, 1896, 1 S. & A. 42).

The expression, "the inhabitants," in this Order, does not mean necessarily the whole or even a majority of the inhabitants, it is held to be satisfied by a petition signed by a sufficient body of them to be fairly representative of the town or district, but not if the signatories are an insignificant minority in no way representative of the locality. Thus a petition signed by 950 only out of 270,000 inhabitants was rejected as not sufficiently representative, where the local authorities had petitioned, and there was no reason for supposing that they did not adequately represent the interests of the inhabitants (*Tottenham and Forest Gate Railway Bill*, 1890, R. & S. 72).

The object of S. O. 134 is the protection of the public, and the Court of Referees in deciding upon *locus standi* under it, will consider whether the interest claiming to be heard is so abundantly represented as to make further representation unnecessary (*Manchester Ship Canal Bill*, 1885, R. & M. 49).

A *locus standi* will not be allowed under S. O. 134, if the petition contains no allegation that the town or district is injuriously affected by the bill; but the precise expression "injuriously affected" need not be used, if in some equivalent language a statement to the effect that the town or district is thus injured is made in the petition; the safer course is, however, to follow the precise language of the order in framing the petition (*Isle of Wight and Cowes Railway Bill*, 1871, 2 C. & S. 211, 213; *South London Gas Bill*, 1872, 2 C. & S. 218: *Lambeth Water Bill*, 1883, 3 C. & R. 292; *Lea Valley Drainage Bill*, 1892, R. & S. 202).

Under the above Order (S. O. 134) the Corporation of Birmingham were allowed to oppose bills dealing with the gun trade, a staple industry of that town (*Birmingham Proof House Bill*, 1868, 1 C. & S. 125; *Gun Barrel Proof Bill*, 1868, 1 C. & S. 136), and in the case of a bill to transfer the undertaking of the Shoreham Waterworks to the Corporation of Brighton, a *locus standi* was allowed under it to the Corporation of Worthing upon the ground that their town was injuriously affected by the powers in the bill enabling the Corporation of Brighton to use in Brighton, if they thought fit, any surplus water not required for Shoreham, which the petitioners alleged would affect a natural watershed from which they might otherwise have procured in the future water for Worthing (*Brighton Corporation Water Bill*, 1896, 1 S. & A. 47). It may be noticed that the bill was not a " Water Bill " within S. O. 134A.

A local authority will be allowed a *locus standi* against a bill or clause enabling a neighbouring authority to purchase and work tramways within its district (*Edinburgh Improvement and Tramways Bill*, 1896, 1 S. & A. 82).

The Corporation of Inverness were allowed a *locus standi* against a bill to construct a railway to compete with the existing railway to that place, upon an allegation that the prosperity of the town of Inverness was largely dependent on the existing railway, and that anything affecting its interests prejudicially, must prejudice those of the town (*Great North of Scotland Railway Bill*, 1890, R. & S. 34).

Upon mere extension of time bills public authorities are not allowed to oppose, any more than private individuals, with a view to alter past legislation (*London Riverside Fish Market (Extension of Time) Bill*, 1885, R. & M. 43); but where a local authority alleged in their petition that the proposed extension of time for making a railway, which interfered with several highways in their district, would prevent them from dealing with their sewers, roads, &c., and that the development of their district would be retarded, and improvements postponed, a *locus standi* was allowed them to oppose the extension of time (*London and South-Western, and Metropolitan District Railway Cos. Bill*, 1884, 3 C. & R. 422).

By S. O. 134A (*post*, p. 131), the municipal or other local authority of any town or district alleging in their petition that their town or district may be injuriously affected by the provisions of any bill relating to the lighting or water supply of their area, or the raising of capital for such purpose is entitled to be heard against such bill. This order is mandatory (*Bradford Corporation Water Bill*, 1892, R. & S. 169; *Bilston Improvement Bill*, 1896, 1 S. & A. 42, 44). It is mandatory to the extent of entitling petitioners to a *locus standi* against the provisions in the bill relating to the lighting or supply of their town or district which may injuriously affect their town or district (see *Birmingham (Consolidation) Bill*, 1883, 3 C. & R. 257). The petitioners must allege that their town or district may be injuriously affected by the provisions of the bill (*Lambeth Water Bill*, 1883, 3 C. & R. 292 ; *Worthing Gas Bill*, 1875, 1 C. & R. 201).

By S. O. 134B (*post*, p. 131), County Councils may be admitted to oppose if they allege in their petition that the whole or some part of their area is injuriously affected by the bill.

This order is not mandatory, it will be observed, in its terms, and it will also be noticed that the petition must allege, like the previous orders, injurious affection.

By S. O. 134C (*post*, p. 131), County Councils, making the allegation in their petitions as to injurious affection required by that Order, have a right to be heard against bills relating to the water supply of any town or district, whether within or without their county.

This Order would seem to be mandatory to the extent of entitling a County Council, upon its allegation in regard to a bill relating to the water supply of any town or district that its provisions in regard to that matter may injuriously affect their county, or some part of it, to a *locus standi* against those provisions.

In the case of *Falkirk Water Bill*, 1896, 1 S. & A. 85, 89, it was held that this Order did not entitle a local authority to oppose upon the ground that the promoters did not include a certain district within the limits for compulsory supply of water.

By S. O. 135 (*post*, p. 131), the owner, lessee, or occupier of any house, shop, or warehouse in a " street " through which it is proposed to construct a tramway, and who alleges in his petition against a bill or provisional order that the construction or use of the tramway will injuriously affect him in the use or enjoyment of his premises, or in the conduct of his trade or business, is entitled to be heard on such allegations.

The word " street " in this Order may include a continuous line of suburban villas with gardens in front, but it has been held not to cover the case of a hundred houses scattered over a mile and a half of road (see *Lea Bridge, Leyton and Walthamstow Tramways Bill*, 1881, 3 C. & R. 73: *London South District Tramways Order*, 1882, 3 C. & R. 242).

It has been held to include a thoroughfare with continuous houses on one side, and on the other only a sea wall (*Edinburgh Northern Tramways Bill*, 1884, 3 C. & R. 397). It has also been held to include a village street or road through a country village (*Tramways Order Confirmation (Somerton, &c.), No. 2, Bill*, 1893, R. & S. 310; and see *Brentford and District Tramways Bill*, 1885, R. & M. 8).

S. O. 135 is not limited to owners, &c., whose houses, shops, or manufactories actually open on to the road. It is enough if their yard, or road, or means of access opens on to it (*North Metropolitan Tramways Bill*, 1886, R. & M. 125, 126: *Clyde, &c., Railway Bill*, 1887, R. & M. 145).

The effect of it is, to confer a *locus* limited to such of the allegations in the petition as show that the construction or use of the tramway would injuriously affect the petitioners individually in the use or enjoyment of their premises, or in the conduct of their trade or business, and it does not extend to permit them to raise mere general objections to tramways. They are not, however, confined to showing that the front of their particular premises will be obstructed, but may show that higher up the street, for instance, the tramway will so contract the street as to prevent carriages going up to their premises or shops (*King's Cross and City Tramways Bill*, 1878, 2 C. & R. 106).

The petition must state that the petitioners are injuriously affected, and should show in what way this is so.

Consumers of water and gas, as a class, and as individuals, are in general allowed to oppose water and gas bills affecting them injuriously, and that notwithstanding that the corporation of their town, or local authority of their district has obtained a *locus standi* (*Walton-on-Thames Gas Bill*, 1887, R. & M. 191 ; *South London Gas Bill*, 1872, 2 C. & S. 220 ; *Pontypool Gas and Water Bill*, 1893, 1 C. & R. 51 ; *Alliance Gas Bill*, 1871, 2 C. & S. 176 ; *Basingstoke Gas Bill*, 1887, R. & M. 137 ; *Partick Gas and Electricity Bill*, 1890, R. & S. 53). But petitioners who were merely affected in common with the ratepayers of the town in general have been disallowed a *locus standi* against a bill promoted by the corporation of their town to acquire the water supply of the district (*Birmingham Water Bill*, 1875, 1 C. & R. 144).

Where a local authority elected by the ratepayers is proposing by a bill to do anything affecting their district, it is a general rule that ratepayers, as such, have no *locus standi* to oppose, but they may be allowed a *locus* as owners (*Hornsey Local Board Bill*, 1893, R. & S. 276, 278 ; *St. Andrews Links Bill*, 1894, R. & S. 349, 353 ; *Hove Improvement Bill*, 1873, 1 C. & R. 30). The doctrine of representation applies to ratepayers and not to owners (*Huddersfield Water, &c., Bill*, 1876, 1 C. & R. 229).

Traders, freighters, and others, injuriously affected by the tolls, rates, or other provisions of bills have in numerous instances been permitted a *locus standi* against the bills, or so much thereof as injuriously affected them, when petitioning as a class, and, where their interests seemed of sufficient importance, when petitioning as individuals ; Indeed, a *locus standi* has been granted upon a petition signed by one of such persons alone (*Lancashire and Yorkshire Railway (Steam Vessels) Bill*, 1892, R. & S. 199 ; *Manchester, Sheffield and Lincolnshire Railway (Steamboats) Bill*, 1889, R. & M. 271 ; *London and North-Western, &c., Railway Bill*, 1877, 2 C. & R. 34.)

Persons in the position of traders, freighters, or ship-owners will not usually be regarded as so represented in their special interests by the corporation of their town, or other public authority, as to be refused a *locus standi* upon

the ground that they are sufficiently represented by such
corporation or authority (see *Glasgow and South-
Western Railway Bill*, 1895, 1 S. & A. 9, 11; and *Manchester, Sheffield and Lincolnshire Railway Bill*, 1892,
R. & S. 212, 213). See further S. O. 133A, *post*, p. 130.

S. O. 14 (*post*, p. 92) requires notice of the application
for the bill to be given to all owners, lessees, and occupiers of
mills, manufactories, or other works using the waters of
the stream for a distance of twenty miles, or, if that is less,
to where it falls into a navigable river, below the point of
abstraction in the case of any bill for abstracting water
from a stream for the purpose of supplying any cut, canal,
reservoir, aqueduct, navigation or waterwork.

S. O. 15 (*post*, p. 92) makes similar provision for burial
ground, gas, sewage, and infectious hospital bills requiring
notices of the application for such bills to be given to all
owners, lessees, and occupiers within 300 yards of the burial
ground, hospital works, &c. These provisions resemble
those of S. O. 11, 14 (*post*, pp. 91, 92) in regard to notices to
owners, lessees, and occupiers of land proposed to be taken
compulsorily, and to frontagers on streets where it is proposed to lay tramways; and it would appear that persons
entitled to notice under S. O. 14 or 15 will, on a petition
showing that they are injuriously affected by provisions in
the bill, be entitled to be heard against them, and that
others even beyond the prescribed limits, and who consequently are not entitled to notice under these orders, who
have been so injuriously affected have been, in some cases,
given a *locus standi* (*Local Government Provisional
Order (No. 23) Confirmation Bill*, 1896, 1 S. & A. 116,
119).

S. O. 17 (*post*, p. 93,) requires notice of the application
for a bill repealing or altering statutory provisions for the
protection of the owner, lessee, or occupier of any property,
or for the protection or benefit of any public trustees or
commissioners, corporation, or person, specifically men-

tioned in such provision, to be served upon every such owner, lessee, or occupier, public trustees, or commissioners, corporation or person. The effect of this is that the persons thus entitled to notice are allowed a *locus standi* against the portion of the bill which thus proposes to affect them, and that even persons or bodies not specifically mentioned are in general allowed a similar *locus standi* where the statutory provision was one for their protection or benefit (*Croydon Corporation Bill*, 1896, 1 S. & A. 5). In the case last cited a waterworks company were given a *locus standi* on a bill which proposed to repeal a clause for their protection in which they were not specifically named.

A *locus standi* is somewhat more readily given on an amalgamation bill than in most other cases, though the general principles applicable are not departed from. This is in consequence of the recommendation contained in the report of the Committee of both Houses of 1872, that special latitude should be given to traders to appear against railway amalgamation bills which injuriously affected their interests. Following this recommendation, upon the *London and North-Western, and Whitehaven, &c., Railway Bill*, 1877, 2 C. & R. 34; the court allowed (1) ironmasters, traders, and freighters of Westmoreland, (2) iron ore smelters, mineral proprietors, and other traders in Cumberland to oppose the bill which would put an end to competition between the amalgamating companies (see also *Highland Railway Bill*, 1884, 3 C. & R. 404; *Ayr Harbour Bill*, 1890, R. & S. 5; *North-Eastern Railway (Hull Docks) Bill*, 1892, R. & S. 217: *Great Western and Midland Railways Bill*, 1894, R. & S. 334).

When a road is proposed to be interfered with, a body which has merely a statutory easement in it, as, for instance, a right to lay pipes therein, does get, not an unlimited *locus standi* as though they were owners, but merely a limited *locus* to oppose the bill so far as it

authorises interference with their pipes or easement
(*Hindley Local Board Bill*, 1878, 2 C. & S. 229).

Where it is proposed by a bill to remove a market or
interfere with it, either permanently or temporarily, a
locus standi has been granted to individual traders carrying on business therein (*Metropolitan and Metropolitan
District Railway Companies Bill*, 1879, 2 C. & R. 190;
North Metropolitan Tramways Bill, 1870, 2 C. & S. 90.)

Where a bill authorises a railway company to destroy
houses so that there will be caused a substantial loss of
rates, a *locus standi* is given to the rating authority (see
S. O. 134; *Metropolitan, &c., Railway Bill*, 1879. 2 C. & R.
201; *Manchester, Sheffield and Lincolnshire Railway Bill*,
1894, R. & S. 341), but not where the loss is not substantial
in amount (*South-Eastern Railway Bill*, 1888, R. & M.
227; *London and North-Western Railway Bill*, 1887,
R. & M. 173).

A loss of £800 a year has been held to be a substantial
loss where the rates of the whole area were very large
(*South-Eastern Railway B ll*, 1890, R. & S. 68.)

The general practice is to require the petitions of corporate bodies to be sealed with their corporate seal where
they have one, but petitions, though not thus sealed, have
been considered sufficient when signed by the chairman,
secretary, or other officer of the corporate body on behalf
of the corporation, where it was proved that they were
authorised so to sign by a resolution of the board, or by
some other sufficient authority (*Dunkinfield Local Boards
Bill*, 1877, 2 C. & R. 9; *Maryport and Carlisle Railway
Bill*, 1883, 3 C. & R. 316, 318).

It has been already noted that a corporator, as such, is,
as a general rule, treated as bound by the seal, that is, by
act of the proper majority; and the rights of dissentient
shareholders have been already referred to; but an instance
may be usefully cited of the practical application of the
general rule. Thus, where it was proposed by a bill to

alter the constitution of a harbour commission, a commissioner petitioning alone was refused a *locus standi* in that capacity, because the commission had by an agreement come to with the promoters agreed with the promoters on the proposal, and the petitioner was allowed a *locus* as owner, only against that portion of the bill which related to the extension of the borough so as to include his property (*Newport Corporation Bill*, 1889, R. & M. 288).

Where Parish Councils have no power to oppose at the charge of the rates bills for altering their boundaries, it would seem that the County Council may obtain a *locus standi* as representing them (*Edinburgh Extension Bill*, 1896, 1 S. & A. 72, and see S. O. 134, 13). Ratepayers as well as owners may be allowed to object to being placed under a new rating authority (*Sunderland Corporation Bill*, 1885, R. & M. 77).

Before the Court of Referees, the petitioners begin, and then the promoters bring forward their objections. The paragraphs in the petition are numbered, and the grounds of objection are likewise numbered, each ground being separately and distinctly, as far as practicable, stated and numbered.

The Court can rehear a petition, and will do so, if it is shown that the decision was come to under a misapprehension (*Southampton Harbour Bill*, 1882, C. & R. 277.)

Estate bills deal only with the rights of parties named in them, and consequently parties not named are not, it is said, given a *locus standi* to oppose in the House of Commons (*Leeds Coloured Cloth Hall Estate Bill*, 1885, R. & M. 38).

CHAPTER VIII.

House of Lords.

THE House of Lords treats a local bill in a slightly different manner according to whether it has come from the Commons or whether by arrangement between the chairmen of both Houses it is first to be considered in the House of Lords.[1] In the former case, as has already been stated, the bill is sent to the Lords with a message: in the latter it is presented to the House by one of the Lords, no petition for leave to bring in the bill being necessary where one has been presented to the Commons.[2] In either case, the bill is read a first time after the certificate of the Examiner has been laid on the table of the House, and that whether the Examiner has certified that the Standing Orders have, or that they have not been complied with. The first reading, if the bill originates in the Lords, must not be later than three clear days after such certificate has been laid on the table.[3] It has been already pointed out [4] that the Examiners examine as to compliance with Standing Orders, 3–59, of both Houses (which are practically identical) simultaneously, before the introduction of the bill into either House, and the proceedings before the

---

[1] S. O. 79. *post*, p. 121 ; and see *ante*, p. 8.
[2] S. O., H. L., 86.
[3] S. O., H. L., 86, A.
[4] *Ante*, p. 11.

Standing Orders Committee of the Lords upon the Examiner's certificate have been described.([1]) In the Lords, as in the Commons, compliance must be shown with certain other Standing Orders in the case of bills promoted by companies before the second reading.([2]) Other orders apply specially to bills brought from the Commons,([3]) and no such bill is to be read a second time until the Examiner has certified whether any further Standing Orders are applicable, and, if so, whether or not they have been complied with.([4]) Before a charity bill is read a second time, the House must have received a report from the Attorney-General,([5]) and before a bill which may increase railway rates can be read a second time the Board of Trade must have reported.([6]) The time for the second reading of a local bill is fixed by the Standing Orders,([7]) or by Sessional Orders passed from time to time.([8])

If the bill has originated in the Lords, petitions praying to be heard against it must be deposited in the Private Bill Office before three o'clock in the afternoon on or before the seventh day after the second reading; ([9]) if the bill is one which has been brought from the Commons, petitions must be deposited not later than the same period after the first reading.([10]) The Chairman of Committees may report that an unopposed bill should be treated as an opposed bill.([11]) An opposed local bill is referred to a Select Committee nominated by the Committee of Selection : ([12]) unopposed bills are considered by the Chairman of Committees, practically alone save for the assistance of his counsel.([13]) Petitions praying to be heard against a bill must be printed and copies deposited in the Parliament Office at such time

([1]) Ante. p. 15.

([2]) S. O., H. L., 62-68.

([3]) S. O., H. L., 60-61.

([4]) S. O., H. L., 87.

([5]) S. O., H. L., 89.

([6]) S. O., H. L., 90.

([7]) S. O.. H. L., 91.

([8]) 127 L. J., 88, e.g.

([9]) S. O., H. L., 92.

([10]) S. O., H. L., 93.

([11]) S. O., H. L., 95.

([12]) S. O., H. L., 96, 97.

([13]) May, p. 801 ; S. O., H. L., 102.

and in such numbers as the Chairman of Committees may direct.([1])

The functions of the committee on the bill are similar to those in the Commons, with this important exception, that questions of *locus standi* which the House of Commons has delegated to the Court of Referees are still determined by the Lords' Committees, whose decision may be, and sometimes, though rarely, is, different from that of the Referees. After the Committee have considered the bill, they report to the House, and in this and in the subsequent proceedings no very material difference exists between the practice in the two Houses.

Provision is made by the Standing Orders for shareholders in companies, &c., who have dissented at a meeting called in pursuance of the Standing Orders, being given a *locus standi* to oppose.([2]) And provision is also made by Standing Orders, very similar to those of the other House for permitting in certain cases Chambers of Commerce or Agriculture, Shipping, Mining or Miners' Associations, and Councils of Administrative Counties or Boroughs to oppose.([3]) As to estate, divorce, naturalization and name bills, see " PERSONAL BILLS," *post*, p. 68.

([1]) 97 L. J., 26, Resolution of Lords.

([2]) S. O., H. L., 105, which is identical with S. O., 132, of the House of Commons, which see *post*, p. 130.

([3]) S. O , H. L. 105 A, B and C; and see S. O. 133 A and B, 134, 134 A, B, and C of the House of Commons, *post*, pp. 130, 131; and LOCUS STANDI, *ante*, pp. 52 57.

CHAPTER IX.

Personal Bills.

PERSONAL bills,(¹) though before the passing of the Settled Land Acts, the Divorce Act, and the Naturalization Act, very frequent, are now of rare occurrence. They are introduced, as has been stated,(²) in the House of Lords, and upon a petition, with a printed copy of the bill annexed.(³) The formal parts of the petition are similar to those of petitions for other private bills in the House of Commons,(⁴) except that the petition is addressed to the Right Honourable the Lords Spiritual and Temporal in Parliament assembled. One or more of the parties principally concerned in the consequences of the bill must sign the petition,(⁵) and a copy of the bill must be delivered to every person concerned in the bill before the second reading ; (⁶) but, where necessary, upon petition or application for the purpose, leave may be given to dispense with personal service, and an order for substituted service made by the House.(⁷) Certain of the Standing Orders of the House of Lords, with reference to local bills, are, so far as applicable, directed to be observed in reference to personal bills also,(⁸) and, in addition, Part V. of the Standing Orders is exclusively devoted to them.

(¹) See *ante*, p. 6.
(²) See *ante*, p. 6.
(³) S. O. H. L. 150.
(⁴) See *ante*, p. 9.
(⁵) S. O. H. L. 151.

(⁶) S. O. H. L. 152.
(⁷) See *Gifford's Divorce Bill*, L. R. 12, App. Cas. 361 : *Joynt's Divorce Bill*, L. R. 13 App. Cas. 741.
(⁸) S. O. H. L. 181.

Petitions for estate bills are, on presentation to the House of Lords, referred to two Judges for their opinion,([1]) and no such bill is read a first time until the Chairman of Committees has received a copy of their report.([2]) Notice of the bill is required to be given to every mortgagee upon the estate affected, before the second reading.([3])

The committee on an estate bill do not sit until ten days after the second reading.([4]) Estate bills are not generally opposed, but provision is made for the presentation of petitions in opposition, according to the directions of the Chairman of Committees on each particular case.([5])

The committee and subsequent stages are similar to those in the case of local bills, and are governed by the same rules, so far as they are applicable;([6]) and, in addition, provision has been made with regard to the contents of the bill, consents and acceptance of trusts.([7]) The committee may admit affidavits in proof of the allegations made in the preamble.([8]) In the Commons, estate bills pass through the House in much the same way as other private bills, except that there need be only three days instead of six between the second reading and the committee stage;([9]) that the committee report specially on the bill in certain cases:([10]) and that the promoters are only charged half the usual fees.([11])

Divorce bills are now necessary only in the case of Irish divorces, the power of the Courts in Ireland being limited to pronouncing a decree of divorce *a mensa et thoro*. The principle upon which Parliament proceeds in passing these bills was declared in *Westropp's Divorce Bill*([12]) to be, that the same evidence which since the Divorce Act, 1857, enables the Divorce Court in England to pronounce a

---

([1]) S. O. H. L. 153—155.

([2]) S. O. H. L. 156.

([3]) S. O. H. L. 157.

([4]) S. O. H. L. 158.

([5]) S. O. H. L. 159.

([6]) S. O. H. L. 181.

([7]) S. O. H. L. 160—173.

([8]) S. O. H. L. 174.

([9]) S. O. 211, *post*. p. 159.

([10]) S. O. 188(*b*). *post*, p. 152.

([11]) See Table of Fees, *post*, p. 290.

([12]) L. R. 11 App. Cas. 294.

decree for dissolution of marriage, will be considered by the House of Lords sufficient ground for passing a Divorce Bill relating to Ireland, where that Act does not apply.

No petition for a Divorce Bill may be presented to the House of Lords unless an official copy of the proceedings in the Divorce Court having jurisdiction over the petitioner be presented on oath at the bar of the House of Lords.[1] Whether this Standing Order requires proceedings to be taken in a court of law as a condition precedent to relief, was canvassed in a recent case.[2] No opinion was given upon the point, but it was laid down that it was not necessary that a petition below should be successful in order that the House should receive the bill. Every Divorce Bill must contain a clause prohibiting the offending parties from intermarrying;[3] this clause, however, is generally struck out by the House. The petitioner must attend upon the second reading to be examined at the will of the House as to collusion and other like matters.[4] Divorce Bills are referred to a Committee of the whole House, and not to a Select Committee. Where upon a bill for divorce by a husband it appears that the wife has no means, the House will order the husband to pay her a small sum that she may make her defence.[5]

In the Commons there is a Committee designated the Select Committee on Divorce Bills[6], to whom all Divorce Bills are referred[7], and the Standing Orders provide for the evidence which is to be given, for the attendance of the petitioner in cases where he has attended the House of Lords, and for reporting every Divorce Bill to the House.[8] The petitioner is only charged one half of the usual fees.[9]

---

[1] S. O. H. L. 175.
[2] *Sinclair's Divorce Bill*, 1897, A. C. 469.
[3] S. O. H. L. 176.
[4] S. O. H. L. 178.

[5] *As Divorce Bill*, L. R. 12, App. Cas. 365.
[6] S. O. 189, *post*, p. 152.
[7] S. O. 208, *post*, p. 158.
[8] S. O. 190, 191, 192, *post*, p. 152.
[9] See Table of Fees, *post*, p. 290.

F

Naturalization bills have been regarded with increasing disfavour during late years, and successive Ministers of the Crown have declared that they are no longer to be permitted merely for purposes of private convenience, and that if any case can be dealt with under the ordinary law, a bill should not be allowed to pass; ([1]) indeed, in the last recorded case, a clause was inserted in the bill embodying the conditions presented by the Naturalization Act of 1870, as to residence and otherwise.

No naturalization bill can be read a second time in the Lords until the petitioner has produced a certificate of conduct from a Secretary of State, and has taken the oath of allegiance at the bar of the House.([2]) The consent of the Crown must also have been previously signified.([3])

In the Commons the only distinctive rule with regard to naturalization bills is, that, as in the case of estate bills, there need only be three clear days between the second reading and Committee.([4]) The promoters in Estate, Divorce, Naturalization, and Name Bills in the Commons escape with payment of half fees.([5])

([1]) Parl. Deb. 3rd series, vol. 346, p. 1717; ib. vol. 347, p. 205; ib. 4th series. vol. 28, p. 1216.

([2]) S. O. H. L. 179.

([3]) S. O. H. L. 180.

([4]) S. O. 211, post, p. 159.

([5]) See Table of Fees, post, p. 290.

CHAPTER X.

Provisional Orders.

A COURSE of procedure somewhat similar to that by private bill, but far less costly, has been authorised by numerous statutes of the present reign which have enabled various public departments to make what are known as Provisional Orders. The object of these statutes appears to be to facilitate the execution of schemes of public utility specially affecting particular localities or interests, and requiring the authority of Parliament, while at the same time preserving to those persons whose individual interests may be specially affected the right to secure a hearing of their particular objections. There are differences of more or less importance in the mode of obtaining a Provisional Order under each particular Act, but the general nature of the steps which usually have to be taken may be indicated as follows:—The parties applying for the Provisional Order (who are termed the promoters) first give notice in the prescribed manner of their application and its objects; they then present a petition to the public department or body having jurisdiction in the matter. That body considers the question, and any objections made by persons interested, and if it does not, as it may, dismiss the application, it will, in a proper case, direct a local inquiry to be held at which both sides may appear. After the inquiry the Provisional Order is either refused or granted, but if granted it is of no force until confirmed by Parliament, and

to obtain this confirmation the public department concerned introduces a public bill containing the order in a
schedule. If there are still private objectors to the order
they may petition Parliament, and in this event the bill
will, after the second reading in either House, be referred
to a select committee, before whom the opponents are
allowed to appear and oppose as in the case of private
bills.

In the House of Commons no fees are charged to the
promoters,([1]) but the opponents are subject to the same fees
as the opponents of private bills, whilst in the House of
Lords fees are only charged to either side at the committee
stage in the case of opposed bills, and then they are the
same for both promoters and opponents as in the case of
local bills.([2])

In both Houses after the bill has been read a first time
it is referred to the Examiners,([3]) and two clear days'
notice is given by them of the day on which it will be
examined.([4]) This notice is not to be given until after the
bill has been printed and circulated. The only Standing
Orders compliance with which has to be proved at this
stage are 38, 39, and 62 to 67 of both Houses: the rest of
the first sixty-eight Standing Orders being inapplicable, as
their functions are fulfilled by the provisions of the special
statute under which the Provisional Order has been
granted and the regulations of the department which has
granted it.

The opponents may by a memorial call attention to
non-compliance with Standing Orders,([5]) and thereupon
they may be heard as upon a private bill.

When the bill has been referred to a select committee,
the proceedings of the committee, and in the Commons

([1]) S. O. 151, *post*, p. 134.
([2]) H. L. Schedule of Fees, *post*, p. 295.
([3]) S. O. 72, *post*, p. 119; S. O. 70A. H. L.
([4]) S. O. 73, *post*, p. 120; S. O. 72. H. L.
([5]) S. O. 232, *post*, p. 163.

those of the Referees, are conducted in the same manner as in the case of private bills, and are subject to the same rules and orders of the House so far as they are applicable.([1]) The petition against the bill in the Commons must be presented not later than seven clear days' after notice of the day of examination by the Examiners.([2]) In the Lords, if the bill originated in that House, the petition must be presented on or before the seventh day after the second reading ([3]) ; if the bill came from the Commons, on or before the seventh day after the first reading.([4])

No bill for confirming a Provisional Order may be read the first time in the Commons after June 1.([5]) Somewhat similar to Provisional Orders, and governed by the same Standing Orders, are the Provisional Certificates issued by the Board of Trade to railway companies and their promoters under the Railway Companies Powers Act, 1864, the Railways Construction Facilities Act, 1864, and various Acts amending those Acts.([6]) The Provisional Certificates only require parliamentary confirmation if notice of opposition has been lodged by a railway or canal company with the Board of Trade. In such case, the Board introduce a public bill into Parliament to confirm the certificate, and if a petition is presented to Parliament against the certificate, the bill is referred to a select committee and treated in exactly the same way as a Provisional Order Confirmation Bill. Below will be found a table showing the various bodies authorised to grant Provisional Orders, the principal Acts giving them the power, the persons who are entitled to apply for orders, and the objects for which the orders are granted.

([1]) S. O. 151, *post*. p. 134 ; S. O. 89, *post*, p. 123.

([2]) S. O. 210, *post*, p. 159.

([3]) S. O. 92, H. L.

([4]) S. O. 93, H. L.

([5]) S. O. 193ᴀ, 153.

([6]) 27 & 28 Vict. c. 120 ; 27 & 28 Vict. c. 121 ; 31 & 32 Vict. c. 119 ; 33 & 34 Vict. c. 19 ; 37 & 38 Vict. c. 40.

Authority.	Act.	Applicant.	Object.
1. Secretary of State.	(i.) Housing of Working Classes, 1890.	Local authority in London.	Improvement scheme in unhealthy districts in London.
„	(ii.) Explosives Act, 1875.	Local authority or person making, &c., explosives.	Repealing Acts as to manufacture or sale of explosives.
„	(iii.) Police Act, 1890.	Police authority.	Dealing with excess of pension fund.
„	(iv.) Police Act, 1893.	Secretary of State.	Repealing, &c., local Acts as to fire brigade or fire police.
„	(v.) Metropolitan Police Act, 1886.	Police receiver.	Compulsory acquisition of land.
„	(vi.) Military Lands Act, 1892.	Volunteer corps, or County Council, or Secretary of State.	Compulsory acquisition of land for military purposes.
II. Board of Trade.	(i.) General Pier and Harbour Act, 1861.	Any person.	Construction of piers or harbours.
„	(ii.) Railway and Canal Traffic Act, 1888.	Board of Trade.	Revised classification of traffic and schedule of rates.
„	(iii.) Merchant Shipping Act, 1894.	Persons interested in pilotage of district.	Alterations in pilotage jurisdiction and rules.
„	(iv.) Sea Fisheries Act, 1868.	Any person.	Establishment, &c., of oyster and mussel fishery on seashore.
„	(v.) Salmon Fishery Act, 1873.	Board of Conservators or proprietor of fishery.	Compulsory acquisition of land for removing obstructions and other purposes.
„	(vi.) Tramways Act, 1870.	Local authority or any person with their consent, or that of road authority.	Construction of tramway.
„	(vii.) Military Tramways Act, 1887.	(a) Secretary of State.	(a) „
„	„	(b) Local authority or any person.	(b) Using tramway so made.
„	(viii.) Gas and Water Facilities Acts, 1870 and 1873.	Any person with consent of local and road authority.	Construction, &c., of gasworks or waterworks.

Authority.	Act.	Applicant.	Object.
II. Board of Trade—*cont.*	(ix.) Electric Lighting Acts, 1882 and 1888.	Local authority or other person.	Supply of electricity in any area.
III. Local Government Board.	(i.) Public Health Act, 1875.	(*a*) Local authority.	(*a*) Repeal, &c., of local Acts.
"	"	(*b*) "	(*b*) Settlement, &c., of differences arising out of transfer of powers, &c., from or to local authority.
"	"	(*c*) Local Government Board.	(*c*) Altering areas and dissolving sewerage boards.
"	"	(*d*) Urban authority or ten ratepayers.	(*d*) altering mode of defraying sanitary expenses of urban authority.
"	"	(*e*) Local author ity.	(*e*) Compulsory acquisition of land for purposes of the Act.
"	"	(*f*) Urban authority.	(*f*) Supply of gas.
"	(ii.) Housing of Working Class Act, 1890.	(*a*) Local authority out of London.	(*a*) Improvement scheme in unhealthy districts.
"	"	(*b*) Local authority.	(*b*) Compulsory acquisition of land under improvement scheme where houses closed by closing order.
"	"	(*c*) Local authority.	(*c*) Compulsory acquisition of land for lodging-houses.
"	(iii.) Poor Law Amendments Acts, 1867 and 1868.	Local authority.	Amending local Acts for the relief of the poor.
"	(iv.) Alkali Works Regulation Act, 1881.	Local Government Board.	Preventing discharge of noxious gases from salt works.
"	(v.) Brine Pumping Act, 1891.	Owners of land or sanitary authority.	Formation of compensation districts where subsidence caused by brine pumping.
"	(vi.) Redistribution of Seats Acts, 1885.	Any voter.	Settling doubts as to limits of parliamentary division.

Authority.	Act.	Applicant.	Object.
III. Local Go- vernment Board—*cont.*	(vii.) Local Go- vernment Act, 1888.	Local Govern- ment Board or County Coun- cil or other lo- cal authority.	Transfer of powers to County Council, altering boun- daries, and other similar matters.
IV. Board of Agriculture.	(i.) Commons Act, 1876.	Any person.	Inclosure or regula- tion of commons.
„	(ii.) Land Drain- age Act, 1861.	(a) Commission ers of Sewers.	(a) Compulsory ac- quisition of land.
„	„	(b) Owners of bog-land.	(b) Constituting a drainage district.
V. Education Department	(i.) Education Act, 1870.	School board.	Compulsory acqui- sition of land for school accommoda- tion.
„	(ii.) Education Act, 1876.	School board.	Compulsory acqui- sition of land for an office.
VI. Railway and Canal Com- mission.	Telegraph Act, 1892.	Postmaster Gen- eral.	Construction of works on private land.
VII. County Au- thority.	Allotments Acts, 1887 and 1890.	Sanitary author- ity or County Council.	Compulsory acqui- sition of land for allotments.

It may be mentioned that the power to grant Provisional Orders is in Scotland vested in the Secretary for Scotland, the Scotch Education Department, the Boundary Commissioners, and the local authority; while in Ireland orders may be granted by the Lord Lieutenant, the Irish Local Government Board, and the Public Works Commissioners. It is not, however, thought necessary to mention in detail the provisions of the statutes applying the system of Provisional Orders to Scotland and Ireland.

It should be noted that the requirements in. the Standing Orders of both Houses for provision for the housing of persons belonging to the labouring class evicted under a bill apply to Provisional Orders.[1]

[1] See S. O. 183A, *post*, p. 150; S. O. 111. H. L.

CHAPTER XI.

Costs.

A LIMITED power of awarding costs to promoters of bills to be paid by opponents, and to opponents to be paid by promoters, is given by statutes to committees, whether of Lords or Commons, on private bills.([1]) But this power only arises where the committee unanimously report that the promoters have been vexatiously subjected to expense in the promotion of the bill by their opponents, or that the opponents have been unreasonably or vexatiously subjected to expense in defending their rights proposed to be interfered with by the bill.([2])

Notwithstanding the above power, no landowner, *bona fide* at his own risk, opposing a bill proposing to take his land, is to be liable to costs in respect of his opposition.([3])

The Committee may, where they have power to award costs, award costs to be taxed by the Taxing Officer of the House, or they may, with the consent of the parties affected, name a sum for costs, and thus avoid the necessity for a taxation.([4])

The Taxing Officer afterwards will, on application, certify the amount he finds due on taxation, or the amount named as above stated by the Committee; and on non-

---

([1]) 28 Vict. c. 27, *post*, p. 344.
([2]) 28 Vict. c. 27, ss. 1, 2, *post*, p. 344.
([3]) 28 Vict. c. 27, s. 2, *post*, p. 344.
([4]) 28 Vict. c. 27, ss. 1, 2, *post*, p. 344.

payment of the amount thus certified, an action may, after demand thereof, be brought in the High Court to recover the amount from the person or persons liable.(¹)

The certificate thus given may not be called in question in any court, and special provision is made simplifying the procedure to recover the amount.(²)

The plaintiff may specially endorse the writ with a statement of his claim, which is the equivalent of the "declaration" under the system of pleading in force at the time the Statute (28 Vict. c. 27) was passed; and upon filing such statement of his claim, together with the certificate of the Taxing Officer and an affidavit showing demand of payment, sign judgment and issue execution for the amount, or he may make use of the ordinary procedure and seek a summary judgment under O. xiv. of the Rules under the Judicature Acts.(³)

Where the special procedure is adopted, the defendant can not, without leave of the Court or a Judge, put in a defence to the claim upon the certificate. The only defences available against a claim upon such a certificate would seem to be defences showing that the certificate was made without jurisdiction, or that it was not given in accordance or conformity with the Act of Parliament, or that it was obtained under, or was being attempted to be enforced under circumstances which would formerly have been ground for injunction to restrain the claimant from continuing his action or enforcing the certificate, and which consequently now, under the Judicature Acts, afford ground for a stay of proceedings.(¹)

If judgment has been signed in an action upon the certificate, in accordance with the special procedure thus

---

(¹) 28 Vict. c. 27, ss. 3, 4, 5, *post*, p. 345.

(²) 28 Vict. c. 27, ss. 5, 6, *post*, p. 345.

(³) Mallet *v.* Hanly, 18 Q. B. D. 303, 310.

(⁴) Williams *v.* Swansea Canal Company, L. R. 3 Ex 158; Swansea Canal *v.* Great Western Railway Company, L. R. 5, Eq. 444; Mallet *v.* Hanly, 18 Q. B. D. 303. 308, 312, 787, 793.

given, it is open to the Court or a Judge to set aside such judgment absolutely, if it is shewn that the certificate was made without jurisdiction, or where the absence of jurisdiction, though not absolutely proved appears probable, to set aside the judgment and admit the defendant to plead a defence to the claim.(¹)

Where a certificate was made—not against the petitioners whose names appeared in the petition against a bill, but against persons held by the Committee to have been the real petitioners, though not named as such in the petition—it was decided by the Court of Appeal that such a certificate was one without jurisdiction and unenforceable.(²)

The certificate of the Taxing Officer would appear to be a condition precedent to the right to sue the opposite party for the costs.(³)

The fees chargeable to promoters, or to petitioners against bills, are governed in each House by a Table of Fees put out by such House.(⁴)

The costs payable by promoters or opponents of bills to their agents or solicitors for Parliamentary work done for them on their retainer, or at their request, are, in regard to the Commons, regulated by a list of charges prepared by the Speaker, so far as regards matters comprised in such list; in regard to the House of Lords, by a similar list prepared by the Clerk of the Parliaments.(⁵) Provision is made by statute for the delivery of a signed bill of costs one calendar month before any action is brought in respect of costs against the client, and for taxation of such bill at the instance of the agent or solicitor, or of the person upon

---

(¹) Mallet *v.* Hanly, 18 Q. B. D. 303, 787.

(²) Mallet *v.* Hanly, 18, Q. B. D. 787.

(³) See Guardians of West Ham *v.* Churchwardens of Bethnal Green [1896], A. C. 477, 485, 488.

(⁴) See Table of Fees (Commons), *post*, p. 290.

(⁵) 10 & 11 Vict. c. 69, s. 4, *post*, p. 334; 12 & 13 Vict. c. 78, s. 4, *post*, p. 338; List of Charges, *post*, p. 296.

whom the demand for payment has been made.([1])   A
taxation at the instance of the client must be applied for
before a verdict has been obtained upon the bill, and, except
where there are special circumstances, before the expiration
of six calendar months from the date of the delivery of the
signed bill.([2])   See further as to the taxation of costs on
private bills the two Statutes 10 & 11 Vict. c. 69 (applicable to the Commons), and 12 & 13 Vict. c. 78 (applicable to
the Lords),([2]) and as to the appeal, in the Commons to the
Speaker, and in the Lords to the Clerk of the Parliaments,
from the Taxing Officer, and as to the certificate of the
Speaker or Clerk of the Parliaments being *conclusive* as
to the amount, and in certain cases having the effect of a
warrant of attorney to confess judgment, see section 9 of
those Statutes.([3])

([1]) 10 & 11 Vict. c. 69, s. 8, *post*, p. 336 ; 12 & 13 Vict. c. 78, s. 8, *post*,
p. 340.

([2]) *Post*, pp. 335–337 ; 339–343.

([3]) *Post*, pp. 337, 341, 342 ; and see as to the somewhat similar certificate
under 28 Vict. c 27, s. 3, *ante*, p. 78.

CHAPTER XII.

Parliamentary Agents and Drafting of Bills.

BEFORE 1836 the officers of the two Houses not only acted for those Houses, but also acted as agents for the parties in the conduct of the private bill business in those Houses, receiving payment for so doing. At that date the private business of Parliament having very largely increased, this was found inconvenient, and the option was given to the officials either of resigning their posts as such officers and acting merely as agents outside the Houses, or of retaining their official positions and confining themselves to their public duties. One portion of the officers elected to retain their posts and confine themselves to their public duties, the other portion elected to retire, and commenced to practise as parliamentary agents, thus founding the profession as it now exists.(¹)

At the present time any person who is either a solicitor, a writer to the signet, or who produces to the clerk at the Private Bill Office, when he for the first time applies to qualify himself to act as parliamentary agent, a certificate of his respectability from, a member of Parliament, or a justice of the peace, or a barrister-at-law, or a solicitor, may be registered as a parliamentary agent if he is actually employed in promoting or opposing some private bill or petition pending in Parliament.(²) The application must be in writing.(²)

(¹) See Report of the Select Committee (of both Houses) of 1876 on Parliamentary Agency.

(²) See Rules for Agents, *post*, p. 328.

Agents have to sign a declaration at the Private Bill Office engaging to observe the rules and to pay the fees chargeable by Parliament on any petition or bill on which they may appear, and, if required, they have further to enter into a recognisance in the penal sum of £500, with two sureties of £250 each, to observe such declaration, and thereupon they are, if otherwise qualified, registered in a book at the Private Bill Office.([1])

The only persons disqualified seem to be, solicitors who have been struck off the rolls, barristers who have been disbarred, and parliamentary agents who have been suspended or prohibited for wilful violation of the rules or practice, or other wilful misconduct in their business, none of whom can be registered without the express authority of the Chairman of Committees or Speaker.([2])

It would seem that the only disciplinary power exercised over parliamentary agents is that of the Chairman of Committees in the Lords, and of the Speaker in the House of Commons, either of whom can prohibit or suspend an agent from practising in their respective Houses for wilful violation of rules, or wilful misconduct in his business.([3])

The agent is personally liable to Parliament for the fees chargeable by Parliament on business he conducts.

It will thus be seen that the profession of agent is open to any person of respectability who can obtain employment in that capacity, though, as will be obvious from a consideration of the foregoing pages, the successful exercise of that profession involves careful attention to the Standing Orders and requirements of Parliament, and a competent skill in framing documents of a semi-legal character, so that practically agents have for the most part been persons possessed of a legal education, or persons who

([1]) See Rules for Agents, *post*, p. 328 ; S. O. 227, *post*, p. 162.
([2]) See Rules for Agents, *post*, p. 328.
([3]) See Rules for Agents, *post*, p. 328.

have had long experience as clerks or the like in the offices of parliamentary agents.

As to the charges agents may make, and as to the taxation of their bills of costs, see "Costs," *ante*, p. 79.

Model Bills and Clauses have been put out, with the authority of the officials responsible to Parliament for private bill legislation, to serve as precedents for promoters in regard to the clauses proper to be inserted in bills of certain kinds, and in framing bills of such kinds these clauses should, so far as applicable, be, in general, adopted. ([1])

A list of the Model Bills and Clauses thus given will be found in the Appendix, *post*, p. 333.

The Standing Orders contain express provisions as to bills of certain specified kinds with regard to the insertion or non-insertion of particular matters or clauses; thus, in all bills for carrying on any work by means of a company, commissioners, or trustees, provision must be made for compelling persons subscribing money therefor to pay the money thus subscribed; ([2]) in railway, tramway, and subway bills various restrictions must be inserted and clauses of various kinds are required, whilst it is forbidden to give powers to effect certain objects, as for example to give powers to railway companies to purchase, hire, or provide steam vessels otherwise than to connect various portions of their line, or to give to a local authority power to construct, acquire, or work a tramway outside its district, except under certain circumstances; ([3]) in bills promoted by or conferring powers on local authorities, the clauses are to be considered in reference to various matters affecting local government([4]);

([1]) The forms may be purchased at the price of 1*s.* 2½*d.* from Messrs. Eyre and Spottiswoode, or at the office for the sale of papers at the Houses of Parliament; see List of Model Bills and Clauses, *post*, p. 333.

([2]) S. O. 144, *post*, p. 133.

([3]) S. O. 153–156, 158, 159–171, *post*, pp. 134–146. S. O. 112 133D, H. L.

([4]) S. O. 173A, *post*, p. 146.

in inclosure bills, provision is to be made for leaving an open space for purposes of exercise and recreation of the neighbouring population; (¹) in bills giving power to take land, clauses must be inserted which, under certain conditions, compel the promoters to make a provision for re-housing persons of the labouring class who may be deprived under the bill of their houses; (²) in bills for gas works, burial grounds and cemeteries, certain clauses must occur. (³)

Special provision is made as to certain bills promoted by the London County Council. (⁴)

In the case of Private Bills, all charges in any way affecting the public revenue which occur in any of the clauses must be printed in italics in such bills when presented to the House. (⁵)

In the preparation of Private Bills it will be found expedient, when no sufficient assistance can be obtained from the Model Bills and Clauses mentioned above, to consult, where possible, similar or analogous bills which have passed into law, and to copy as closely as may be the wording of such clauses of those bills as carry out the required purposes, since Parliament and Parliamentary Committees are more ready to sanction clauses to which they have. in other cases given their sanction, than to adopt entirely new forms of expression, or novel methods of carrying out a desired purpose, but, of course, as new needs arise, new clauses must be framed; though even then there may be advantage in retaining, as far as possible, familiar forms of expression.

(¹) S. O. 179, *post*, p. 148 ; S. O. 138, H. L.

(²) S. O. 183A, *post*, p. 150 ; S. O. 111, H. L.

(³) S. O. 188, 188A, *post*, p. 152 ; S. O. 139–140A, H. L.

(⁴) S. O. 194–194D, *post*, p. 153 ; S. O. 69–69C, H. L.

(⁵) S. O. 202, *post*, p. 157.

(85)

APPENDIX.

STANDING ORDERS OF THE HOUSE OF COMMONS.

I.—THE TWO CLASSES OF PRIVATE BILLS.

1. For the purposes of the Standing Orders of this House, all private bills to which the Standing Orders are applicable shall be divided into the two following classes, according to the subjects to which they respectively relate :— *Private bills divided into two classes.*

1*st Class :—* 1st class.

Burial ground, making, maintaining, or altering.

Charters and corporations, enlarging or altering powers of.

Church or chapel, building, enlarging, repairing, or maintaining.

City or town, paving, lighting, watching, cleansing, or improving.

Company, incorporating, regulating, or giving powers to.

County rate.

County or Shire Hall, Court House.

Crown, Church, or Corporation property, or property held in trust for public or charitable purposes.

Ferry, where no work is to be executed.

Fishery, making, maintaining, or improving.

Gaol or House of Correction.

Gas work.

Improvement charge, unless proposed in connection with a second class work to be authorised by the bill.

Land, inclosing, draining, or improving.

Letters patent.

Local court, constituting.

Market or market place, erecting, improving, repairing, maintaining, or regulating.

Police.

Poor, maintaining or employing.

Poor rate.

Powers to sue and be sued, conferring.

Stipendiary magistrate, or any public officer, payment of.

G

And continuing or amending an Act passed for any of the purposes included in this or the second class, where no further work than such as was authorised by a former Act is proposed to be made.

2nd Class :—

Making, maintaining, varying, extending, or enlarging any

Aqueduct.

Archway.

Bridge.

Canal.

Cut.

Dock.

Drainage—where it is not provided in the bill that the cut shall not be more than eleven feet wide at the bottom.

Embankment for reclaiming land from the sea or any tidal river.

Ferry, where any work is to be executed.

Harbour.

Navigation.

Pier.

Port.

Public carriage road.

Railway.

Reservoir.

Sewer.

Street.

Subway—to be used for the conveyance of passengers, animals, or goods, in carriages or trucks drawn or propelled on rails.

Tramway—by which term, as used in these Orders, is meant a tramway to be laid along a street or road. "Tramroad," by which term, as used in these Orders, is meant any tramway other than a tramway to be laid along a street or road.

Tunnel.

Waterwork.

APPOINTMENT OF EXAMINERS.

2. There shall be one or more officers of this House, to be called "The Examiners of Petitions for Private Bills," who shall be appointed by Mr. Speaker.

II.—STANDING ORDERS, COMPLIANCE WITH WHICH IS TO BE PROVED BEFORE THE EXAMINERS.

[In these Orders (3 to 68 inclusive), unless the context otherwise requires—

the term "railway" includes "tramroad" ;

the term "lessee" includes a person holding an agreement for a lease ;

Standing Orders, compliance with which is to be proved before Examiners.

the term "occupier" applies only to ratepayers, and to other persons not being ratepayers, whose interest in the premises occupied is not less than that of a quarterly tenant;

the term "parish" means (as respects England and Wales) a place for which a separate poor rate is or can be made or for which a separate overseer is or can be appointed;

the term "district," with respect to the administrative county of London, means any parish in Schedule A, and any district in Schedule B, of The Metropolis Management Act, 1855, as amended by any subsequent Act.)

Compliance with the following Standing Orders shall be proved before one of the examiners; viz.—

1. *Notices by Advertisement.*

3. In all cases where application is intended to be made for leave to bring in a bill relating to any of the subjects included in either of the two classes of private bills, notice shall be given stating the objects of such intended application, and the time at which copies of the bill will be deposited in the Private Bill Office; and if it be intended to apply for powers for the compulsory purchase of lands or houses, or for extending the time granted by any former Act for that purpose, or to amalgamate with any other company, or to sell or lease the undertaking, or to purchase or take on lease the undertaking of any other company, or to enter into working agreements or traffic arrangements, or to dissolve any company, or to amend or repeal any former Act or Acts, or to levy any tolls, rates, or duties, or to alter any existing tolls, rates, or duties, or to confer, vary, or extinguish any exemptions from payment of tolls, rates, or duties, or to confer, vary, or extinguish any other rights or privileges, or to impose on any lands or houses, or to render any lands or houses liable to the imposition of, any charge in respect of any improvement, the notice shall specify such intention, and shall also specify the company, person, or persons with, to, from, or by whom it is intended to be proposed that such amalgamation, sale, purchase, lease, working agreements, or traffic arrangements shall be made; and the whole of the notice relating to the same bill shall, except as provided by Standing Order 9, be included in the same advertisement, which shall be headed by a short title, descriptive of the undertaking or bill, and shall be subscribed with the name and address of the person, company, corporation, or firm responsible for the publication of the notice.

Notices to state objects of application when bills will be deposited in Private Bill Office, and intention to seek for powers to purchase lands, or to amalgamate, &c., or to levy or alter tolls, to be stated, and also the companies, &c., with whom any amalgamation, &c., is proposed.

4. In cases of bills included in the second class, and of bills of the first class, in respect to which plans are required to be deposited,

In second class bills, notices to contain names of parishes, &c.

Standing
Orders, com-
pliance with
which is to be
proved before
Examiners.

such notices shall also contain a description of all the termini,
together with the names of the parishes, townlands, and extra-
parochial places from, in, through, or into which the work is
intended to be made, maintained, varied, extended, or enlarged, or
in which any land or houses intended to be taken are situate, and
where any common or commonable land is intended to be taken,
such notice shall contain the name of such common or commonable
land (if any), and the name of any parish in which such land is
situate, together with an estimate of the quantity of such common
or commonable land proposed to be taken, and shall state the time
and place of deposit of the plans, sections, books of reference, and
copies of the Gazette notice respectively, with the clerks of the
peace and sheriff clerks, and also with the officers respectively
mentioned in Standing Order 29, as the case may be.

Notices to
specify limits
of burial
ground, of gas
works, &c.

5. In cases of bills for constructing gas works, or sewage
works, or works for the manufacture or conversion of the residual
products of gas or sewage, or for making or constructing a sewage
farm, cemetery, burial ground, crematorium, destructor, hospital
for infectious disease, or station for generating electric power, the
notices shall set forth and specify the lands in or upon which such
gas works, sewage works, works for the manufacture or conversion
of residual products, farm, cemetery, burial ground, crematorium,
destructor, hospital, or generating station, is intended to be made
or constructed.

Street
tramways.

6. In cases of bills for laying down a tramway, the notice shall
specify at what point or points, and on which side of the street or
road it is proposed to lay such tramway, so that for a distance of
30 ft. or upwards a less space than 9 ft. 6 in., or if it is
intended to run thereon carriages or trucks adapted for use
upon railways, a less space than 10 ft. 6 in. shall intervene
between the outside of the footpath on the side of the street or
road and the nearest rail of the tramway; the notice shall also
specify the gauge to be adopted and what power it is intended to
employ, and in the case of mechanical power the mode in which
such power is to be applied, for moving carriages or trucks upon
the tramway.

Subways.

6a. In the case of bills for constructing a subway, the notice
shall specify the gauge to be adopted and the motive power to be
employed, and in the case of mechanical power the mode in which
such power is to be applied.

Tramroads.

Notices in the
case of tram-
road bills.

6b. In the case of a bill for constructing a tramroad, the
notice shall specify the gauge to be adopted, and the motive power

to be employed, and in the case of mechanical power the mode in which such power is to be applied.

7. In all cases where it is proposed to divert into any existing or intended cut, canal, reservoir, aqueduct or navigation, or into any intended variation, extension or enlargement thereof respectively, any water from any existing cut, canal, reservoir, aqueduct, or navigation, whether the water is to be abstracted directly or indirectly from any such cut, canal, reservoir, aqueduct or navigation, or from any feeder thereof, and whether under any agreement with the proprietors thereof or otherwise, the notices shall contain the name of every such last-mentioned cut, canal, reservoir, aqueduct or navigation.

8. In cases of bills relating to letters patent, each notice shall have prefixed to it in capital letters the name by which the invention is usually distinguished, and shall contain a distinct description of the invention for which such letters patent have been obtained, and also an account of the term of their duration.

8a. In addition to the ordinary notices, notice of the intention to apply to Parliament for a bill relating to letters patent shall be published twice in the official journal of the Patent Office, before the introduction of the bill in this House.

9. In the months of October and November, or either of them, immediately preceding the application for a bill, the notice shall be published once in the London, Edinburgh, or Dublin *Gazette*, as the case may be, and in the following newspapers, namely :—

(1.) In the case of a bill relating specially to any particular city, borough, town, or urban district, the notice shall be published once in each of two successive weeks, with an interval between such publications of not less than six clear days, in some one and the same newspaper published in such city, borough, town, or district, or if there be no newspaper published therein, then in some one and the same newspaper published in the county in which such city, borough, town, or district, or any part thereof is situate ;

(2.) In the case of a bill authorising the construction of works or the taking of lands, or extending the time granted by a former Act for the construction of works or taking of lands, situate in one county only, or relating to an undertaking situate in one county only, or promoted by a company or companies, or other parties possessed of an undertaking situate in one county only, the notice shall be published once in each of two successive weeks, with an interval between

Standing Orders, compliance with which is to be proved before Examiners.

Cuts, Canals, Navigations, &c.

When it is intended to divert water from an existing cut, &c.

Letters Patent.

Name of invention to be prefixed in capitals to notice.

Notice in official journal of Patent Office.

Publication of notices in gazettes and newspapers.

such publications of not less than six clear days, in some one and the same newspaper published in that county, or if there be no newspaper published therein, then in some one and the same newspaper published in some county adjoining or near thereto ;

(3.) In the case of a bill authorising the construction of works or the taking of lands, or extending the time granted by a former Act for the construction of works or the taking of lands, in more than one county, or relating to an undertaking situate in more than one county, or promoted by a company or companies, or other parties possessed of an undertaking situate in more than one county, the notice shall be published once in each of two successive weeks, with an interval between such publications of not less than six clear days, in some one and the same newspaper of the county in which the principal office of the company or companies, or other parties who are the promoters of the bill is situate, and in some one and the same newspaper published in each county in which any new works are proposed to be constructed, or in which any lands are intended to be taken, or in which any works or lands are situate, in respect of which any new or further powers for the completion or taking thereof are intended to be applied for, or if there be no newspaper published therein, then in some one and the same newspaper published in some county adjoining or near thereto : Provided always, that, if the bill relates to lands or works, situate in more than one county, it shall be sufficient (at the option of the promoters) to publish in each of such counties so much only of the notice as relates specifically to the lands or works situate in that county, together with the short title of the notice and an intimation that the notice has been published in full or sent for publication in full in the *Gazette ;*

(4.) No publication under this Order shall be made after the 27th day of November.

10. In the months of October and November, or one of them, immediately preceding the application for any bill for laying down a tramway, or constructing an underground railway or subway, when such bill contains powers authorising any alteration or disturbance of the surface of any street or road, notice thereof shall be posted for fourteen consecutive days in every such street or road in such manner as the authority having the control of such street or road shall direct, and if after such application to such

authority no such direction shall be given, then in some conspicuous position in every such street or road, and such notice shall also state the place or places at which the plans of such tramway, railway, or subway, will be deposited.

2. *Notices and Applications to Owners, Lessees, and Occupiers of Lands and Houses.*

11. On or before the fifteenth day of December immediately preceding the application for a bill for power to take any lands or houses compulsorily, or for an extension of the time granted by any former Act for that purpose, or to impose an improvement charge on any lands or houses, or to render any lands or houses liable to the imposition of an improvement charge, application in writing shall be made to the owners or reputed owners, lessees or reputed lessees, and occupiers of all such lands and houses, inquiring whether they assent, dissent, or are neuter in respect of such application; and in cases of Bills included in the second class, such application shall be, as nearly as may be, in the form set forth in the Appendix marked (A).

12. Separate lists shall be made of the names of such owners, lessees and occupiers, distinguishing those who have assented, dissented or are neuter in respect to such application, or who have returned no answer thereto; and where no written acknowledgment has been returned to an application forwarded by post, or where such application has been returned as undelivered at any time before the making up of such lists, the direction of the letter in which the same was so forwarded shall be inserted therein.

13. On or before the fifteenth day of December immediately preceding the application for a bill for the laying down a tramway, notice in writing shall be given to the owners or reputed owners, lessees or reputed lessees, and occupiers of all houses, shops, or warehouses abutting upon any part of any street or road where, for a distance of 30 ft. or upwards, it is proposed that a less space than 9 ft. 6 in. shall intervene between the outside of the footpath on either side of the road and the nearest rail of the tramway, or a less space than 10 ft. 6 in., if it is intended to run on the tramway carriages or trucks adapted for use upon railways. On or before the fifteenth day of December immediately preceding the application for any Bill for laying down a tramway crossing any railway or tramway on the level, or crossing any railway, tramway, or canal by means of a bridge, or otherwise affecting or interfering with such railway, tramway, or canal, notice in writing of such

Standing Orders, compliance with which is to be proved before Examiners.

application shall be served upon the owner or reputed owner, and upon the lessee or reputed lessee of such railway, tramway, or canal, and such notice shall state the place or places at which the plans of the tramway to be authorised by such bill have been or will be deposited.

Notices when it is proposed to abstract water from any stream.

14. On or before the fifteenth day of December immediately preceding the application for a bill, whereby it is proposed to abstract water from any stream for the purpose of supplying any cut, canal, reservoir, aqueduct, navigation, or waterwork, notice in writing of such bill shall be given to the owners or reputed owners, lessees or reputed lessees, and occupiers of all mills and manufactories or other works using the waters of such stream for a distance of 20 miles below the point at which such water is intended to be abstracted, such distance to be measured along the course of such stream, unless such waters shall, within a less distance than 20 miles, fall into or unite with any navigable stream, and then only to the owners or reputed owners, lessees or reputed lessees, and occupiers of such mills and manufactories, or other works as aforesaid, which shall be situate between the point at which such water is proposed to be abstracted, and the point at which such water shall fall into or unite with such navigable stream ; and such notice shall state the name (if any) by which the stream is known at the point at which such water shall be immediately abstracted, and also the parish in which such point is situate, and the time and place of deposit of plans, sections, and books of reference and copies of the *Gazette* notice respectively with the clerks of the peace and sheriff clerks, as the case may be.

Burial Grounds and Gas Works, &c.

Notice to owners and occupiers of houses.

15. On or before the fifteenth day of December immediately preceding the application for a bill for constructing gas works or sewage works, or works for the manufacture or conversion of the residual products of gas and sewage, or for making or constructing a sewage farm, cemetery, burial ground, crematorium, destructor, or hospital for infectious disease, notice shall be served upon the owner, lessee, and occupier of every dwelling house situated within 300 yards of the lands in or upon which such gasworks, sewage works, works for the manufacture of residual products, farm, cemetery, burial ground, crematorium, destructor, or hospital may be made or constructed.

Relinquishment of Works.

Notice to owners, &c. when the Bill

16. On or before the fifteenth day of December immediately preceding the application for a bill whereby the whole or any part of a work authorized by any former Act is intended to be relinquished, notice in writing of such bill shall be served upon

the owners or reputed owners, lessees or reputed lessees, and occupiers of the lands in which any part of the said work intended to be thereby relinquished is situate.

17. On or before the twenty-first day of December immediately preceding the application for a bill, whereby any express statutory provision then in force for the protection of the owner, lessee, or occupier of any property, or for the protection or benefit of any public trustees or commissioners, corporation or person, specifically named in such provision, is sought to be altered or repealed, notice in writing of such Bill, and of the intention to alter or repeal such provision, shall be served upon every such owner, lessee, or occupier, public trustees or commissioners, corporation or person.

18. On or before the twenty-first day of December immediately preceding the application for a bill whereby any compulsory running powers are proposed to be taken over any railway, notice in writing of such bill, and of the intention to apply for such running powers, shall be served upon every company owning or working such railway.

19. All applications shall be made, and notices served, either by delivering the same personally to the party entitled to such application or notice, or by leaving the same at his usual place of abode, or, in his absence from the United Kingdom, with his agent, or by forwarding the same by post in a registered letter, addressed with a sufficient direction to his usual place of abode, and posted on or before the third day previously to the day required for delivery of the same personally, at such places, at such hours, and according to such regulations as the Postmaster General shall from time to time appoint, for the posting and registration of such letters, and shall be accompanied by a copy of the Standing Orders which regulate the time and mode of presenting petitions in opposition to Bills.([1])

20. In all cases the written acknowledgment of the party applied to shall, in the absence of other proof, be sufficient evidence of such application having being made, or notice given ; and in case of an application or notice having been forwarded by post, in a registered letter, the production of the Post Office receipt for such letter, duly stamped, in such form as the Postmaster General shall have appointed, shall be sufficient evidence of the due delivery of such letter : Provided it shall appear that the same was properly and sufficiently directed, and that the same was not returned by the Post Office as undelivered.

([1]) These are S. O. 129, *post*, and S. O. 92, 93, H. L.

Marginal notes:

Standing Orders, compliance with which is to be proved before Examiners.

is to abridge any public works.

Notice to owners, &c. in cases of alteration or repeal of provisions.

Notice in case of application for compulsory running powers.

How application to be made, and notices served.

Written acknowledgment of party applied to, and, in case of application or notice by post, Post Office receipt sufficient evidence of application.

Standing
Orders, com-
pliance with
which is to be
proved before
Examiners.

21. No notice served or application made on Sunday, Christmas
Day, Good Friday, or Easter Monday, or before eight o'clock in
the forenoon, or after eight o'clock in the afternoon of any day, shall
be deemed valid, except in the case of delivery of letters by post.

Notices not to
be given on
Sunday, &c.

Consents in
case of Tram-
ways Bill.

22. In cases of bills to authorize the laying down of a tramway, the promoters shall obtain the consent of the local authority
of the district or districts through which it is proposed to construct
such tramway, and where in any district there is a road authority
distinct from the local authority, the consent of such road authority
shall also be necessary in any case where power is sought to break
up any road, subject to the jurisdiction of such road authority.
For the purposes of this Order, the local and road authorities in
England and Scotland shall be the local and road authorities mentioned in Section 3 and Schedule A. of "The Tramways Act,
1870," except that in the case of such schedule the London County
Council shall be substituted for the Metropolitan Board of Works,
Urban District Council for Local Board, and Rural District
Council for Vestry, Select Vestry, or other body of persons acting
by virtue of any Act of Parliament, prescription, custom, or otherwise, as or instead of a vestry or select vestry, and in Ireland shall
be the grand jury of the county in respect to any highway, or
portion of highway, within the jurisdiction of such grand jury;
and in respect to highways wholly or partly within any city,
borough, town corporate, or other place or district in which the
public roads are not under the control of the grand jury of the
county, shall be the respective local and road authorities of such
city, borough, town corporate, or other place or district mentioned
in Section 38 of "The Tramways (Ireland) Act, 1860": Provided that where it is proposed to lay down a continuous line of
tramway in two or more districts, and any local or road authority
having jurisdiction in any such districts does not consent thereto,
the consents of the local and road authority, or the local and road
authorities having jurisdiction over two-thirds of the length of
such proposed line of tramway, shall be deemed to be sufficient.

3. *Documents required to be deposited, and the times and places of deposit.*

Deposit not
to be made on
Sunday, &c.

23. No deposit required by the following orders shall be deemed
valid if made on Sunday, Christmas Day, Good Friday, or Easter
Monday, or before eight o'clock in the forenoon, or after eight
o'clock in the afternoon of any day.

Deposits on or before the 30th November.

24. In cases of bills of the second class, a plan and also a duplicate thereof, together with a book of reference thereto, and a section and also a duplicate thereof, as hereinafter described, and in cases of bills of the first class, under the powers of which any lands or houses may be taken compulsorily, and in the case of all bills by which any charge is imposed upon any lands or houses or any lands or houses are rendered liable to have a charge imposed upon them in respect of any improvement, a plan and duplicate thereof, together with a book of reference thereto, shall be deposited for public inspection at the office of the clerk of the peace for every county, riding or division in England or Ireland, or in the office of the principal sheriff clerk of every county in Scotland, and where any county in Scotland is divided into districts or divisions, then also in the office of the principal sheriff clerk in or for each district or division, in or through which the work is proposed to be made, maintained, varied, extended or enlarged, or in which such lands or houses are situate, on or before the 30th day of November immediately preceding the application for the bill; and in the case of railway bills, the Ordnance map, on the scale of one inch to a mile, or where there is no Ordnance map, a published map, to a scale of not less than half an inch to a mile (or in Ireland, to a scale of not less than a quarter of an inch to a mile), with the line of railway delineated thereon, so as to show its general course and direction, shall be deposited with such plans, sections and book of reference; and the clerks of the peace or sheriff clerks, or their respective deputies, shall make a memorial in writing upon the plans, sections and books of reference so deposited with them, denoting the time at which the same were lodged in their respective offices, and shall at all seasonable hours of the day permit any person to view and examine one of the same, and to make copies or extracts therefrom; and *one* of the two plans and sections so deposited shall be sealed up and retained in the possession of the clerk of the peace or sheriff clerk until called for by order of one of the two Houses of Parliament. In cases of bills whereby it is proposed to alter or extend the municipal boundary of any city, borough, or urban district, a map on a scale of not less than three inches to a mile, and also a duplicate thereof, showing as well the present boundaries of the city, borough, or urban district as the boundaries of the proposed extension, shall be deposited with the town clerk of such city or

Standing Orders, compliance with which is to be proved before Examiners.

Plans and books of reference, and sections, to be deposited with clerk of the peace, &c.

In cases of railways, Ordnance or published map to be deposited with clerk of peace, &c.

Clerks of peace to indorse a memorial on plans, &c.

In case of proposed alteration or extension of municipal boundaries, map and duplicate to be deposited with Town Clerk, &c.

Standing
Orders, com-
pliance with
which is to be
proved before
Examiners.

Deposit of
plans, &c. in
Private Bill
Office.

Deposit of
tramway map
at the office of
Board of
Trade.

When works
on tidal lands,
plans, sections,
and map, to be
deposited at
the office of the
Harbour De-
partment,
Board of
Trade.

When works on
banks, &c. of
any river,
plans, sections,
and map to be
deposited at the
office of the
conservators
of the river.

borough, or clerk of such urban district, who shall at all seasonable hours of the day permit any person to view and examine such map, and to make copies thereof.

25. On or before the 30th day of November, a copy of the said plans, sections and books of reference, and in the case of railway bills, also a copy of the said Ordnance or published map, with the line of railway delineated thereon, shall be deposited in the Private Bill Office of this House.

25a. In the case of bills for laying down a tramway, a published map of the district on a scale of not less than six inches to a mile (or if no map on such a scale be published, then the best map obtainable), with the line of the proposed tramway marked thereon, and a diagram on a scale of not less than two inches to a mile, prepared in accordance with the specimen to be obtained at the Office of the Board of Trade, must also be deposited at that office on or before the 30th November.

26. In cases where the work is to be situate on tidal lands within the ordinary spring tides, a copy of the plans and sections shall, on or before the 30th day of November immediately pre- ceding the application for the bill, be deposited at the office of the Harbour Department, Board of Trade, marked "TIDAL WATERS," and on such copy all tidal waters shall be coloured blue, and if the plans include any bridge across tidal waters, the dimensions, as regards span and headway of the nearest bridges, if any, across the same tidal waters above and below the proposed new bridge, shall be marked thereon ; and in all such cases, such plans and sections shall be accompanied by an Ordnance or published map of the country over which the works are proposed to extend, or are to be carried, with their position and extent, or route accurately laid down thereon.

26a. And, in cases where the work is to be situate on the banks, foreshore, or bed of any river having a Board of Conservators con- stituted by Act of Parliament, a copy of the plans and sections shall, on or before the 30th day of November immediately pre- ceding the application for the bill, be deposited at the office of the conservators of the river, and if the plans include any tunnel under or bridge over the river, the dimensions as regards depth below bed of the river, and span and headway, shall be marked thereon ; and such plans shall be accompanied by an Ordnance or published map of the country over which the works are proposed to extend or are to be carried, with their position and extent or route accurately laid down thereon.

27. In the case of railway, tramway, subway, and canal bills, a copy of all plans, sections, and books of reference, required to be deposited in the office of any clerk of the peace or sheriff clerk, on or before the 30th day of November immediately preceding the application for the bill (and in the case of railway bills also a copy of the said Ordnance or published map, with the line of railway delineated thereon), shall on or before the same day be deposited in the office of the Board of Trade.

Standing Orders, compliance with which is to be proved before Examiners.

Deposit of plans, &c. at the office of the Board of Trade.

28. Where the work or any part thereof will be situate within the administrative county of London, or where powers are sought to take any lands within the said county, a copy of so much of the plans, sections, and book of reference as relates to lands within the said county shall, on or before the 30th day of November, be deposited at the office of the London County Council.

Deposit of plans and sections with London County Council.

29. Where, under the powers of any bill, any work is intended to be made, maintained, varied, extended, or enlarged, or any lands or houses may be taken compulsorily, or an improvement charge may be imposed, a copy of so much of the said plans and sections as relates to any of the areas hereinafter mentioned, together with a copy of so much of the book of reference as relates to such area, shall on or before the 30th day of November be deposited with the officer respectively hereinafter mentioned, that is to say, in the case of—

Deposit of plans, sections, and books of reference.

(*a*) Any parish in the City of London, with the parish clerk of that parish ;

(*b*) Any district of the administrative County of London (outside the City of London), with the clerk of the Vestry or District Board, as the case may be ;

(*c*) Any county borough or other borough in England or Wales, with the town clerk ;

(*d*) Any urban district in England or Wales, not being a borough, with the clerk of the District Council ;

(*e*) Any parish in England or Wales having a Parish Council, with the clerk of the Parish Council, or, if there is no clerk, with the chairman of that Council ;

(*f*) Any parish in England or Wales comprised in a Rural District, and not having a Parish Council, with the clerk of the District Council ;

(*g*) Any parish in Scotland, with the clerk of the Parish Council ;

Standing
Orders, com-
pliance with
which is to be
proved before
Examiners.

(*h*) Any royal or parliamentry burgh in Scotland, with the town clerk;

(*i*) Any police burgh in Scotland, with the clerk to the burgh commissioners;

(*j*) Any parish in Ireland, with the clerk of the union within which that parish is included;

(*k*) Any urban sanitary authority in Ireland, with the clerk of the sanitary authority.

Deposit of
plans, &c. at
the Home De-
partment and
the Board of
Agriculture.

30. Where by any bill power is sought to take any churchyard, burial ground, or cemetery, or any part thereof, or to disturb the bodies interred therein, or where power is sought to take any common or commonable land as the case may be, a copy of so much of the plans, sections, and books of reference required by these orders to be deposited in the Private Bill Office in respect of such bill as relates to such churchyard, burial ground, or cemetery, common or commonable land, shall, on or before the thirtieth day of November, be deposited at the office of the Secretary of State for the Home Department, and a copy of so much of the said plans, sections, and books of reference as relates to such common or commonable land shall, on or before the said day, be deposited at the office of the Board of Agriculture.

Gazette notice
to be deposited
with plans, &c.

31. Wherever any plans, sections, and books of reference, or parts thereof, are required to be deposited, a copy of the notice published in the *Gazette* of the intended application to parliament shall be deposited therewith.

Deposits on or before the 21st December.

32. Every petition for a private bill, headed by a short title descriptive of the undertaking or bill, corresponding with that at the head of the advertisement, with a declaration, signed by the agent, and a printed copy of the bill annexed, shall be deposited in the Private Bill Office on or before the 21st day of December; and such petition, bill and declaration shall be open to the inspection of all parties; and printed copies of the bill shall also be delivered therewith for the use of any member of the house or agent who may apply for the same. Such declaration shall state

Declaration of
agent as to
class of bill,
and powers
thereof, to be
annexed to
petition.

to which of the two classes of bills such bill in the judgment of the agent belongs; and if the proposed bill shall give power to effect any of the following objects; that is to say:—

Power to take any lands or houses compulsorily, or to extend the time granted by any former Act for that purpose:

Power to levy tolls, rates or duties, or to alter any existing tolls, rates or duties ; or to confer, vary or extinguish any exemption from payment of tolls, rates or duties, or to confer, vary or extinguish any other right or privilege:

Power to amalgamate with any other company, or to sell or lease their undertaking, or to purchase or take on lease the undertaking of any other company :

Power to interfere with any crown, church or corporation property, or property held in trust for public or charitable purposes :

Power to relinquish any part of a work authorized by a former Act :

Power to divert into any existing or intended cut, canal, resevoir, aqueduct or navigation, or into any intended variation, extension or enlargement thereof respectively, any water from any existing cut, canal, reservoir, aqueduct or navigation, whether directly or derivatively, and whether under any agreement with the proprietors thereof, or otherwise :

Power to make, vary, extend or enlarge any cut, canal, reservoir, aqueduct or navigation :

Power to make, vary, extend or enlarge any railway.

Standing Orders, compliance with which is to be proved before Examiners.

The said declaration shall state which of such powers are given by the bill, and shall indicate in which clauses of the bill (referring to them by their number) such powers are given, and shall further state that the bill does not give power to effect any of the objects enumerated in this Order, other than those stated in the declaration.

If the proposed bill shall not give power to effect any of the objects enumerated in the preceding Order, the said declaration shall state that the bill does not give power to effect any of such objects.

The said declaration shall also state that the bill does not give any powers other than those included in the notices for the bill.

33. On or before the 21st day of December, a printed copy of every private bill shall be deposited at the office of Her Majesty's Treasury and at the General Post Office ; a printed copy of every bill relating to railways, tramways, subways, canals, gas, water, patents, or electric lighting, or for incorporating or giving powers to any company, shall be deposited at the office of the Board of Trade ; a printed copy of every bill relating to any dock, harbour, navigation, pier or port, shall be deposited at the office of the Harbour Department of the Board of Trade, marked " Tidal waters " ; a printed copy of every bill containing provisions with respect to the use of weights and measures, or the inspection or verification of the same, shall be deposited at the Standard Depart-

Deposit of private bills at Treasury and other public departments.

ment of the Board of Trade; a printed copy of every bill relating to a local court or stipendiary magistrate, and of every bill whereby power is sought to take any churchyard, burial ground, or cemetery, or any part thereof, or to disturb the bodies interred therein, or to take any common or commonable land, at the office of the Secretary of State for the Home Department; a printed copy of every bill relating to any company, body, or person carrying on business in any colony or British possession, at the office of the Secretary of State for the Colonies; a printed copy of every Bill relating to Scotland, at the office of the Secretary for Scotland: a printed copy of every bill relating to any matter in England or Wales within the jurisdiction of the Local Government Board, or to which Standing Order 38 applies at the office of that Board; a printed copy of every bill which proposes to alter the boundary of the area of any county, urban district, parish, or any other administrative area, or which relates to any matter to which the Birth and Deaths Registration Acts, 1836 to 1874, and any Act amending the same, relate, at the General Register Office, Somerset House; a printed copy of every private bill whereby the boundaries of any school district or the jurisdiction of any school board are affected at the office of the Education Department; a printed copy of every bill affecting Crown property at the office of the Commissioners of Her Majesty's Works and Public Buildings, and at the office of Her Majesty's Woods, Forests, and Land Revenues; a printed copy of every bill affecting charities or charitable trusts at the office of the Charity Commission; and a printed copy of every bill affecting the Duchy of Cornwall or the Duchy of Lancaster at the office of such Duchy respectively.

33*a*. On or before the 21st day of December, a printed copy of every private bill promoted by municipal or other local authorities, by which it is proposed to create powers relating to police or sanitary regulations which deviate from, or are in extension of, or repugnant to, the general law, shall be deposited at the office of the Secretary of State for the Home Department.

33*b*. On or before the 21st day of December, a printed copy of every local bill which relates to the drainage of land in England or Wales, or which relates to the improvement of land in England, Wales, or Scotland, or to the erection, improvement, repair, maintenance, or regulation of any market or market place at which cattle are exposed for sale, or to any matter within the jurisdiction of the Board of Agriculture, or which proposes to alter the boundary of any county, urban district, urban sanitary district, parish, or any other administrative area in the United Kingdom, or whereby power is sought to take any common or commonable land, shall be deposited at the office of the Board of Agriculture.

34. On or before the 21st day of December, a printed copy of every bill of the second class whereby any work shall be authorized within the limits of the administrative County of London, shall be deposited at the office of the London County Council.

34a. On or before the 21st day of December, a printed copy of every bill of the second class, whereby it is intended to authorize the construction of any work on the banks, foreshore, or bed of any river having a board of conservators constituted by Act of Parment, shall be deposited at the office of the conservators of the river.

Standing Orders, compliance with which is to be proved before Examiners.

Deposit of bills with the London County Council.

Deposit of bills with the conservators of rivers.

Deposits on or before the 31st December.

35. All estimates and declarations, and lists of owners, lessees and occupiers, which are required by the Standing Orders of this House shall be deposited in the Private Bill Office on or before the 31st day of December.

35a. As respects all bills for the incorporation of joint stock companies, or proposed companies for carrying on any trade or business, or for conferring upon such companies the power of suing and being sued, there shall be deposited in the Private Bill Office, on or before 31st December, a copy of the deed or agreement of partnership (if any) under which the company or proposed company is acting, and in all cases other than those of companies registered under the "Companies Act, 1862," a declaration stating the following matters :—

Deposit of estimates, &c., in Private Bill Office.

Documents to be deposited in Private Bill Office in regard to joint stock companies bills.

1st.—The present and proposed amount of the capital of the company.

2nd.—The number of shares, and the amount of each share.

3rd.—The number of shares subscribed for.

4th.—The amount of subscriptions paid up.

5th.—The names, residences, and descriptions of the shareholders or subscribers (so far as the same can be made out), and of the actual or provisional directors, treasurers, secretaries or other officer, if any.

And such documents shall be verified by the signature of some authorized officer of the company or proposed company (if any), and by some responsible party promoting the Bill ; and copies of such declarations shall be printed at the expense of the promoters

H

Standing
Orders. com-
pliance with
which is to be
proved before
Examiners.

Copies of
estimate and
declaration
to be printed,
and delivered
in at Private
Bill Office.

Form of
estimate.

of the bill, and delivered at the Vote Office for the use of the Members of the House, and at the Private Bill Office for the use of any agent who may apply for the same.

36. On or before 31st December, copies of the estimate of expense of the undertaking; and where a declaration alone, or declaration and estimate of the probable amount of rates and duties are required, copies of such declaration, or of such declaration and estimate, shall be printed at the expense of the promoters of the bill, and delivered at the Vote Office for the use of the Members of the House, and at the Private Bill Office for the use of any agent who may apply for the same.

37. The estimate for any works proposed to be authorized by any railway, tramway, tramroad, subway, canal, dock, or harbour bill, shall be in the following form, or as near thereto as circumstances may permit:—

ESTIMATE of the proposed   (Railway).

Line, No.

Miles. fur. chs.   Whether Single or Double.

Length of Line   -   -   -

Cubic yds. Price per yd. £ s. d. | £ s. d.

Earthworks :
   Cuttings—Rock   -
          Soft Soil -
          Roads   -

     TOTAL   -

Embankments, including roads   -   Cubic yds.   -   -
Bridges—Public roads   -   -   -   Number   -   -
     Accommodation bridges and works   -   -   -
Viaducts   -   -   -   -   -   -   -   -
Culverts and drains   -   -   -   -   -   -
Metallings of roads and level crossings -   -   -   -
Gatekeepers' houses at level crossings   -   -   -
Permanent way, including fencing :

                 Cost per mile.
       Miles. fur. chs.
               £ s. d.
           at

Permanent ways for sidings, and cost of junctions -   -   -
Stations   -   -   -   -   -   -   -   -

     Contingencies   -   -   -   -   - per cent.

Land and buildings :
            A. R. P.
               TOTAL -   -   -

The same details for each branch, and general summary of total cost.

38. In the case of any Bill which contains power to take compulsorily or by agreement, in any parish in the Metropolis, twenty or more houses, or as regards England and Wales, exclusive of the Metropolis, in any city, borough, or other urban district, or in any parish, or part of a parish, not being within an urban district, or in Scotland in any district within the meaning of "The Public Health (Scotland) Act, 1867," or in Ireland in any urban sanitary district as defined by "The Public Health (Ireland) Act, 1878," ten or more houses, occupied either wholly or partially by persons belonging to the labouring class, as defined by Order 183*a*, as tenants or lodgers, or which revives or extends any such power, the promoters shall deposit in the Private Bill Office, and at the office of the central authority, as defined in Order 183*a*, on or before the 31st day of December, a statement of the number, description, and situation of such houses, the number (so far as can be ascertained) of persons residing therein, and a copy of so much of the plan (if any) as relates thereto ; this Standing Order shall not apply where a statement in pursuance of this Standing Order was deposited in respect of the Act the powers of which are proposed to be revived or extended. [*See also* Standing Order 183*a*.]

Standing Orders, compliance with which is to be proved before Examiners.

Statement relating to houses inhabited by labouring classes to be deposited in Private Bill Office and office of central authority.

39. Whenever plans, sections, books of reference, or maps are deposited in the case of an application to any public department or county council, for a provisional order or provisional certificate, duplicates of the said documents shall also be deposited in the Private Bill Office ; provided that with regard to such deposits as are so made at any public department, or with any county council, after the prorogation of Parliament, and before the 30th day of November in any year, such duplicates shall be so deposited on or before the 30th day of November.

Deposit of plans, &c., in case of Provisional Orders in Private Bill Office.

4. *Form in which Plans, Books of Reference, Sections and Cross Sections are to be prepared.*

Plans.

40. Every plan required to be deposited shall be drawn to a scale of not less than four inches to a mile, and shall describe the lands which may be taken compulsorily, or on which an improvement charge may be imposed, or which are rendered liable to the imposition of an improvement charge, and in the case of bills of the second class, shall also describe the line or situation of the whole of the work (no alternative line or work being in any case permitted), and the lands in or through which it is to be made,

Description of plans.

Standing Orders. compliance with which is to be proved before Examiners.

Lands within deviation to be on plan.

Buildings, &c. on enlarged scale.

maintained, varied, extended, or enlarged, or through which any communication to or from the work may be made; and where it is the intention of the promoters to apply for powers to make any lateral deviation from the line of the proposed work, the limits of such deviation shall be defined upon the plan, and all lands included within such limits shall be marked thereon; and unless the whole of such plan shall be upon a scale of not less than a quarter of an inch to every 100 feet, an enlarged plan shall be added of any building, yard, courtyard, or land within the curtilage of any building, or of any ground cultivated as a garden, either in the line of the proposed work, or included within the limits of the said deviation, upon a scale of not less than a quarter of an inch to every 100 feet.

In case of cut, canals, &c. plan to describe brooks, &c. to be diverted.

41. In all cases where it is proposed to make, vary, extend, or enlarge any cut, canal, reservoir, aqueduct, or navigation, the plan shall describe the brooks and streams to be directly diverted into such intended cut, canal, reservoir, aqueduct, or navigation, or into any variation, extension, or enlargement thereof respectively, for supplying the same with water.

In case of railways, distances to be marked in miles and furlongs. and memorandum of curves and tunnelling.

42. In all cases where it is proposed to make, vary, extend, or enlarge any railway, the plan shall exhibit thereon the distances in miles and furlongs from one of the termini; and a memorandum of the radius of every curve not exceeding one mile in length shall be noted on the plan in furlongs and chains; and where tunnelling as a substitute for open cutting is intended, the same shall be marked by a dotted line on the plan, and no work shall be shown as tunnelling in the making of which it will be necessary to cut through or remove the surface soil.

Diversion of roads, &c. to be shown.

43. If it be intended to divert, widen, or narrow any public carriage road, navigable river, canal, or railway, the course of such diversion, and the extent of such widening or narrowing, shall be marked upon the plan.

In case of junctions, course of existing line to be shown on deposited plan.

44. When a railway is intended to form a junction with an existing or authorized line of railway, the course of such existing or authorized line of railway shall be shown on the deposited plan for a distance of 800 yards on either side of the proposed junction, on the same scale as the scale of the general plan.

Street Tramways.

Plans in the case of Street Tramway Bills.

45. In cases of bills for laying down a tramway, the plans shall indicate whether it is proposed to lay such tramway along the centre of any street, and if not along the centre, then on which side of, and at what distance from an imaginary line drawn along the centre of such street, and whether or not, and if so, at what

point or points it is proposed to lay such tramway, so that for a distance of 30 ft., or upwards, a less space than 9 ft. 6 in., or if it is intended to run thereon carriages or trucks adapted for use upon railways, a less space than 10 ft. 6 in. shall intervene between the outside of the footpath on either side of the road, and the nearest rail of the tramway.

Standing Orders, compliance with which is to be proved before Examiners.

All lengths shall be stated on the plan and section in miles, furlongs, chains, and decimals of a chain. The distances in miles and furlongs from one of the termini of each tramway shall be marked on the plan and section. Each double portion of tramway, whether a passing-place or otherwise, shall be indicated by a double line. The total length of the road upon which each tramway is to be laid shall be stated (*i.e.*, the length of route of each tramway).

The length of each double and single portion of such tramway, and the total length of such double and single portions respectively shall also be stated.

In the case of double lines (including passing-places), the distance between the centre lines of each line of tramway shall be marked on the plans. This distance must in all cases be sufficient to leave at least fifteen inches between the sides of the widest carriages and engines to be used on the tramways when passing one another. The gradients of the road on which each tramway is to be laid shall be marked on the section. Every crossing of a railway, tramway, river, or canal shall be shown, specifying in the case of railways and tramways whether they are crossed over, under, or on the level.

All tidal waters shall be coloured blue.

All places where for a distance of 30 ft. and upwards there will be a less space than 9 ft. 6 in. between the outside of the footpath on either side of the road and the nearest rail of the tramway shall be indicated by a thick dotted line on the plans on the side or sides of the line of tramway where such narrow places occur, as well as noted on the plans, and the width of the road at those places should also be marked on the plans.

The preceding paragraph shall apply, in the case of a tramroad, wherever it is carried along a street or road.

Tramroads.

45a. In the case of bills for constructing a subway the plans and sections shall indicate the height and width of the proposed subway and the nature of the approaches by which it is proposed to afford access to such subway.

Plans, &c. in the case of subway bills.

Standing Orders, compliance with which is to be proved before Examiners.

45b. In the case of bills containing power to impose on any lands or houses, or to render any lands or houses liable to the imposition of any charge in respect of any improvement, the plan shall define the improvement, and also the improvement area (being the limits within which the charge may be imposed).

Book of Reference.

Definition of improvement and limits of improvement area.
Contents of book of reference.

46. The book of reference shall contain the names of the owners or reputed owners, lessees or reputed lessees, and occupiers of all lands and houses which may be taken compulsorily, or upon which any improvement charge is imposed, or which are rendered liable to have an improvement charge imposed upon them, and shall describe such lands and houses respectively.

Sections.

Section.

47. The section shall be drawn to the same horizontal scale as the plan, and to a vertical scale of not less than one inch to every 100 feet, and shall show the surface of the ground marked on the plan, the intended level of the proposed work, the height of every embankment, and the depth of every cutting, and a datum horizontal line, which shall be the same throughout the whole length of the work, or any branch thereof respectively, and shall be referred to some fixed point (stated in writing on the section), near some portion of such work, and in the case of a canal, cut, navigation, public carriage road or railway, near either of the termini.

Improvement, &c. of navigations.

48. In cases of bills for improving the navigation of any river, there shall be a section which shall specify the levels of both banks of such river; and where any alteration is intended to be made therein, it shall describe the same by feet and inches, or decimal parts of a foot.

Line of railway on section to correspond with upper surface of rails.
Vertical measures to be marked at change of gradient.

49. In every section of a railway the line of the railway marked thereon shall correspond with the upper surface of the rails.

50. Distances on the datum line shall be marked in miles and furlongs to correspond with those on the plan; a vertical measure from the datum line to the line of the railway shall be marked in feet and inches, or decimal parts of a foot, at the commencement and termination of the railway, and at each change of the gradient or inclination thereof; and the proportion or rate of inclination between every two consecutive vertical measures shall also be marked.

51. Wherever the line of the railway is intended to cross any public carriage-road, navigable river, canal, or railway, the height of the railway over or depth under the surface thereof, and the height and span of every arch of all bridges and viaducts, by which the railway will be carried over the same, shall be marked in figures at every crossing thereof; and where the railway will be carried across any such public carriage-road or railway, on the level thereof, such crossing shall be so described on the section; and it shall also be stated if such level will be unaltered.

52. If any alteration be intended in the water level of any canal, or in the level or rate of inclination of any public carriage-road or railway, which will be crossed by the line of railway, then the same shall be stated on the section, and each alteration shall be numbered; and cross sections, in reference to the numbers, on a horizontal scale of not less than one inch to every 330 feet, and on a vertical scale of not less than one inch to every 40 feet, shall be added, which shall show the present surface of such road, canal or railway, and the intended surface thereof when altered: and the greatest of the present and intended rates of inclination of the portion of such road or railway intended to be altered shall also be marked in figures thereon; and where any public carriage-road is crossed on the level, a cross section of such road shall also be added, and all such cross sections shall extend for 200 yards on each side of the centre line of the railway.

53. Wherever the extreme height of any embankment, or the extreme depth of any cutting shall exceed five feet, the extreme height over or depth under the surface of the ground shall be marked in figures upon the section; and if any bridge or viaduct of more than three arches shall intervene in any embankment, or if any tunnel shall intervene in any cutting, the extreme height or depth shall be marked in figures on each of the parts into which such embankment or cutting shall be divided by such bridge, viaduct, or tunnel.

54. Where tunnelling, as a substitute for open cutting, or a viaduct as a substitute for solid embankment, is intended, the same shall be marked on the section, and no work shall be shown as tunnelling, in the making of which it will be necessary to cut through or remove the surface soil.

55. When a railway is intended to form a junction with an existing or authorized line of railway, the gradient of such existing or authorized line of railway shall be shown on the deposited section, and in connection therewith, and on the same scale as the

general section, for a distance of 800 yards on either side of the point of junction.

5. *Estimates and Deposit of Money, and Declarations in Certain Cases.*

56. An estimate of the expense of the undertaking under each bill of the second class shall be made and signed by the person making the same.

57. In the case of a railway bill, tramway bill, or subway bill, authorizing the construction of works by other than an existing railway company, tramway company, or subway company, incorporated by Act of Parliament, possessed of a railway, tramway, or subway already opened for public traffic, and which has during the year last past paid dividends on its ordinary share capital, and which does not propose to raise under the bill a capital greater than its existing authorized capital, a sum not less than five per cent. on the amount of the estimate of expense, or in the case of substituted works, on the amount by which the expense thereof will exceed the expense of the works to be abandoned, and in the case of all bills other than railway bills, tramway bills, and subway bills, a sum not less than four per cent. on the amount of such estimate, or of such excess as aforesaid, shall, previously to the 15th day of January, be deposited with the Paymaster-General for and on behalf of the Supreme Court of Judicature in England, if the work is intended to be done in England, or with the Paymaster-General for and on behalf of the Supreme Court of Judicature in England, or with the Queen's and Lord Treasurer's Remembrancer on behalf of the Court of Exchequer in Scotland, if the work is intended to be done in Scotland, or with the Accountant General of the Supreme Court of Judicature in Ireland, if the work is intended to be done in Ireland.

58. Where the work is to be made, wholly or in part, by means of funds, or out of money to be raised upon the credit of present surplus revenue, belonging to any society or company, or under the control of directors, trustees, or commissioners, as the case may be, of any existing public work, such parties being the promoters of the bill, a declaration stating those facts, and setting forth the nature of such control, and the nature and amount of such funds or surplus revenue, and showing the actual surplus of such funds or revenue, after deducting the funds required for purposes authorized by any Act or Acts of Parliament, and also the funds which

may be required for any other work to be executed under any bill in the same session, and given under the common seal of the society or company, or under the hand of some authorized officer of such directors, trustees, or commissioners, may be deposited, and in such case no deposit of money shall be required in respect of so much of the estimate of expense as shall be provided for by such surplus funds.

Standing Orders, compliance with which is to be proved before Examiners.

59. In cases of any bill under which no private or personal pecuniary profit or advantage is to be derived, and where the work is to be made out of money to be raised upon the security of the rates, duties, or revenue already belonging to or under the control of the promoters, or to be created by or to arise under the bill, a declaration stating those facts, and setting forth the means by which funds are to be obtained for executing the work, and signed by the party or agent soliciting the bill, together with an estimate of the probable amount of such rates, duties, or revenue, signed by the person making the same, may be deposited, and in such case no money deposit shall be required.

Cases in which declaration and estimate of amount of rates may be deposited.

Bills brought from the House of Lords.

60. A copy of every railway bill, tramway bill, subway bill, and canal bill, brought from the House of Lords shall be deposited in the office of the Board of Trade, not later than two days after the bill is read a first time.

Copy of railway, &c. bill to be deposited at Board of Trade.

60*a*. In the case of bills brought from the House of Lords, a copy of every bill whereby application is made by or on behalf of any county council, municipal corporation, district council, or other local authority in England or Wales, for power in respect of any matter within the jurisdiction of the Local Government Board, and of every bill whereby any powers, rights, duties, capacities, liabilities, or obligations are sought to be conferred or imposed on any local authority in England or Wales in respect of any matter within the jurisdiction of the Local Government Board, and of every bill relating to turnpike roads or trusts, highways, or bridges, and of every bill to which Standing Order 38 applies, shall be deposited at the office of the Local Government Board not later than two days after the bill is read a first time. A copy of every bill which proposes to alter the boundary of the area of any county, urban district, parish, or any other administrative area, or which relates to any matter to which the Births and Deaths Registration Acts, 1836 to 1874, and any Act amending

Copy of Bill for conferring powers, &c. on municipal corporation, local board, or any local authority. to be deposited at office of the Local Government Board, &c.

Standing
Orders, com-
pliance with
which is to be
proved before
Examiners.

the same, relate, shall be deposited at the General Register Office,. Somerset House, not later than two days after the bill is read a first time. A copy of every bill required to be deposited at the office of the Secretary of State for the Home Department under Standing Orders 33 and 33a shall be deposited at that office not later than two days after the bill is read a first time. A copy of every bill required to be deposited at the office of the Board of Agriculture under Standing Order 33b shall be deposited at that office not later than two days after the bill is read a first time.

Notices to be
given and de-
posits made in
cases where
work is altered
while Bill is in
Parliament.

61. Whenever during the progress through the House of Lords of any bill of the second class originating in that House, any alteration has been made in any work authorized by such bill, proof shall be given before the Examiners that a plan and section of such alteration, on the same scale, and containing the same particulars as the original plan and section, together with a book of reference thereto, has been deposited in the Private Bill Office, and with the clerk of the peace of every county, riding, or division in England or Ireland, and in the office of the sheriff clerk of every county in Scotland, in which such alteration is proposed to be made, and where any county in Scotland is divided into districts or divisions then also in the office of the principal sheriff clerk in and for each district or division in which such alteration is proposed to be made; and that a copy of such plan and section, so far as relates to any of the areas mentioned in Standing Order 29, together with a book of reference thereto, has been deposited with the officers respectively mentioned in that Order, as the case may be, two weeks previously to the introduction of the bill into this House; and that the intention to make such alteration has been published previously to the introduction of the bill into this House once in the London, Edinburgh, or Dublin *Gazette*, as the case may be,. and for two successive weeks in some one and the same newspaper of the county in which such alteration is situate, and that application in writing, as nearly as may be in the form set forth in the Appendix, marked (A), was made to the owners or reputed owners,. lessees or reputed lessees, or in their absence from the United Kingdom, to their agents respectively, and to the occupiers of lands through which any such alteration is intended to be made; and the consent of such owners or reputed owners, lessees or reputed lessees, and occupiers, to the making of such alteration, shall be proved before the examiner. Compliance with this order shall not be necessary in the case of alterations made on petition or additional provision in the House of Lords.

Provisions relating to the Consents of Proprietors or Members of Companies already constituted, and of Persons named as Directors.

Standing Orders, compliance with which is to be proved before Examiners.

62. Every bill originating in this House, promoted by a company already constituted by Act of Parliament, shall after the first reading thereof be referred to Examiners, who shall report as to compliance or non-compliance with the following Order :—

Meeting of proprietors in the case of certain bills originating in this House.

The bill, as introduced, or proposed to be introduced, in this House, shall be submitted to the proprietors of such company at a meeting held specially for that purpose.

Such meeting shall be called by advertisement inserted once in each of two consecutive weeks in some one and the same newspaper published in London, Edinburgh, or Dublin, as the case may be, and in some one and the same newspaper of the county or counties in which the principal office or offices of the company is or are situate; and also by a circular addressed to each proprietor at his last known or usual address, and sent by post, or delivered at such address, not less than ten days before the holding of such meeting, enclosing a blank form of proxy, with proper instructions for the use of the same ; and the same form of proxy and the same instructions, and none other, shall be sent to every such proprietor; but no such form of proxy shall be stamped before it is sent out, nor shall the funds of the company be used for the stamping any proxies, nor shall intimation be sent as to any person in whose favour the proxy may be granted, and no other circular or form of proxy relating to such meeting shall be sent to any proprietor from the office of the company, or by any director or officer of the company so describing himself.

Such meeting shall be held not earlier than the seventh day after the last insertion of such advertisement, and may be held on the same day as an ordinary general meeting of the company.

At such meeting the said bill shall be submitted to the proprietors aforesaid then present, and approved of by proprietors present in person or by proxy, holding at least three-fourths of the paid-up capital of the company represented by the votes at such meeting, such proprietors being qualified to vote at all ordinary meetings of the company in right of such capital. The votes of proprietors of any paid-up shares or

Standing
Orders, com-
pliance with
which is to be
proved before
Examiners.

stock other than debenture stock, not qualified to vote at ordinary meetings, whose interests may be affected by the bill, if tendered at the meeting shall be recorded separately. The names of the proprietors present in person at the meeting shall be recorded by the company. For this purpose the meeting, and any other consecutive meetings, whether general or special, and whether preceding or following it, shall be deemed to be the same meeting. A poll may be demanded by any proprietor present in person at the meeting.

There shall be deposited at the Private Bill Office a statement of the number of votes if a poll was taken, and of the number of votes recorded separately.

So far as any such bill relates to a separate undertaking in any company as distinct from the general undertaking, separate meetings shall be held of the proprietors of the company and of the separate undertaking, and the provisions of this order applicable to meetings of proprietors of the company shall, *mutatis mutandis*, apply to meetings of proprietors of the separate undertaking.

Meeting of
members of
limited com-
panies, &c., in
the case of
certain bills
originating in
this House.

63. Every bill originating in this House, promoted by any company, society, association, or co-partnership formed or registered under the Companies Act, 1862, or constituted by Act of Parliament, royal charter, letters patent, deed of settlement, contract of co-partnery, cost book regulations, or other instrument, and under the management of a committee, or directors or trustees (and not being a company to which the preceding Order applies) shall, after the first reading thereof, be referred to the Examiners, who shall report as to compliance or non-compliance with the following order :

In the case of a company formed or registered under the Companies Act, 1862,

The bill as introduced or proposed to be introduced in this House shall be approved by a special resolution of the company.

In the case of any other such company, society, association, or co-partnership as aforesaid,

The bill as introduced or proposed to be introduced in this House shall be consented to by a majority of three-fourths in number and (where applicable) in value of the proprietors or members of such company, society, association, or co-partnership present, in person or by proxy, at a meeting convened, with notice of the business to be transacted, and voting at such meeting; such consent to be certified in writing by the chairman of the meeting.

A copy of such special resolution or certificate of consent shall be deposited in the Private Bill Office.

The names of the proprietors or members present in person at the meeting shall be recorded by the company, society, association or co-partnership. For this purpose the meeting, and any other consecutive meetings, whether general or special, and whether preceding or following it, shall be deemed to be the same meeting.

A poll may be demanded by any one proprietor or member present in person at the meeting, notwithstanding any provision to the contrary contained in any instrument constituting or regulating the company, society, association, or co-partnership.

If a poll is taken, there shall be deposited in the Private Bill Office a statement of the number of votes.

So far as any such bill relates to a separate class of proprietors or members of any company, society, association, or co-partnership, as distinct from the proprietors or members generally, such bill shall be approved or assented to by the proprietors or members generally, and also by the separate class of proprietors or members, and the provisions of this Order applicable to the proprietors or members generally, shall, *mutatis mutandis*, apply to the separate class of proprietors or members.

64. In the case of every bill brought from the House of Lords in which provisions have been inserted in that House, empowering the promoters thereof, being a company already constituted by Act of Parliament, to execute, undertake, or contribute towards any work other than that for which it was originally established, or to sell or lease their undertaking, or any part thereof, or to enter into any agreements with any other company for the working, maintenance, management, or use of the railway or works of either company, or any part thereof, or to amalgamate their undertaking, or any part thereof with any other undertaking, or to purchase any other undertaking, or part thereof, or any additional lands, or to abandon their undertaking, or any part thereof, or to dissolve the said company, or in which any such provisions originally contained in the bill have been materially altered in that House, or in which any such powers are conferred on any company not being the

Standing Orders, compliance with which is to be proved before Examiners.

Meeting of proprietors in the case of certain bills originating in the House of Lords.

Standing
Orders, com-
pliance with
which is to be
proved before
Examiners.

promoters of the bill, the Examiner shall report as to compliance or non-compliance with the following Order :—

The bill as introduced or proposed to be introduced into this House, shall be submitted to the proprietors of any such company, at a meeting held specially for that purpose.

Such meeting shall be called by advertisement, inserted once in each of two consecutive weeks in some one and the same newspaper published in London, Edinburgh, or Dublin, as the case may be, and in some one and the same newspaper of the county or counties in which the principal office or offices of the company is or are situate; and also by a circular addressed to each proprietor at his last known or usual address, and sent by post, or delivered at such address, not less than ten days before the holding of such meeting, enclosing a blank form of proxy, with proper instructions for the use of the same; and the same form of proxy, and the same instructions, and none other, shall be sent to every such proprietor; but no such form of proxy shall be stamped before it is sent out, nor shall the funds of the company be used for the stamping any proxies, nor shall intimation be sent as to any person in whose favour the proxy may be granted, and no other circular or form of proxy relating to such meeting shall be sent to any proprietor from the office of the company, or by any director or officer of the company so describing himself.

Such meeting shall be held not earlier than the seventh day after the last insertion of such advertisement, and may be held on the same day as an ordinary general meeting of the company.

At such meeting the said bill shall be submitted to the proprietors aforesaid then present, and approved by proprietors present in person or by proxy, holding at least three-fourths of the paid-up capital of the company represented by the votes at such meeting, such proprietors being qualified to vote at all ordinary meetings of the company in right of such capital. The votes of proprietors of any paid-up shares or stock other than debenture stock, not qualified to vote at ordinary meetings, whose interests may be affected by the bill, if tendered at the meeting, shall be recorded separately. The names of the proprietors present in person at the meeting shall be recorded by the company. For this purpose the meeting, and any other consecutive meetings, whether general or special, and whether preceding or following it, shall be deemed to be the same meeting. A poll may be demanded by any proprietor present in person at the meeting.

There shall be deposited at the Private Bill Office a statement of the number of votes if a poll was taken, and of the number of votes recorded separately.

So far as any such bill relates to a separate undertaking in any company as distinct from the general undertaking, separate meetings shall be held of the proprietors of the company and of the separate undertaking, and the provisions of this Order applicable to meetings of proprietors of the company shall, *mutatis mutandis,* apply to meetings of proprietors of the separate undertaking.

65. In the case of every bill brought from the House of Lords, in which provisions have been inserted in that House empowering or requiring any company, society, association, or co-partnership, formed or registered under the Companies Act, 1862, or constituted by Act of Parliament, royal charter, letters patent, deed of settlement, contract of co-partnery, cost book regulations, or other instrument or instruments, and under the management of a committee, or directors or trustees, and not being a company to which the preceding Order applies, to do any act not authorized by the memorandum and articles of association of such company, or other instrument constituting or regulating such company, society, association, or co-partnership, or authorizing or enacting the abandonment of the undertaking, or any part of the undertaking, of any such company, society, association, or co-partnership, or the dissolution thereof, or in which any such provisions originally contained in the bill have been materially altered in that House, or by which any such powers are conferred on any company, society, association, or co-partnership, not being the promoters of the bill, the Examiner shall report as to compliance and non-compliance with the following Order :

In the case of a company formed or registered under the Companies Act, 1862.

The bill as introduced or proposed to be introduced into this House shall be approved by a special resolution of the company.

In the case of any other such company, society, association, or co-partnership as aforesaid,

The bill as introduced or proposed to be introduced in this House shall be consented to by a majority of three-fourths in number and (where applicable) in value of the proprietors or

Standing Orders, compliance with which is to be proved before Examiners.

Separate undertakings.

Meeting of members of limited companies, &c., in the case of certain bills originating in the House of Lords.

Standing
Orders, com-
pliance with
which is to be
proved before
Examiners.

members of such company, society, association, or co-partnership present, in person or by proxy, at a meeting convened
with notice of the business to be transacted and voting at
such meeting, such consent to be certified in writing by the
chairman of the meeting.

A copy of such special resolution or certificate of consent
shall be deposited in the Private Bill Office.

Provided always, that if by the terms of such special
resolution or consent the bill as introduced or proposed to
be introduced into the House of Lords shall have been
approved or consented to, subject to such additions, alterations, and variations as Parliament may think fit to make
therein, then it shall not be necessary for the purposes of
this order to obtain any further approval or consent in
respect of any provisions inserted in the bill in the House
of Lords : Provided nevertheless that it shall be competent
for the committee on the bill, if they think fit, having regard
to the nature and effect of such provisions, to require any
further evidence of the approval or consent to such provisions on the part of the shareholders or members of the
company, society, association, or co-partnership.

The names of the proprietors or members present in
person at the meeting shall be recorded by the company,
society, association, or co-partnership. For this purpose the
meeting, and any other consecutive meetings, whether
general or special, and whether preceding or following it,
shall be deemed to be the same meeting.

A poll may be demanded by any one proprietor or member
present in person at the meeting, notwithstanding any provision to the contrary contained in any instrument constituting
or regulating the company, society, association, or co-partnership.

If a poll is taken, there shall be deposited in the Private
Bill Office a statement of the number of votes.

So far as any such bill relates to a separate class of proprietors or members of any company, society, association, or
co-partnership as distinct from the proprietors or members
generally, such bill shall be approved or assented to by the
proprietors or members generally, and also by the separate
class of proprietors or members; and the provisions of this
order applicable to the proprietors or members generally

shall, *mutatis mutandis*, apply to the separate class of proprietors or members.

66. When any bill as introduced into Parliament, or as amended, or proposed to be amended, on petition for additional provision, contains a provision authorizing any company incorporated by Act of Parliament, or any class of holders of share or loan capital in any such company, to subscribe or to alter the terms or conditions of any subscription towards, or to guarantee or to raise any money in aid of the undertaking of another company (which bill is not brought in by the company so authorized, or of which such company is not a joint promoter), proof shall be required before the Examiner before the second reading in this House, if such provision is contained in the bill as introduced into Parliament, that the company, or the class of holders of share or loan capital, so authorized has consented to such subscription, alteration, guarantee, or raising of money, at a meeting of the proprietors of the company, or of any such class of holders of share or loan capital, as the case may be, held specially for that purpose, in the same manner and subject to the same provisions as the meeting directed to be held under Standing Order 64 ; and in case such provision is contained in the bill as introduced into Parliament, that the notices for the bill state the specific sum, if any, proposed to be subscribed, or guaranteed or raised, or the alteration of the terms or conditions of the subscription, as the case may be, or in case such provision shall be proposed to be inserted in the bill, on a petition for additional provision that notices stating the specific sum, if any, proposed to be subscribed, or guaranteed or raised, or the alteration of the terms or conditions of the subscription, as the case may be, and stating that the consent of the company, or of such class of holders of share or loan capital, has been given as aforesaid, have been published once in the London, Edinburgh, or Dublin *Gazette*, as the case may be, and in the county newspapers in which the notices for the bill were published, for two successive weeks during the six weeks immediately preceding the presentation of such petition for additional provision ; in any case in which such consent has been given, it shall not be necessary to submit the bill, in respect of such provision as aforesaid, to the approval of a meeting to be held in accordance with Standing Order 64.

67. When in any railway bill originating in this House a provision is contained by which the payment of any moneys is directly or contingently charged upon grand jury cess, or any other local rate in Ireland, by means of a guarantee or otherwise,

Side notes:

Standing Orders, compliance with which is to be proved before Examiners.

Consent of proprietors of any company to sum authorized to be raised in aid of undertaking of another company.

Petition for additional provision.

Railway Bills charging payments on grand jury cess or local rate in

I

Standing Orders, compliance with which is to be proved before Examiners.

Ireland to be submitted to and approved by grand jury or local authority.

Notice of bill to grand jury or local authority.

Limit of time for bill to be submitted, and presentment or resolution to be deposited in Private Bill Office.

Consent of directors, &c., who are named in a Bill, to be proved.

such bill shall, after the first reading thereof, be referred to the Examiners, who shall report as to compliance or non-compliance with the following order :—

A copy of the bill, as deposited in the Private Bill Office, shall be submitted to the grand jury or other authority empowered to present such grand jury cess, or to make such local rate, and according as the payment of any moneys is by the said bill proposed to be charged upon a county at large, or upon one or more baronies in any county, or upon any part or parts of any barony or baronies, such bill shall also be submitted to the presentment sessions for such county at large, or for such barony or baronies, as the case may be, and also to the poor law guardians of every union in which any lands proposed to be charged with the payment of any moneys are situate.

Notice of the intention to submit a copy of such bill to such grand jury or other authority, and to such presentment sessions and board of guardians, shall be given ten days previously to submitting the same to the secretary or clerk of such grand jury or authority, or presentment sessions and board of guardians, and shall be advertised once in each of two consecutive weeks in some one and the same morning newspaper published in Dublin, and in some one and the same newspaper published in the county upon which, or upon any barony or baronies in which it is proposed by the bill to impose any local rate or charge, or if in such county no newspaper is published, then in some one and the same newspaper published in any adjoining county.

A copy of such bill shall be so submitted not earlier than six months before the time fixed for the deposit of such bill, and not earlier than the seventh day after the last insertion of such advertisement ; and shall be approved by a majority of the members of the grand jury or authority, presentment sessions, and board of guardians respectively, then present and voting thereon, and the presentment or resolution of each of the said bodies approving the same shall be deposited at the Private Bill Office, together with a statement under the hand of the foreman, chairman, or other person presiding when such presentment was made, or such resolution was passed, of the number of the members then present and voting.

68. When in any bill brought from the House of Lords for the purpose of establishing a company for carrying on any work or undertaking, any person is specified as manager, director, proprietor, or otherwise concerned in carrying such bill into effect, proof shall

be required before the Examiner that such person has subscribed his name to the petition for the bill, or to a printed copy of the bill, as brought up to this House.

III.—PROCEEDINGS OF, AND IN RELATION TO, THE EXAMINERS.

Proceedings of Examiners.

REFERENCE OF BILLS, &C., TO, AND DUTIES OF, AND PRACTICE BEFORE EXAMINERS.

69. The examination of the petitions for private bills which shall have been duly deposited in the Private Bill Office, shall commence on the 18th day of January, in such order and according to such regulations as shall have been made by Mr. Speaker.(¹)

When examination of petitions to commence.

70. One of the Examiners shall give at least seven clear days' notice in the Private Bill Office of the day appointed for the examination of each petition which shall have been duly deposited in the Private Bill Office; and in case the promoters shall not appear at the time when the petition shall come on to be heard, the Examiner to whom the case shall have been allotted shall strike the petition off the general list of petitions, and shall not re-insert the same, except by order of the House.

Notice to be given by one of the Examiners of day appointed for examination.

71. The examiner shall certify by indorsement on each petition whether the Standing Orders have or have not been complied with; and, when they have not been complied with, he shall also report to the House the facts upon which his decision is founded, and any special circumstances connected with the case.

Examiner to indorse petition, and when Standing Orders not complied with, to report.

72. All petitions for additional provision in private bills, with the proposed clauses annexed, and all private bills brought from the House of Lords, and all bills introduced by leave of the House in lieu of other bills which shall have been withdrawn, and all bills to confirm any provisional order or provisional certificate, after having been read a first time, shall be referred to the Examiners, and the Examiner shall report to the House whether the Standing Orders have or have not been complied with, and when they have not been complied with, the facts upon which his decision is founded, and any special circumstances connected with the case, and in the case of any bill which, in pursuance of any report from the chairman of the Committee of Ways and Means, has originated

Petitions for additional provision and estate bills from Lords, &c. to be referred to Examiner of petitions.

(¹) See the Regulations and Notice, *post*, pp. 322, 323, and the Resolutions, *post*, p. 324, put out by the Select Committee on Standing Orders. These and the Standing Orders regulate the practice.

Proceedings of Examiners.

in the House of Lords, the compliance with such Standing Orders only as shall not have been previously inquired into shall be proved.

Notice in cases of petitions for additional provision in Private Bills. &c.

73. In all cases of petitions for additional provision in private bills and of private bills brought from the House of Lords, and of bills introduced by leave of this House in lieu of other bills which shall have been withdrawn, and of bills for confirming any provisional order or certificate, the Examiner shall give at least two clear days' notice in the Private Bill Office of the day on which the same will be examined; but, in the case of a bill for confirming any provisional order or certificate, he shall not give such notice until after the bill has been printed and circulated.

Memorial complaining of non-compliance.

74. Any parties shall be entitled to appear and to be heard, by themselves, their agents and witnesses, upon a memorial addressed to the Examiner, complaining of a non-compliance with the standing orders, provided the matter complained of be specifically stated in such memorial, and the party (if any) who may be specially affected by the non-compliance with the Standing Orders have signed such memorial and shall not have withdrawn his signature thereto, and such memorial have been duly deposited in the Private Bill Office.

Proprietors dissenting at meeting under Orders 62 to 66 may petition and be heard.

75. In case any proprietor, shareholder, or member of or in any company, society, association, or co-partnership shall by himself, or any person authorised to act for him in that behalf, have dissented at any meeting called in pursuance of standing orders 62 to 66, such proprietor, shareholder, or member shall be permitted to be heard by the Examiner of Petitions, on the compliance with such Standing Order, by himself, his agents and witnesses, on a memorial addressed to the Examiner, such memorial having been duly deposited in the Private Bill Office.

Proof by affidavit.

76. The Examiner may admit affidavits in proof of the compliance with the Standing Orders, or may require further evidence; and such affidavit shall be sworn, if in England, before a justice of the peace, or a commissioner to administer oaths in the Supreme Court of Judicature; if in Scotland, before any sheriff depute or his substitute, or a justice of the peace; and if in Ireland, before any judge or assistant barrister of that part of the United Kingdom, or before a justice of the peace.

To report in cases of bills originating in the Lords.

77. The Examiner shall make a report on the several cases in which he shall have certified that the Standing Orders have or have not been complied with in respect of any bills which, in pursuance of any report from the chairman of the Committee of Ways and

Means, under Standing Order 79, shall originate in the House of Lords ; and where they have not been complied with, he shall also report, separately, the facts upon which his decision is founded, and any special circumstances connected with the case.

78. In case the Examiner shall feel doubts as to the due construction of any Standing Order in its application to a particular case, he shall make a special report of the facts, without deciding whether the Standing Order has or has not been complied with ; and in such case he shall indorse the petition with the words " special report," either alone, or if non-compliances with other Standing Orders shall have been proved, in addition to the words " Standing Orders not complied with."

PROCEEDINGS OF, AND IN RELATION TO, THE CHAIRMAN OF THE COMMITTEE OF WAYS AND MEANS, AND THE COUNSEL TO MR. SPEAKER.

79. The Chairman of the Committee of Ways and Means shall, at the commencement of each session, seek a conference with the Chairman of Committees of the House of Lords for the purpose of determining in which House of Parliament the respective private bills should be first considered, and such determination shall be reported to the House.

80. The Chairman of the Committee of Ways and Means, with the assistance of the counsel to Mr. Speaker, shall examine all private bills, whether opposed or unopposed, and call the attention of the House, and also of the Chairman of the Committee on every opposed private bill, to all points which may appear to him to require it ; and copies of all such bills shall be laid by the agent before the said chairman and counsel not later than the day after the Examiner of Petitions shall have indorsed the petition for the bill.

81. The Chairman of the Committee of Ways and Means shall make a report to the House previously to the second reading of any private bill by which it is intended to authorize, confirm, or alter any contract with any department of the Government whereby a public charge has been or may be created ; and such report, together with a copy of the contract, and of any resolution to be proposed in relation thereto, shall be circulated with the votes two clear days at least before the day on which the resolution is to be considered in a committee of the whole House, which consideration shall not take place until after the time of private business ; nor shall the report of any such resolution be considered until three clear days at least after the resolution shall have been agreed to by the committee.

82. Two clear days at least before the day appointed for the consideration of any private bill by a committee, there shall be laid before the Chairman of Ways and Means and the counsel to Mr. Speaker, by the agent, copies of every such bill as proposed to be submitted to the committee, and such copies shall be signed by the agent for the bill.

83. The Chairman of the Committee of Ways and Means shall be at liberty, at any period after any private bill shall have been referred to a committee, to report to the House any special circumstances relative thereto which may appear to him to require it, or to inform the House that in his opinion any unopposed private bill should be treated as an opposed private bill.

84. Three clear days at least before the consideration of any private bill ordered to lie upon the table, a copy of every such bill, as amended in committee, shall be laid by the agent before the Chairman of the Committee of Ways and Means and the counsel to Mr. Speaker, and deposited at the office of Her Majesty's Treasury, at the General Post Office, and at the office of the Board of Trade; and in the case of every bill required by Standing Orders 33, 33a, and 60a, to be deposited on or before the 21st day of December at the office of the Secretary of State for the Home Department, at the office of the Secretary of State for the Colonies, at the office of the Secretary for Scotland, at the office of the Local Government Board, at the office of the Board of Agriculture, at the office of the Education Department, or of the Scotch Education Department, at the office of the Commissioners of Her Majesty's Works and Public Buildings, at the office of Her Majesty's Woods, Forests, and Land Revenues, and at the office of the Duchy of Cornwall or the Duchy of Lancaster, a copy of such bill, as amended in committee, shall also be deposited at those offices respectively.

85. When it is intended to bring up any clause, or to propose any amendment on the consideration of any private bill ordered to lie upon the table, or any verbal amendment on the third reading of any private bill, the same shall be submitted by the agent to the Chairman of the Committee of Ways and Means and the counsel to Mr. Speaker, on the day on which notice is given thereof in the private bill office.

86. A copy of all amendments made in the House of Lords to any private bill, and of all amendments to such amendments intended to be proposed in this House, shall be laid by the agent before the Chairman of the Committee of Ways and Means and

the counsel to Mr. Speaker, before two o'clock on the day previous to that on which the same are respectively appointed for consideration by the House.

Amendments thereto, to be laid before Chairman of Ways and Means, &c.

PROCEEDINGS OF, AND IN RELATION TO, THE REFEREES ON PRIVATE BILLS.

Proceedings of Referees on Private Bills.

87. The Chairman of Ways and Means, with not less than three other persons, who shall be appointed by Mr. Speaker for such period as he shall think fit, shall be Referees of the House on private bills; such Referees to form one or more courts; three at least to be required to constitute each court: provided that the chairman of any second court shall be a member of this House; and provided that no such Referee, if he be a member of this House, shall receive any salary.

Referees on Private Bills to be constituted.

88. The practice and procedure of the Referees, their times of sitting, order of business, and the forms and notices required in their proceedings, shall be prescribed by rules, to be framed by the Chairman of Ways and Means, subject to alteration by him as occasion may require, but only one counsel shall appear before such Referees in support of a private bill, or in support of any petition in opposition thereto, unless specially authorized by the Referees. All such rules and alterations, when made, to be laid on the table of the House.(¹)

Rules of practice and procedure to be made by Chairman of Ways and Means.

89. The Referees shall decide upon all petitions against private bills, or against Provisional Orders, or Provisional Certificates, as to the rights of the petitioners to be heard upon such petitions, without prejudice, however, to the power of the select committee to which the bill is referred to decide upon any question as to such rights arising incidentally in the course of their proceedings.

Referees on Private Bills to decide as to rights of petitioners to be heard upon their petitions, &c.

PROCEEDINGS OF AND IN RELATION TO THE SELECT COMMITTEE ON STANDING ORDERS.

91. There shall be a committee, to be designated "The Select Committee on Standing Orders," to consist of eleven members, who shall be nominated at the commencement of every session, of whom five shall be a quorum.

Committee on Standing Orders.

92. When any report of the Examiner of petitions for private bills, in which he shall report that the Standing Orders have not been complied with, shall have been referred to the Select Committee on Standing Orders, and after the petition for the bill shall

To report whether Standing Orders ought or ought not to be dispensed with.

(¹) See Rules for Referees, *post*, p. 326.

Proceedings of Standing Orders Committee.

have been duly presented, they shall report to the House whether such Standing Orders ought or ought not to be dispensed with, and whether in their opinion the parties should be permitted to proceed with their Bill, or any portion thereof, and under what (if any) conditions.

In cases of bills originating in Lords.

93. The Select Committee on Standing Orders shall have power to report on the cases referred to them in respect of private bills originating in the House of Lords, notwithstanding that the petitions for the same shall not have been presented to the House.

Proceeding in case of special report.

94. When any special report from the Examiner of Petitions as to the construction of a Standing Order shall have been referred to the Select Committee on Standing Orders, they shall determine, according to their construction of the Standing Order, and on the facts stated in such report, whether the Standing Orders have or have not been complied with, and they shall then either report to the House that the Standing Orders have been complied with, or shall proceed to consider the question of dispensing with the Standing Orders, as the case may be.

To report whether Sessional or Standing Orders ought or ought not to be dispensed with.

95. When any petition, praying that any of the Sessional or Standing Orders of the House relating to private bills may be dispensed with, shall stand referred to the Select Committee on Standing Orders, they shall report to the House whether such Sessional or Standing Orders ought or ought not to be dispensed with.

To report whether petition ought or ought not to be re-inserted in the General List.

96. When any petition for the re-insertion of any petition for a private bill in the general list of petitions shall stand referred to the Select Committee on Standing Orders, they shall report to the House whether in their opinion such petition ought or ought not to be re-inserted, and, if re-inserted, under what (if any) conditions.

To report whether Clause or Amendment on consideration of bill should be adopted by House or not, or whether Bill should be re-committed.

97. When any clause or amendment proposed on the consideration of any private bill ordered to lie upon the table shall have been referred to the Select Committee on Standing Orders, they shall report to the House whether such clause or amendment should be adopted by the House or not, or whether the Bill should be re-committed.

PROCEEDINGS OF AND IN RELATION TO THE COMMITTEE OF SELECTION, AND OF THE GENERAL COMMITTEE ON RAILWAY AND CANAL BILLS.

Committee of Selection.

98. There shall be a committee, to be designated "The Committee of Selection," to consist of the Chairman of the Select

Committee on Standing Orders, who shall be ex-officio chairman thereof, and seven other members, who shall be nominated at the commencement of every session, of which committee three shall be a quorum.

99. There shall be a committee, to be designated "The General Committee on Railway and Canal Bills," which shall be nominated at the commencement of every Session by the Committee of Selection, of which committee three shall be a quorum.

100. The Committee of Selection may, from time to time, discharge members from further attendance on such General Committee, and add other members in their room, and shall appoint the chairman of such committee.

101. The General Committee on Railway and Canal Bills shall appoint from among themselves the chairman of each committee on a railway or canal bill, or on a group of such bills, and may change the chairman so appointed from time to time.

102. Printed copies of all private bills, not being railway or canal bills, shall be laid before the Committee of Selection, and printed copies of all railway and canal bills before the General Committee on Railway and Canal Bills, by the parties promoting the same, at the first meeting of the said committees respectively.

103. The Committee of Selection may, if they think fit, form into groups all private bills, not being railway or canal bills, and the General Committee on Railway and Canal Bills may form into groups all railway and canal bills, which, in their opinion, it may be expedient to submit to the same committee, and such groups shall be published in the votes.

104. The General Committee on Railway and Canal Bills may, whenever they shall think fit, refer any unopposed railway or canal bill to the Chairman of the Committee of Ways and Means, together with two other members not locally or otherwise interested, or one such member and a referee, to be nominated by the Committee of Selection.

105. The Committee of Selection in the case of all private bills other than railway and canal bills, and the General Committee on Railway and Canal Bills in the case of such bills, shall, subject to the Order in regard to the interval between the second reading of every private bill and the sitting of the committee thereupon, fix the time for holding the first sitting of every committee on a private bill which shall have been referred to either of the said committees.

(marginal notes)
Proceedings of Committee of Selection, &c.

General Committee on Railway and Canal Bills.

Committee of Selection may discharge members and add others.

General Committee to appoint Chairman.

Printed copies of bills to be laid before Committee of Selection and General Committee.

Committee of Selection and General Committee to group private bills.

Railway and canal unopposed bills.

Committee of Selection and General Committee on railway, &c. bills to appoint first sitting of committee.

106. The Committee of Selection shall name the bill or bills which shall be taken into consideration on the first day of the meeting of the committee on any group of bills not being railway or canal bills; and the General Committee on Railway and Canal Bills shall name the bill or bills which shall be taken into consideration on the first day of the meeting of each committee on any group of such bills.

107. The Committee of Selection shall consider no bill as an opposed private bill, unless, not later than ten clear days after the first reading thereof, a petition shall have been presented against it, in which the petitioner or petitioners shall have prayed to be heard, by themselves, their counsel or agents, or unless, where no such petition shall have been presented, the Chairman of the Committee of Ways and Means shall have reported to the House that in his opinion any bill ought to be so treated.

108. The Committee of Selection shall refer every opposed private bill which shall have been referred to them, or any group of such bills, to a chairman and three members, and a referee or a chairman and three members, not locally or otherwise interested therein.

109. The Committee of Selection shall refer every unopposed private bill, which shall have been referred to them, not being a road bill, to the Chairman of the Committee of Ways and Means, together with one of the members ordered to prepare and bring in the same, and one other member not locally interested therein, or a referee, if the bill shall have originated in this House; and if the bill shall have been brought from the House of Lords, to the Chairman of the Committee of Ways and Means, together with two other members, of whom one at least shall not be locally or otherwise interested therein, or one member and a referee.

110. The Committee of Selection shall refer all road bills, whether opposed or unopposed, to a committee, consisting of a chairman and three other members not locally or otherwise interested therein.

111. The Committee of Selection shall give each member not less than seven days' notice, by publication in the votes or otherwise, of the week in which it will be necessary for him to be in attendance for the purpose of serving, if required, as a member, not locally or otherwise interested, of a committee on a private bill.

112. The Committee of Selection shall give to each member sufficient notice of his appointment as a member of a committee on

any private bill, or group of such bills, and, in every case where a declaration is required to be signed and returned by such member, shall transmit to him a blank form of the declaration required, with a request that it may forthwith be returned properly filled up and signed.

113. The Committee of Selection shall report to the House the name of every member from whom they shall not have received in due time such declaration, so filled up and signed, or, in lieu thereof, an excuse which they shall deem sufficient.

114. The Committee of Selection shall have the power of discharging any member or members of a committee, and of substituting other members.

115. The Committee of Selection shall have power, in the execution of their duties, to send for persons, papers, and records.

PROCEEDINGS OF COMMITTEES ON OPPOSED BILLS.

116. The committee on every opposed railway and canal bill, or group of railway and canal bills, shall be composed of four members and a referee, or four members not locally or otherwise interested in the bill or bills referred to them ; the chairman to be appointed by the General Committee on Railway and Canal Bills, and three other members by the Committee of Selection.

117. The committee on every opposed private bill (not being a railway, canal or divorce bill), or group of bills, and the committee on any bill to confirm any provisional order or provisional certificate, shall be composed of a chairman and three members and a referee, or a chairman and three members not locally or otherwise interested in the bill or bills referred to them, to be appointed by the Committee of Selection.

118. Each member of a committee on an opposed private bill, or group of such bills, shall, before he be entitled to attend and vote on such committee, sign the following declaration :

> I do hereby declare, that my constituents have no local interest, and that I have no personal interest, in such bill ; and that I will never vote on any question which may arise without having duly heard and attended to the evidence relating thereto.

And no such committee shall proceed to business until the said declaration shall have been so signed by each of such members.

119. Committees shall not be allowed to proceed if more than one of their members be absent, unless by special leave of the House.

Proceedings of Committee of Selection, &c.

to be transmitted to members.

Members returning no answer to be reported.

Committee of Selection may substitute members for others.

Committee of Selection to send for persons, &c.

Committees on railway and canal bills.

Committees on opposed private bills.

Declaration of members.

Quorum to be always present.

120. No member of a committee on an opposed private bill shall absent himself from his duties thereon, except in the case of sickness, or by order of the House.

121. If the chairman shall be absent from the committee, the member next in rotation on the list of members who shall be present shall act as chairman, but in the case of railway and canal bills only until the general committee on such bills shall have appointed, if they shall so think fit, another chairman.

122. If at any time during the sitting of any committee more than one of the members be absent, the chairman shall suspend the proceedings of such committee; and if at the expiration of one hour from the time fixed for the meeting of the committee, or from the time when the chairman shall so have suspended the proceedings, more than one member be absent, the committee shall be adjourned to the next day on which the House shall sit, and then shall meet at the hour on which such committee would have sat, had no such adjournment taken place.

123. If any of the members shall not be present within one hour after the time appointed for the meeting of the committee, or if any member shall absent himself from his duties on such committee, every such member shall be reported to the House at its next sitting.

124. If, at any time after the committee on a bill shall have been formed, a quorum of members required by the Standing Orders cannot attend in consequence of any of the members who shall have duly qualified to serve on such committee having become incompetent to continue such service by death or otherwise, the chairman shall report the circumstances of the case to the House, in order that such measures may be taken by the House as shall enable the members still remaining on the committee to proceed with the business referred to such committee, or as the emergency of the case may require.

125. All questions before committees on private bills shall be decided by a majority of voices, including the voice of the chairman; and whenever the voices are equal, the chairman shall have a second or casting vote.

126. The committee on each group of bills shall take the bill or bills first into consideration which shall have been named by the Committee of Selection, or by the General Committee on Railway and Canal Bills; and the committee shall, from time to time, appoint the day on which they will enter upon the consideration of each of the remaining bills, and on which they will require the parties

severally promoting or opposing the same to enter appearances; and two clear days' notice, at the least, of such appointment, shall be given by the clerk attending the committee to the clerks in the Private Bill Office; and in case the committee shall postpone the consideration of any bill, notice shall be given of the day to which the same is postponed.

127. Every committee on an opposed private bill shall report specially to the House the cause of any adjournment over any day on which the House shall sit.

128. No petition against a private bill, or bill to confirm any provisional order or provisional certificate, shall be taken into consideration by the committee on such bill, which shall not distinctly specify the ground on which the petitioners object to any of the provisions thereof; and the petitioners shall be only heard on such grounds so stated; and if it shall appear to the said committee that such grounds are not specified with sufficienct accuracy, the committee may direct that there be given in to the committee a more specific statement, in writing, but limited to such grounds of objection so inaccurately specified.

129. No petitioners against any private bill, or any bill to confirm any provisional order or provisional certificate, shall be heard before the committee on the bill, unless their petition shall have been prepared and signed in strict conformity with the rules and orders of this House, and shall have been presented to this House by having been deposited in the Private Bill Office, in the case of private bills, not later than ten clear days after the first reading of such bill, and in the case of bills to confirm any provisional order or provisional certificate, not later than seven clear days after the Examiner shall have given notice of the day on which the bill will be examined, except where the petitioners shall complain of any matter which may have arisen during the progress of the bill before the said committee, or of any proposed additional provision, or of the amendments as proposed in the filled-up bill deposited in the Private Bill Office.

130. It shall be competent to the referees on private bills to admit petitioners to be heard upon their petitions against a private bill, on the ground of competition, if they shall think fit.

131. Where a bill is promoted by an incorporated company, shareholders of such company shall not be entitled to be heard before the committee against such bill, unless their interests, as affected thereby, shall be distinct from the general interests of such company.

132. In case any proprietor, shareholder, or member of or in any company, society, association, or co-partnership, shall by himself or any person authorized to act for him in that behalf, have dissented at any meeting called in pursuance of Standing Orders 62 to 66, or at any meeting called in pursuance of any similar Standing Order of the House of Lords, such proprietor, shareholder, or member shall be permitted to be heard by the committee on the bill on a petition presented to the House, such petition having been duly deposited in the Private Bill Office.

133. Where a railway bill contains provisions for taking or using any part of the lands, railway, stations, or accommodations of another company, or for running engines or carriages upon or across the same, or for granting other facilities, such company shall be entitled to be heard upon their petition against such provisions or against the preamble and clauses of such bill.

133a. Where a chamber of commerce or agriculture, or other similar body, sufficiently representing a particular trade or business in any district to which any railway bill relates, petition against the bill, alleging that such trade or business will be injuriously affected by the rates and fares proposed to be authorized by the bill, or is injuriously affected by the rates and fares already authorized by Acts relating to the railway undertaking, it shall be competent to the referees on private bills, if they think fit, to admit the petitioners to be heard, on such allegation, against the bill, or any part thereof, or against the rates and fares authorized by the said Acts, or any of them.

The provisions of this Order relative to rates and fares already authorized, extend to traders and freighters, and to a single trader, in any case where a *locus standi* would have been allowed to them or him, if this Order had not been made.

Nothing in this Order shall authorize the referees to entertain any question within the jurisdiction of the railway commissioners.

133b. Where a chamber of agriculture, commerce, or shipping, or a mining or miners' association, sufficiently representing the agriculture, trade, mining, or commerce in any district to which any bill relates, petition against the bill, alleging that such agriculture, trade, mining, or commerce will be injuriously affected by the provisions contained therein, it shall be competent to the referees on private bills, if they think fit, to admit the petitioners to be heard on such allegations against the bill or any part thereof.

134. It shall be competent to the referees on private bills to admit the petitioners, being the municipal or other authority

having the local management of the Metropolis, or of any town, or the inhabitants of any town or district alleged to be injuriously affected by a bill, to be heard against such bill, if they shall think fit.

134*a.* The municipal or other local authority of any town or district alleging in their petition that such town or district may be injuriously affected by the provisions of any bill relating to the lighting or water supply thereof, or the raising of capital for any such purpose, shall be entitled to be heard against such bill.

134*b.* It shall be competent to the referees on private bills to admit the petitioners, being the council of any administrative county or county borough, the whole or any part of which is alleged to be injuriously affected by a bill, to be heard against such bill if they think fit.

134*c.* The council of any administrative county alleging in their petition that such administrative county, or any part thereof, may be injuriously affected by the provisions of any bill relating to the water supply of any town or district, whether situate within or without such county, shall be entitled to be heard against such bill.

135. The owner, lessee, or occupier of any house, shop, or warehouse in any street through which it is proposed to construct any tramway, and who alleges in any petition against a private bill or provisional order that the construction or use of the tramway proposed to be authorized thereby will injuriously affect him in the use or enjoyment of his premises, or in the conduct of his trade or business, shall be entitled to be heard on such allegations before any select committee to which such private bill, or the bill relating to such provisional order is referred.

136. In all cases of opposed private bills, in which no parties shall have appeared on the petitions against such bills, or having appeared shall have withdrawn their opposition before the evidence of the promoters shall have been commenced, the committees on such bills shall forthwith refer them back, with a statement of the facts, if not railway or canal bills, to the committee of selection, and if railway or canal bills, to the general committee on railway and canal bills, who shall deal with them as unopposed bills.

COMMITTEES ON UNOPPOSED BILLS.

137. The committee on every unopposed private bill (not being a railway, canal or divorce bill), shall, if the same shall have originated in this House, be composed of the chairman of the

Committee of Ways and Means, who, when present, shall be *ex-officio* chairman of every such committee, together with one of the members ordered to prepare and bring in the bill, and one other member not locally or otherwise interested therein, or a referee, such members of the committee to be appointed by the Committee of Selection, and shall, if such bill shall have been brought from the House of Lords, be composed of the chairman, as aforesaid, and two other members, of whom one at least shall not be locally or otherwise interested in the bill, or one member and a referee, to be appointed by the Committee of Selection, and two shall be the quorum thereof.

PROCEEDINGS OF, AND IN RELATION TO, COMMITTEES ON BILLS, WHETHER OPPOSED OR UNOPPOSED.

138. At the first meeting of the committee, copies of the bill, as proposed to be submitted to them, and signed by the agent, shall be laid by him before each member of the committee.

139. No member, locally or otherwise interested, of a committee on any unopposed private bill, shall have a vote on any question that may arise, but every such member shall be entitled to attend and take part in the proceedings of the committee.

140. The names of the members attending each committee shall be entered by the clerk on the minutes of the committee; and if any division shall take place in the committee, the clerk shall take down the names of members voting in any such division, distinguishing on which side of the question they respectively vote, and that such lists be given in with the report to the House.

141. No committee shall have power to examine into the compliance or non-compliance with such Standing Orders as are directed to be proved before the Examiner of Petitions for private bills, unless by special order of the House.

142. The committee on any private bill may admit affidavits in proof of the compliance with such Standing Orders of the House as are directed to be proved before them, or may require further evidence; and such affidavits shall be sworn, if in England, before a justice of the peace, or a commissioner to administer oaths in the Supreme Court of Judicature; if in Scotland, before any sheriff-depute or his substitute, or a justice of the peace; and if in Ireland, before any judge or assistant-barrister of that part of the United Kingdom, or before a justice of the peace.

143. The committee may admit proof of the consents of parties concerned in interest in any private bill, by affidavits sworn as aforesaid, or by the certificate in writing of such parties, whose

signatures to such certificate shall be proved by one or more witnesses, unless the committee shall require further evidence.

143a. A petitioner against a bill originating in the House of Lords who has discussed clauses in that House, shall not on that account be precluded from opposing the preamble of the bill in this House.

144. In all bills presented to the House for carrying on any work by means of a company, commissioners or trustees, provision shall be made for compelling persons who have subscribed any money towards carrying any such work into execution, to make payment of the sums severally subscribed by them.

145. Where the level of any road shall be altered in making any public work, the ascent of any public carriage road, or of any road in Ireland so defined in the Railway Clauses Consolidation Act, 1845, shall not be more than one foot in 30 feet, and of any other public carriage road not more than one foot in 20 feet; and a good and sufficient fence, of four feet high at the least, shall be made on each side of every bridge which shall be erected.

145a. In the case of any bill relating to a railway, tramway, canal, dock, harbour, navigation, pier, or port, seeking powers to levy tolls, rates, or duties in excess of those already authorized for that undertaking, or usually authorized in previous years for like undertakings, the bill shall not be reported by the committee until a report from the Board of Trade on the powers so sought has been laid before the committee; and the committee shall report specially to the House in what manner the recommendations or observations in the report of the Board of Trade, and also in what manner the clauses of the bill relating to the powers so sought, have been dealt with by the committee.

146. Every plan, and book of reference thereto, which shall be produced in evidence before the committee upon any private bill (whether the same shall have been previously lodged in the Private Bill Office or not), shall be signed by the chairman of such committee, with his name at length; and he shall also mark with the initials of his name every alteration of such plan and book of reference, which shall be agreed upon by the said committee; and every such plan and book of reference shall thereafter be deposited in the Private Bill Office.

147. The chairman of the committee shall sign, with his name at length, a printed copy of the bill (to be called the Committee Bill), on which the amendments are to be fairly written; and also

Side notes:

Proceedings of Committees on Bills.

Petitioner who has discussed clauses of bill in House of Lords not precluded from opposing preamble in this House.

Clause compelling payment of subscriptions.

Level of roads.

Fence to bridge.

Committee to report specially to House on railway, &c. bills, seeking powers to levy tolls, &c. in excess of those already authorized.

Plan, &c., to be signed by chairman.

Committee bill and clauses to be signed by chairman.

K

sign, with the initials of his name, the several clauses added in the committee.

148. The chairman of the committee shall report to the House that the allegations of the bill have been examined; and whether the parties concerned have given their consent (where such consent is required by the Standing Orders) to the satisfaction of the committee.

149. The chairman of the committee shall report the bill to the House, whether the committee shall or shall not have agreed to the preamble, or gone through the several clauses, or any of them; or where the parties shall have acquainted the committee that it is not their intention to proceed with the bill; and when any alteration shall have been made in the preamble of the bill, such alteration, together with the ground of making it, shall be specially stated in the report.

150. Whenever a recommendation shall have been made in a report on a private bill from a department of the Government referred to the committee, the committee shall notice such recommendation in their report, and shall state their reasons for dissenting, should such recommendation not be agreed to.

151. Whenever the House shall order that any bill for confirming a provisional order or a provisional certificate be referred to the Committee of Selection with respect to any order or certificate to be confirmed thereby, the proceedings of the Select Committee to which the bill is referred, and of the referees, shall be conducted in like manner as in the case of private bills, and shall be subject to the same rules and orders of the House so far as they are applicable, except those which relate to the payment of fees by the promoters of such provisional order or certificate.

152. The minutes of the committee on every private bill shall be brought up and laid on the table of the House, with the report of the bill.

Railway, Tramway, and Subway Bills.

153. In the case of a railway bill, no company shall be authorized to raise by loan or mortgage, a larger sum than one-third of their capital; and until 50 per cent. on the whole of the capital shall have been paid up, it shall not be in the power of the company to raise any money, by loan or mortgage, unless the committee on the bill shall report that such restrictions, or either of them, ought not to be enforced, with the reasons on which their opinion is founded.

The same rule shall apply in the case of a tramway, tramroad, or subway bill, one-fourth of the capital being substituted for one-third.

Proceedings of Committees on Bills.

154. Where the level of any road shall be altered in making any railway, the ascent of any turnpike road, or of any road in Ireland, so defined in the Railway Clauses Consolidation Act, 1845, shall not be more than one foot in 30 feet, and of any other public carriage road not more than one foot in 20 feet, unless a report thereupon from some officer of the Board of Trade shall be laid before the committee on the bill, and unless the committee, after considering such report, and hearing the officer, if the committee think fit, if they shall disagree with the said report, shall recommend steeper ascents, with the reasons and facts upon which their opinion is founded : also, a good and sufficient fence, of four feet high at the least, shall be made on each side of every bridge which shall be erected.

Limiting ascent of roads where level is altered.

155. No railway whereon carriages are moved by steam, or by any mechanical power, including cable power, shall be authorized to be made across any railway, tramway, tramroad, or public carriage road on the level, unless a report thereupon from some officer of the Board of Trade shall be laid before the committee on the bill, and unless the committee, after considering such report, and hearing the officer, if the committee think fit, if they shall disagree with the said report, shall recommend such level crossing, with the reasons and facts upon which their opinion is founded ; and in every clause authorizing a level crossing, the number of lines of rails authorized to be made at such crossing shall be specified.

Railway not to cross railways or roads on a level unless committee report, &c.

156. No railway company shall be authorized to construct or enlarge, purchase or take on lease, or otherwise appropriate any canal, dock, pier, harbour, or ferry, or to acquire and use any steam vessels for the conveyance of goods and passengers, or to apply any portion of their capital or revenue to other objects, distinct from the undertaking of a railway company, unless the committee on the bill report that such a restriction ought not to be enforced, with the reasons and facts upon which their opinion is founded.

Railway company not to acquire canals, docks, &c. unless Committee report, &c.

157. Every committee on a railway bill shall report specially to the House,—

Reports of Public Departments.

> Whether any report from any public department in regard to the bill, or the objects thereof, has been referred by the House to the committee ; and, if so, in what manner the several recommendations contained in such report have been dealt with by the committee :

Proceedings
of
Committees
on Bills.

Crossing rail-
ways, &c. on a
level.
Other cir-
cumstances.

Clause to be
inserted in
railway,
tramway, and
subway bills,
imposing
penalty, unless
line be opened.

Whether it be intended that the railway shall cross on a level any railway, tramway, tramroad, or highway :

And any other circumstances which, in the opinion of the committee, it is desirable that the House should be informed of.

158 In every railway bill, tramway bill, and subway bill, whereby the construction of any new line of railway, tramway, or subway is authorized, or the time for completing any line already authorized is extended, promoted by an existing railway company, tramway company, or subway company, which is possessed of a railway, tramway, or subway already opened for public traffic, and which has, during the year last past, paid dividends on its ordinary share capital, and which does not propose to raise under the bill a capital greater than its existing authorized capital, there shall be inserted a clause to the following effect, viz. :

(A.) If the company fail within the period limited by this Act to complete the railway, tramway, or subway, authorized to be made by this Act, the company shall be liable to a penalty of £50 a day for every day after the expiration of the period so limited, until the said railway, tramway, or subway is completed and opened for public traffic, or until the sum received in respect of such penalty shall amount to five per cent. on the estimated cost of the works ; and the said penalty may be applied for by any landowner or other person claiming to be compensated or interested in accordance with the provisions of the next following section of this Act, and in the same manner as the penalty provided in the third section of the Act, 17 & 18 Vict. c. 31, known as "The Railway and Canal Traffic Act, 1854," and every sum of money recovered by way of such penalty as aforesaid, shall be paid under the warrant or order of such court or judge as is specified in the said third section of the Act, 17 & 18 Vict. c. 31, to an account opened or to be opened in the name and with the privity of the Paymaster-General for and on behalf of the Supreme Court in England [the Queen's Remembrancer of the Court of Exchequer in Scotland, or the Accountant-General of the Supreme Court in Ireland (according as the railway, tramway, or subway is situate in England, Scotland, or Ireland,)] in the bank named in such order, and shall not be paid thereout except as hereinafter pro-vided ; but no penalty shall accrue in respect of any time during which it shall appear, by a certificate to be obtained from the Board of Trade, that the company was prevented from completing or opening such line by unforeseen accident or circumstances beyond their control : Provided, that the want of sufficient funds shall not be held to be a circumstance beyond their control.

Railway, Tramway, or Subway Deposits.

In every railway bill, tramway bill, or subway bill, whereby the construction of any new line is authorized, or the time for completing any line already authorized is extended ; if such bill be promoted by an existing railway company, tramway company, or subway company, which is not possessed of a railway, tramway, or subway, already opened for public traffic, or which has not during the year last past paid dividends on its ordinary share capital ; or by an existing railway company, tramway company, or subway company, when the capital to be raised under the bill is greater than the existing authorized capital of the company, or by persons not already incorporated, a clause to the following effect shall be inserted, viz. :—

(B.) Whereas, pursuant to the Standing Orders of both Houses of Parliament, and to " The Parliamentary Deposits Act, 1846," a sum of £   , being five per cent. upon the amount of the estimate in respect of the railway, tramway, or subway authorized by this Act, has been deposited with the Court, that is to say, the Paymaster-General for and on behalf of the Supreme Court in England [or the Court of Exchequer in Scotland, or the Accountant-General of the Supreme Court in Ireland, as the case may be] ; [or exchequer bills, stocks, or funds to the amount of £   , have been deposited or transferred pursuant to the said Act, as the case may be], in respect of the application to Parliament for this Act (which sum, exchequer bills, stocks, or funds, as the case may be, is or are in this Act referred to as " The Deposit Fund " :) Be it enacted, that notwithstanding anything contained in the said recited Act, the deposit fund shall not be paid or transferred to, or on the application of the person or persons, or the majority of the persons, named in the warrant or order issued in pursuance of the said Act, or the survivors or survivor of them (which persons, survivors, or survivor, are or is in this Act referred to as the " depositors "), unless the company shall, previously to the expiration of the period limited by this Act for completion of the railway [tramway or subway] hereby authorized to be made [or the time for completing which is hereby extended], open the said railway [tramway or subway] for public traffic [or, if a passenger railway, for the public conveyance of passengers], and if the company shall make default in so opening

Proceedings of Committees on Bills.

Clause to be inserted, providing that deposit be impounded as security for completion of the line.

the said railway [tramway or subway] the deposit fund shall be applicable, and shall be applied as provided by the next following section. And to such clause the committee may, if they think fit, add a proviso to the following effect :—Provided, that if within such period as aforesaid the company open any portion of the said railway [tramway or subway] for public traffic [or, if a passenger railway, for the public conveyance of passengers], then on production of a certificate of the Board of Trade, specifying the length of the portion of the said railway [tramway or subway] opened as aforesaid, and the portion of the deposit fund which bears to the whole of the deposit fund the same proportion as the length of the said railway [tramway or subway] so opened bears to the entire length of the said railway [tramway or subway] hereby authorized, the High Court shall, on the application of the depositors, order the said portion of the deposit fund so specified in such certificate as aforesaid to be paid or transferred to them, or as they shall direct ; and the certificate of the Board of Trade shall, if signed by the secretary or by an assistant secretary of the said Board, be sufficient evidence of the facts therein certified ; and it shall not be necessary to produce any certificate of this Act having passed, anything in the recited Act to the contrary notwithstanding.

Application of
deposit or
penalty in
compensation
to parties
injured.

In every railway bill, tramway bill, or subway bill whereby the construction of any new line of railway, tramway, or subway is authorized, or the time for completing any line already authorized is extended, a clause to the following effect shall be inserted :—

(C.) If the company do not, previously to the expiration of the period limited by this Act for the completion of the railway [tramway or subway] hereby authorized to be made (or the time for completion which is hereby extended) complete the said railway [tramway or subway] and open it for public traffic [or, if a passenger railway, for the public conveyance of passengers], then and in every such case the deposit fund, or so much thereof as shall not have been paid to the depositors, or any sum of money recovered by way of penalty as aforesaid shall be applicable, and after due notice in the London *Gazette*, or Edinburgh or Dublin *Gazette*, [as the case may require], shall be applied towards compensating any landowners or other persons whose property may have been interfered with, or otherwise rendered less valuable, by the commencement, construction, or abandonment of the said railway [tramway or subway], or any portion thereof, or who may have been subjected to injury or loss in consequence of the compulsory

powers of taking property conferred upon the company by this Act,
[and also (in the case of a tramway) in compensating all road
authorities for the expense incurred by them in taking up any
tramway, or materials connected therewith, placed by the Company
in or on any road vested in or maintainable by such road authorities respectively, and in making good all damage caused to such
roads by the construction or abandonment of such tramway], and
shall be distributed in satisfaction of such compensation as aforesaid, in such manner and in such proportions as to the court may
seem fit; and if no such compensation shall be payable, or if a
portion of the deposit fund (or of the sum or sums of money recovered by way of penalty as aforesaid) shall have been found sufficient to satisfy all just claims in respect of such compensation,
then the deposit fund (or the sum or sums of money recovered by
way of penalty as aforesaid), or such portion thereof as may not be
required as aforesaid, shall, if a receiver has been appointed, or the
company is insolvent and has been ordered to be wound up or the
undertaking (in the case of a penalty, the railway or railways in
respect of which the penalty has been incurred or any part thereof),
has been abandoned, be paid or transferred to such receiver, or to
the liquidator or liquidators of the company, or be applied, in the
discretion of the court, as part of the assets of the company for the
benefit of the creditors thereof, and subject to such application,
shall be repaid or retransferred to the depositors (company) : Provided, that until the deposit fund shall have been repaid to the
depositors, or shall have become otherwise applicable as hereinbefore
mentioned, any interest or dividends accruing thereon shall from
time to time, and as often as the same shall become payable, be
paid to or on the application of the depositors.

N.B.—If the clause lettered (A) is inserted in the bill, the
proviso at the end of the clause lettered (C) shall be omitted. In
the case of a railway company omit the words "and has been
ordered to be wound up," and "or to the liquidator or liquidators
of the company," and where there is no deposit omit the proviso.

(D.) If the railway [or tramway] authorized by this Act shall
not be completed within the period limited by this Act, then, on the
expiration of such period, the power by this Act granted to the
company for making and completing the said railway [or tram-
way], or otherwise in relation thereto, shall cease to be exercised,
except as to so much thereof as shall then be completed. The
period limited shall not in the case of a new railway line exceed
five years, of a new tramroad three years [or in the case of a new

Proceedings
of
Committees
on Bills.

tramway line two years], and the extension of time for completion shall not in the case of a railway line exceed three years, of a tramroad two years [or in the case of a tramway line one year], unless the committee on the bill think fit, in the special circumstances of the case, to allow a longer period. In the case of extension of time the additional period shall be computed from the expiration of the period sought to be extended.

Where preceding provisions are inapplicable.

In any railway bill or tramway bill to which the preceding provisions are not applicable, the committee on the bill shall make such other provision as they shall deem necessary for ensuring the completion of the line of railway or tramway.

In case of abandonment of railway, tramway or subway bill, and release of deposit money, committee on bill to report to the House how recommendations of Board of Trade on the bill have been dealt with by Committee. Committee to fix the rates and charges.

158a. In the case of every bill authorizing the abandonment of a railway, tramway, or subway, or of any part thereof, and the release of any deposit money impounded as security for the completion thereof, a report from the Board of Trade respecting the bill, and the objects thereof, shall be presented to this House, and be referred to the committee on the bill; and the committee shall report specially to the House in what manner the several recommendations contained in the report from the Board of Trade have been dealt with by the committee.

159. The committee on every railway bill shall fix the maximum rates of charge for the conveyance of passengers, with a due amount of luggage, such rates to include every expense incidental to such conveyance, and shall also fix the charges for the conveyance of parcels by passenger train ; but if the committee shall not deem it expedient to determine such maximum rates of charge, a special report, explanatory of the grounds of their omitting so to do, shall be made to the House, which special report shall accompany the report of the bill.

In bills granting preference in payment of interest, &c., provision to be made that the same shall not prejudice former grants of preference, unless Committee report otherwise.

160. In every railway bill by which it is proposed to authorize the company to grant any preference or priority in the payment of interest or dividends on any shares or stock, there shall be inserted a clause providing that the granting of such preference or priority shall not prejudice or affect any preference or priority in the payment of interest or dividends on any other shares or stock which shall have been granted by the company in pursuance of or which may have been confirmed by any previous Act of Parliament, or which may otherwise be lawfully subsisting, unless the committee on the bill shall report that such provision ought not to be required, with the reasons on which their opinion is founded.

Company not to alter any preference

161. No railway company shall be authorized to alter the terms of any preference or priority of interest or dividend which shall

have been granted by such company in pursuance of or which may have been confirmed by any previous Act of Parliament, or which may otherwise be lawfully subsisting, unless the committee on the bill report that such alteration ought to be allowed, with the reasons on which their opinion is founded, together with the number of preference shareholders who have assented to or dissented from such alteration.

162. No powers of purchasing, hiring, or providing steam vessels shall be contained in a bill by which any other powers are sought to be obtained by a railway company, except when the transit by such steam vessels is required to connect portions of railway belonging to or proposed to be constructed by such company.

163. No powers of purchase, sale, lease or amalgamation shall be given to any railway company, with reference to any other undertaking already authorized by any Act or Acts, nor to any other incorporated company, with reference to any railway, unless, previously to the application to Parliament for such purpose, the several companies who may be parties to such purchase, sale, lease or amalgamation shall have proved to the satisfaction of the Board of Trade, that they have respectively paid up one-half of the capital authorized to be raised by any previous Act or Acts by means of shares, and have expended for the purpose of such Act or Acts a sum equal thereto; and in case such powers shall be applied for in respect of works intended to be authorized by any bill or bills of the same session, it shall be proved to the satisfaction of the Board of Trade that such companies have respectively paid up one-half the amount of their capital, and that the company proposed to be empowered to construct such works have included in such amount the capital proposed to be authorized by such bill or bills; and that no such powers shall be given in respect of works intended to be authorized by any Act or Acts for which it is intended to apply in any subsequent session.

164. No railway company shall be authorized, except for the execution of its original line or lines sanctioned by Act of Parliament, to guarantee interest on any shares which it may issue for creating additional capital, or to guarantee any rent or dividend to any other railway company, until such first-mentioned company shall have completed and opened for traffic such original lines.

165. In bills for the amalgamation of railway companies, the amount of capital created by such amalgamation shall in no case exceed the sum of the capitals of the companies so amalgamated.

Proceedings of Committees on Bills.
———
previously granted.

No powers of purchasing, &c. steam vessels in railway bills.

No powers of purchase, &c. to be given, except after proof of certain matters before Board of Trade, &c.

Railway company not to guarantee interest or dividend before completion of line.

Limitation of capital on amalgamation of companies.

166. In bills for empowering any railway company to purchase any other railway, no addition shall be authorized to be made to the capital of the purchasing company, beyond the amount of the capital of the railway purchased; and in case such railway shall be purchased at a premium, no addition on account of such premium shall be made to the capital of the purchasing company.

166a. In the case of every bill for incorporating a railway, canal, or tramroad company, or for giving any powers to an existing railway, canal, or tramroad company to which no Rates and Charges Order Confirmation Act expressly applies, the Committee on the bill shall fix the rates and charges for merchandise traffic (including small parcels of a perishable nature conveyed by passenger train, exceeding fifty-six pounds in weight) by reference to the Rates and Charges Order Confirmation Act of some other company, which in the opinion of the committee will properly and conveniently apply; and the committee shall in the case of an existing company provide that the rates and charges for merchandise traffic and such small parcels as aforesaid so fixed, shall be in substitution for the rates and charges for similar traffic authorised to be taken by the company under their existing Acts.

If in any such bill other than a railway bill the committee shall be of opinion that no such Act as aforesaid will properly and conveniently apply they shall insert a clause to the following effect :—

Section 24 of " The Railway and Canal Traffic Act, 1888," and any enactment which may be passed in the present or any future session of Parliament extending or modifying that enactment shall, with any necessary modifications, apply to to the company in all respects as if it were one of the companies to which the provisions of the said enactment in terms applied. Provided that the time within which the revised schedule of maximum rates and charges prescribed by the said section shall be submitted to the Board of Trade shall be three years from the date of the passing of this Act, or such further time as the Board of Trade may permit.

167. A clause shall be inserted in every railway bill, prohibiting the payment of any interest or dividend to any shareholder on the amount of the calls made in respect of the shares held by him, except such interest on money advanced by any shareholder beyond the amount of the calls actually made as is in conformity with the Companies Clauses Consolidation Act, 1845, or the Companies Clauses Consolidation (Scotland) Acts, 1845, as the case may be; and except such interest (if any) as the committee on the bill may,

according to the circumstances of the case, think fit to allow, subject always to the following conditions :—

Proceedings of Committees on Bills.

(1.) That the rate of interest allowed by the committee do not in any case exceed three per centum per annum ;

(2.) That interest be allowed to be paid in respect only of the time allowed by the bill for the completion of the railway, or such less time as the committee think fit ;

(3.) That payment of interest be not allowed to begin until the railway company have obtained a certificate of the Board of Trade to the effect that two-thirds at least of the share capital authorized by the bill, in respect whereof interest may be paid, have been actually issued and accepted, and are held by shareholders, who, or whose executors, administrators, successors, or assigns, are legally liable for the same ;

(4.) That interest do not accrue in favour of any shareholder for any time during which any call on any of his shares is in arrear ;

(5.) That the aggregate amount to be so paid for interest be estimated and stated in the bill, and be not deemed capital within Standing Order 153 ;

(6.) That notice of the company having power so to pay interest be given in every prospectus, advertisement, or other document of the company inviting subscriptions for shares, and in every certificate of shares ; and

(7.) That the half-yearly accounts of the company do show the amount on which, and the rate at which, interest has been paid ;—

and the company may be authorized by the bill to pay interest accordingly, but not further or otherwise, and the committee on the bill shall report to the House whether or not they have allowed such interest.

168. A clause shall be inserted in every railway bill by which any money is authorized to be raised, prohibiting the company from paying, out of such money, the deposits required by the Standing Orders to be made for the purposes of any application to Parliament for a bill for the construction of another railway.

Clause as to deposits not to be paid out of capital.

168a. The foregoing Orders, No. 145A and Nos. 158 to 168 inclusive, shall apply *mutatis mutandis* to subways, subway companies, and subway bills, and to tramroads, tramroad companies, and tramroad bills.

Application of Standing Orders, 145a and Nos. 158 to 168 inclusive.

Tramroad Bills.

168b. In every bill for the construction of a tramroad of railway gauge, and intended to communicate with a railway, a clause shall be inserted that the provisions of " The Railway and Canal Traffic Act, 1854," and of the Railway and Canal Traffic Acts, 1873 and 1888, shall apply to the company as if they were a railway or canal company, and to the tramroad to be authorized by the Act as if such tramroad were a railway or canal.

168c. In every tramroad bill the length of so much of any tramroad as is to be constructed along any street or road, or upon any street or road, or upon any waste or open ground by the side of any street or road, shall be set forth in miles, furlongs, chains, and links or yards, or decimals of a chain, in the clause describing the works.

169. The following clause shall be inserted in all railway bills passing through this House :

And be it further enacted, that nothing herein contained shall be deemed or construed to exempt the railway by this or the said recited Acts authorized to be made from the provisions of any general Act relating to railways now in force, or which may hereafter pass during this or any future session of Parliament, or from any future revision and alteration, under the authority of Parliament, of the maximum rates of fares and charges authorized by this Act [or by the said recited acts].

170. In every railway bill, tramway bill, and subway bill, the length of each railway, tramway, and subway be set forth in miles, furlongs, chains, and yards, or decimals of a chain, in the clause describing the works, with a statement in the case of each tramway whether it is a single or a double line.

Tramway Bills.

170a. No powers shall be given to any local authority to construct, acquire, take on lease, or work, any tramway, or portion of tramway, beyond the limits of their district, unless such tramway or portion of tramway is in connection with the tramway belonging to or authorized to be constructed, acquired, or worked, by the local authority, and unless the committee on the bill shall determine that, having regard to the special local circumstances, such construction, acquisition, taking on lease, or working, ought to be sanctioned.

In every case in which the committee shall so determine, they shall specify what portion of the tramway will be situate beyond the district of the local authority to which the power of construction, acquisition, or taking on lease is given, and shall insert a clause for the protection of the local authority of the district in which such tramway or portion of tramway will be situate in the terms *mutatis mutandis* of section 43 of "The Tramways Act, 1870," except that the period of seven years shall be substituted for the period of twenty-one years, and the period of three years for the period of seven years.

171. **Where** a local authority are empowered to work any tramways belonging to, or authorized to be constructed or acquired by them the committee on the bill may, if they think fit under the special circumstances of the case, empower the local authority to enter into agreements for running powers over any tramways in connection with the tramways so worked or to be worked by them, and such running powers shall be deemed to be a purpose of "The Public Health Act, 1875," and the expenses of the exercise of such powers shall, in the event of deficiency in the tramway account, be defrayed out of a local rate, as defined by "The Tramways Act, 1870." Provided that in any such case the committee on the bill shall make provision—

 (1.) That no such agreement shall have effect until approved by the Board of Trade.

 (2.) That all enactments, bye-laws, and regulations relating to the use of or the running of carriages upon the tramways, and the taking of tolls and charges therefor, shall, so far as applicable, extend and apply *mutatis mutandis* to, and shall be observed by the local authority exercising such running powers;

 (3.) That such running powers shall in no case be exclusive, and shall cease unconditionally at the expiration of seven years from the date of the agreement;

 (4.) That further agreements for the exercise of such running powers may be made from time to time with the approval of the Board of Trade for any period not exceeding seven years, provided that such powers shall cease unconditionally at the expiration of the period for which the same are given;

 (5.) That all questions in dispute as to the construction of or arising in consequence of such agreements shall be determined by arbitration.

Proceedings of Committees on Bills.

And the committee shall report the circumstances specially to the House.

Local Government.

Estimates of proposed application of money borrowed by local authorities in certain cases to be recited in the bill, and proved before the Select Committee thereon.

172. In the case of all bills whereby any municipal corporation, district council, joint board, or joint committee, or other local authority in England or Wales, are authorized to borrow money for any matter within the jurisdiction of the Board of Trade or the Local Government Board, estimates showing the proposed application of the money for permanent works shall (except so far as the exercise of the borrowing power is made subject to the sanction of the respective board) be recited in the bill as introduced into Parliament, and proved before the select committee to which the bill is referred.

As to bills relating to Local Government in Ireland.

173. Whenever by any bill application is made by or on behalf of any municipal corporation, municipal commissioners, or town or other commissioners in Ireland for any new powers, or for any increased or additional powers, the promoters shall be required to obtain a certificate under the seal of the Local Government Board of Ireland, setting forth whether such application is made with or without the sanction and approval of the said Local Government Board, which certificate shall be produced before the committee to whom the bill is referred, and shall be reported upon by the said committee.

Committee on Bill to consider its clauses in reference to various matters affecting local government or rating, and report of committee to House to be printed and circulated with the votes.

173a. In the case of any bill promoted by or conferring powers on a municipal corporation or local board, improvement commissioners, town commissioners, or other local authority or public body having powers of local government or rating, the committee on the bill shall consider the clauses of the bill with reference to the following matters :

(a.) Whether the bill gives powers relating to police or sanitary regulations in conflict with, deviation from, or excess of, the provisions of powers of the general law ;

(b.) Whether the bill gives powers which may be obtained by means of bye-laws made subject to the restrictions of general Acts already existing ;

(c.) Whether the bill assigns a period for repayment of any loan or for the redemption of any charge or debt under the bill exceeding the term of sixty years, which term the committee shall not in any case allow to be exceeded, or any period disproportionate to the duration of the works to be executed or other objects of the loan, charge or debt ;

(d.) Whether the bill gives borrowing powers for purposes for which such powers already exist or may be obtained under general Acts, without subjecting the exercise of the powers under the bill to approval from time to time by the proper Government Department.

And the committee shall report specially to the House—

In what manner any clauses relating to the several matters aforesaid have been dealt with by the committee ; and

Whether any report from any Government Department relative to the bill has been referred to the committee ; and

If so, in what manner the recommendations in that report have been dealt with by the committee ; and

Any other circumstances of which, in the opinion of the committee, it is desirable that the House should be informed :

And the report of the committee shall be printed, and shall be circulated with the votes.

Proceedings of Committees on Bills.

Agreements.

174. Where it is sought by any bill to give Parliamentary sanction to any agreement, such agreement shall be annexed to the bill as a schedule thereto, and shall be printed *in extenso* therewith.

Agreement to be annexed to bill.

Letters Patent.

175. When any bill shall be brought into the House for restoring any letters patent, there shall be a true copy of such letters patent annexed to the bill, and the total amount of fees (including the prescribed fee for enlargement under Section 17 of "The Patents, Designs, and Trade Marks Act, 1883"), due and to become due on the patent, shall be deposited with the Comptroller General of Patents, Designs, and Trade Marks, before the meeting of the committee on the bill, and such deposit proved before the committee.

Copy of Letters Patent to be annexed to the bill.

Inclosure and Drainage Bills.

176. In the case of any bill for inclosing lands, the committee may admit proof of the notices required by the Standing Orders, and of the allegations in the preamble of such bill, by affidavit taken and authenticated, according to the form prescribed in the schedule to the General Inclosure Act (41 Geo. 3, c. 109), unless such committee shall otherwise order.

Notices and Allegations.

General Inclosure Act.

Proceedings of Committees on Bills.

Consent bill and statement of property to be delivered in. (Inclosure Bills.)

177. The committee on every bill for inclosing lands shall in the first place require the agent for the same to deliver in to the committee a printed copy of the bill, signed by the lord of the manor (in cases where the lord of the manor has any interest as such in the lands to be inclosed), and by such owners of property within the parish to which the bill relates as shall have assented thereto; but the parties, if they shall think fit, shall be permitted to deliver in different copies of the bill, separately signed by the several parties hereinbefore mentioned, instead of one copy, signed by all of them collectively; together with a list of all the owners of property within such parish, showing the value according to the poor rate or land tax assessment of each owner's property therein, and distinguishing which of them have assented, dissented, or are neuter in respect thereto.

Consent bill and statement of property to be delivered in. (Drainage Bills.)

178. The committee on every bill for draining lands shall in the first place require the agent for the same to deliver in to the committee a printed copy of the bill, signed by such owners and occupiers of property within the drainage district to which the bill relates as shall have assented thereto; but the parties, if they shall think fit, shall be permitted to deliver in different copies of the bill, separately signed by the several parties hereinbefore mentioned, instead of one copy, signed by all of them collectively; together with a list of all the owners of property within such district, showing the value according to the poor rate or land tax assessment of each owner's property therein, or the extent in acres, roods, and perches, and distinguishing which of them have assented, dissented, or are neuter in respect thereto.

Clause for leaving open space for exercise and recreation.

179. In every bill for inclosing lands, provision shall be made for leaving an open space in the most appropriate situation, sufficient for purposes of exercise and recreation of the neighbouring population; and the committee on the bill shall have before them the number of acres proposed to be inclosed, as also of the population in the parishes or places in which the land to be inclosed is situate; and also shall see that provision is made for the efficient fencing of the allotment, for the investment of the same in the churchwardens and overseers of the parish in which such open space is reserved, and for the efficient making and permanent maintenance of the fences by such parish; and in any case where the information hereby required is not given, and the required provisions are not made in the bill, the committee on the same shall report specially to the House the reasons for not complying with such Order.

180. In every bill for inclosing lands, the names of the commissioners proposed to be appointed, and the compensation intended for the lord of the manor and the owners of tithes, in lieu of their respective rights, and also the compensation intended to be made for the enfranchisement of copyholds, where any bargains or agreements have been made for such compensations, shall be inserted in the copy of the bill presented to the House : And all copies of such bills which shall be sent to any of the persons interested in the said manor, tithes, lands, or commons, for their consent, shall contain the names of such proposed commissioners, and also the compensations so bargained or agreed for.

Proceedings of Committees on Bills.

Consent bill to contain names of commissioners and compensations for manorial rights, tithes, and enfranchisements.

181. No person shall be named in any bill for inclosing lands as a commissioner, umpire, surveyor, or valuer, who shall be interested in the inclosure to be made by virtue of such Bill; or the agent ordinarily intrusted with the care, superintendence, or management of the estate of any person so interested.

Disqualification of certain persons as commissioners, surveyors, &c.

182. In every bill for inclosing, draining, or improving lands, there shall be inserted a clause, providing what sum of money in the whole, or by the day, shall be paid to each of the commissioners to be appointed by such bill, in satisfaction of the expense and trouble which he shall incur in the execution of the powers thereby given ; and also a clause, providing that the account of such commissioner or commissioners, containing a true statement of all sums by him or them received and expended, or due to him or them for their own trouble or expenses, shall, at least once in every year, from the date of the passing of the Act till such accounts shall be finally allowed, together with the vouchers relating to the same, be examined by some person or persons to be appointed by the bill, and the balance by him or them stated in the book of accounts required to be kept in the office of the clerk of such commissioners ; and that no charge or item in such accounts shall be binding on the parties concerned, or be valid in law, unless the same shall be duly allowed by such person or persons.

Clause for settling pay of commissioners, and passing their accounts.

Inclosures.

183. Whenever a private bill contains any provisions relating to the inclosure of land, which might be comprised in a provisional order, under the Acts for the Inclosure and Improvement of Land, the committee do make a special report thereon to the House.

Committee on any private bill containing provisions relating to the inclosure of land in certain cases to make a special report.

L

Houses of the Labouring Classes.

183*a.* In the case of every bill which gives, revives, or extends power to take land compulsorily or by agreement, clauses shall be inserted—

(1) Providing that the promoters shall not, in the exercise of such power, purchase or acquire in any parish in the Metropolis twenty or more houses, or as regards England and Wales, exclusive of the Metropolis, in any city, borough, or other urban district, or in any parish or part of a parish not being within an urban district, or in Scotland in any district within the meaning of "The Public Health (Scotland) Act, 1867," or in Ireland in any urban sanitary district as defined by "The Public Health (Ireland) Act, 1878," ten or more houses, occupied either wholly or partially by persons belonging to the labouring class as defined by this Order, as tenants or lodgers, unless and until

(*a*) They shall have obtained the approval of the central authority to a scheme for providing new dwellings for the persons residing in such houses, or for such number or proportion of such persons as the central authority shall, after inquiry, deem necessary, having regard to the number of persons residing in the houses liable to be taken and working within one mile therefrom, and to the amount of vacant suitable accommodation in the immediate neighbourhood of the houses liable to be taken, or to the place of employment of such persons, and to all the other circumstances of the case ; and

(*b*) They shall have given security to the satisfaction of the central authority for the carrying out of the scheme ;

(2) Imposing adequate penalties on the promoters in the event of houses being acquired or appropriated for the purposes of the Bill in contravention of the foregoing provisions ; and

(3) Conferring on the promoters and on the central authority respectively any powers that may be necessary to enable full effect to be given to the said scheme ;

The committee on the bill may provide that the expenses or any part of the expenses incurred by the central authority under this Order shall be defrayed by the promoters of the bill, or out of moneys to be raised under the bill :

In this Standing Order and in Standing Order No. 38,

The expression "labouring class" means mechanics, artizans, labourers, and others working for wages, hawkers, costermongers, persons not working for wages but working at some trade or handicraft without employing others except members of their own family, and persons, other than domestic servants, whose income does not exceed an average of thirty shillings a week, and the families of any of such persons who may be residing with them:

The expression "the Metropolis" means the Metropolis as defined by the Metropolis Management Act, 1855:

The expression "Central Authority" means, as regards the Metropolis, the Secretary of State for the Home Department, and as regards Scotland, the Secretary for Scotland, and as regards England and Wales, exclusive of the Metropolis, the Local Government Board, and as regards Ireland, the Local Government Board for Ireland:

The word "Bill" includes a bill confirming a Provisional Order.

184. In the case of every bill whereby it is proposed to impound the whole or any part of the water of any river or stream, and to give a flow of water in compensation for the water so impounded, the committee on the bill shall inquire into the expediency of making provision, so far as may be practicable, that the whole or a minimum amount of such compensation water shall be given in a continuous flow throughout the twenty-four hours of every day, and shall report to the House accordingly.

Turnpike Roads (Ireland).

187. In every bill for making a turnpike road in Ireland, or for the continuing or amending any Act passed for that purpose, or for the increase or alteration of the existing tolls, rates, or duties upon any such road, or for widening or diverting any such road, a clause shall be inserted to prevent any person who shall be nominated a commissioner from acting or voting in the business of the said turnpike, unless he shall be possessed of an estate in land, or of a personal estate, to such certain value as shall be specified in such bills; and such qualification shall be extended to the heirs apparent of persons possessed of an estate in land to a certain value to be specified.

Margin notes:
Proceedings of Committees on Bills.

Definition of expressions "labouring class," &c.

Compensation water.

Clause for qualification of commissioners.

L 2

Burial Grounds, Cemeteries, and Gas Works.

188. In every bill for making or constructing gas works or sewage works, or works for the manufacture or conversion of the residual products of gas or sewage, or for making or constructing, altering, or enlarging any sewage farm, cemetery, burial ground, crematorium, destructor, hospital for infectious disease, or station for generating electric powers, there shall be inserted a clause defining the lands in or upon which such gas works, sewage works, farm, cemetery, burial ground, crematorium, destructor, hospital, or generating station may be made or constructed.

188*a.* In every bill by which an existing gas or water company is authorized to raise additional capital, provision shall be made for the offer of such capital by public auction or tender at the best price which can be obtained, unless the committee on the bill shall report that such provision ought not to be required, with the reasons on which their opinion is founded.

In the case of every such gas bill it shall be competent to the committee so to regulate the price of the gas to be charged to consumers that any reduction of an authorized standard price shall entitle the company to make a proportionate increase of the authorized dividend, and that any increase above the standard price shall involve a proportionate decrease of dividend.

Estate Bills.

188*b.* In the case of any estate bill, the committee on the bill shall report specially to the House if the bill contains provisions extending either the term or the area of any settlement of land, and the report of the committee shall be printed and circulated with the votes.

See also S. O. 211, and Table of Fees, *p.* 290.

PROCEEDINGS OF SELECT COMMITTEE ON DIVORCE BILLS.

189. There shall be a committee, to be designated "The Select Committee on Divorce Bills," to consist of nine members, who shall be nominated at the commencement of every session, of whom three shall be a quorum.

190. The Select Committee on Divorce Bills shall require evidence to be given before them that an action for damages has been brought in one of Her Majesty's Courts of Record at Westminster, or in one of Her Majesty's Courts of Record in Dublin, or in one

of Her Majesty's Supreme Courts of Judicature of the Presidencies of Calcutta, Madras, Bombay, or the Island of Ceylon, respectively, against the persons supposed to have been guilty of adultery, and judgment for the plaintiff had thereupon ; or sufficient cause to be shown to the satisfaction of the said committee why such action was not brought, or such judgment was not obtained. *Proceedings of Committees on Bills.*

191. The Select Committee on Divorce Bills shall, in all cases in which the petitioner for the bill has attended the House of Lords upon the second reading of the bill, require him to attend before them to answer any questions they may think fit that he should answer. *When petitioner for bill to attend committee.*

192. The Select Committee on Divorce Bills shall report every such bill to the House, whether such committee shall or shall not have agreed to the preamble, or gone through the several clauses or any of them. *Committee to report bill in all cases.*

IV.—THE ORDERS REGULATING THE PRACTICE OF THE HOUSE WITH REGARD TO PRIVATE BILLS.

193. No private bill shall be brought into this House, but upon a petition first presented, which shall have been duly deposited in the Private Bill Office, and indorsed by one of the Examiners, with a printed copy of the proposed bill annexed : And such petition shall be signed by the parties, or some of them, who are suitors for the bill. *Petition for bill, and how to be signed.*

193A. No bill, originating in this House, for confirming a provisional order or provisional certificate shall be read the first time after the first day of June. *Provisional orders and provisional certificates.*

194. All bills promoted by the London County Council, containing power to raise money, by the creation of stock or on loan, shall be introduced as public bills; but after being read a second time by the House, shall be referred to a Select Committee to be nominated by the Committee of Selection, in like manner as private bills. *Procedure in case of bills promoted by the London County Council.*

But this Order shall not apply to a bill promoted by the London County Council for the borrowing of money, which complies with the following conditions:—

(1.) If it authorizes the borrowing and expenditure for the purposes mentioned in the bill of the sum shown by the estimates recited in the preamble to be required for each such purpose, that purpose being the execution of a power conferred or extended either by the bill, or by some public, local, or personal Act ;

Provided that the bill may authorize the borrowing and expenditure for any purpose for which estimates are not recited in the preamble, if it fixes a maximum aggregate sum to be so borrowed, and requires every such borrowing to be sanctioned by the Local Government Board.

(2.) If it is so framed as not to authorize the borrowing and expenditure of any money after the financial period, that is to say, the period ending on the 30th day of September next after the expiration of the then current financial year of the Council ;

(3.) If it is so framed as to provide for the money borrowed being repaid, whether by the creation of a sinking fund, or the redemption of stock, or otherwise, within the period fixed by the bill, or if the borrowing is sanctioned by the Local Government Board fixed by that Board, and the Committee or Board in fixing the period for the repayment of money borrowed for any work shall not fix any period which is in their opinion disproportionate to the duration of such work, and shall in no case fix a period exceeding that prescribed by any public Act relating thereto, or if no period is so prescribed exceeding sixty years ;

(4.) If in the case of any bill conferring or extending any power involving the expenditure of money after the financial period, the recited estimates show the total amount of money required for the execution of the power as well as the particular amount to be borrowed and expended during the financial period.

194A. Where any Act has conferred upon the London County Council any power involving the expenditure of money for any purpose after the then current financial period, or has extended any such power, it shall not be competent for the committee on any bill authorizing the borrowing and expenditure of money for the same purpose during a subsequent financial period, except in pursuance of an express instruction from the House, to reduce the total amount of money shown by the estimates recited in such Act to be required for the execution of the power.

194B. A bill complying with the conditions specified in Standing Order 194, if it contains no powers or provisions except in relation to and consequential on the borrowing and expenditure of

Practice of
the House.

money, or in relation to the Consolidated Loans Fund, or to borrowing by the Council, shall be subject to the following requirements, that is to say :—

(1.) The petition for the bill, with the declaration and printed copy of the bill annexed, shall be deposited in the Private Bill Office on or before the 14th day of April, or the first day on which the House shall reassemble after the Easter recess, whichever shall be the later, instead of the 21st day of December in the previous year;

(2.) Notice of such bill shall be published in the months of February and March, or either of them, instead of in the months of October and November in the previous year;

(3.) Copies of the bill shall be deposited with the Treasury and the Local Government Board on or before the day on which the petition for the bill is deposited in the Private Bill Office;

(4.) The petition for the bill may be presented forthwith and the bill shall be presented for first reading not later than the second sitting day after the presentation of the petition, and shall, after the first reading, be referred to the Examiner, who shall give two clear days' notice at the Private Bill Office of the day appointed for the examination thereof, and the bill shall not be read a second time until the Examiner has reported whether the preceding requirements of this Order have been complied with;

(5.) Whenever the bill is amended at any stage, a copy of the bill as so amended shall be forthwith deposited with the Treasury and the Local Government Board;

(6.) The tables accompanying the bill, as required by Section 12 of "The Metropolitan Board of Works Loans Act, 1875," shall be made up to the 31st day of March preceding the last day allowed for the deposit of the bill, and if printed copies of those tables have been deposited in the Private Bill Office, and at the Vote Office, and with the Treasury and Local Government Board, at least one clear day before the second reading of the bill, it shall be sufficient if those tables are prefixed to the bill as brought up for second reading in this House.

38 & 39 Vict.
c. 65.

194c. No bill promoted by the London County Council shall authorize any alteration of the mode of dealing with the Consolidated Loans Fund, or of borrowing by the Council, unless a report of the Treasury on the proposed alteration is presented to the

House and referred to the committee on the bill. The committee shall consider the report, and may, if they think fit, hear the officers of the Treasury. If the committee disagree with the report, they shall report the fact to the House, with the reasons of their disagreement.

194D. In the case of any bill promoted by the London County Council authorizing the borrowing and expenditure of money, if there is presented to the House and referred to the committee on the bill a report from the Local Government Board or Treasury with respect to the bill or to the borrowing by the County Council and the management of the Consolidated Loans Fund during the previous financial year, the committee shall report specially to the House in what manner the matters contained in such report have been dealt with by the committee, and any circumstances arising out of such report, which, in the opinion of the committee, it is desirable that the House should be informed of. If no such report is referred to the committee, the committee shall report the fact to the House.

194E. The estimates recited in any bill promoted by the London County Council shall be supported by such plans and specifications as the committee think proper.

195. All petitions for private bills shall be presented to the House not later than three clear days after the same shall have been indorsed by the Examiner, or if, when the same is indorsed, the House shall not be sitting, then not later than three clear days after the first sitting thereof subsequent to such indorsement; and if the House shall not be sitting on the latest day on which any petition ought to be presented, then the same shall be presented on the first day on which the House shall again sit.

196. All private bills which have been ordered to be brought in shall be presented to the House by depositing the same in the Private Bill Office, and shall be laid, by one of the clerks of that office, on the table of the House for first reading, together with a list of such bills.

197. No private bill shall be read a first time unless it be presented not later than one clear day after the presentation of the petition for leave to bring in the same; or where the petition has been referred to the select committee on Standing Orders, then not later than one clear day after the House shall have given leave to the parties to proceed with the bill.

198. No petition for additional provision in any private bill will be received by this House, unless a printed copy of the proposed clauses be annexed thereto.

199. All reports of the Examiner of Petitions for private bills, in which he shall report that the Standing Orders have not been complied with, and all special reports of the said Examiner shall be referred to the Select Committee on Standing Orders.

200. All petitions praying that any of the sessional or Standing Orders of the House relating to private bills may be dispensed with, and all petitions for the re-insertion of petitions for private bills in the general list of petitions, and all petitions opposing the same, shall be presented to this House by depositing the same in the Private Bill Office ; and every such petition so deposited shall stand referred to the Select Committee on Standing Orders.

200a. Where a bill having been brought in on motion (not being a bill to confirm a provisional order or certificate) is read the first time, and ordered to be read a second time on a day appointed, and it appears that the Standing Orders relative to private bills may be applicable to the bill, the Examiners of Petitions for private bills shall examine the bill with respect to compliance with the Standing Orders, and shall proceed and report forthwith, and the order of the day relating to the bill shall not be affected thereby ; but if the Examiner report that any Standing Order applicable to the bill has not been complied with, and the Select Committee on Standing Orders report that such Standing Order ought not to be dispensed with, the order of the day relating to the bill shall be discharged.

201. Every private bill, printed on paper, of a size to be determined upon by Mr. Speaker, shall be presented to the House, with a cover of parchment attached to it, upon which the title of the bill is to be written ; and the short title of the bill, as first entered on the votes, shall correspond with that at the head of the advertisement.

202. All charges in any way affecting the public revenue, which occur in the clauses of any private bill, shall be printed in italics in such bill when presented to the House.

203. Every private bill (except name bills) shall be printed ; and printed copies thereof delivered to the Vote Office for the use of the members before the first reading.

204. There shall not be less than three clear days, nor more than seven, between the first and second reading of any private bill, or any bill to confirm any provisional order or provisional

certificate, unless any such private bill have been referred to the
Examiners of Petitions for private bills, in which case such bill
shall not be read a second time later than seven clear days after
the report of the Examiner, or of the Select Committee on Standing
Orders, as the case may be.

Petition relat-
ing to bills to
be presented to
House by being
deposited in the
Private Bill
Office, and
name of bill
to be indorsed
on every peti-
tion.

205. Every petition in favour of or against any private bill, or
any bill to confirm any provisional order or provisional certificate
before the House, or otherwise relating thereto (not being a
petition for additional provision), shall be presented to this House,
by depositing the same in the Private Bill Office, and there shall
be endorsed thereon the name or short title by which such bill is
entered in the votes, and a statement that such petition is in favour
of or against the bill, or otherwise, as the case may be, together
with the name of the member, or party or agent depositing the
same.

206. Any petitioner or memorialist may withdraw his petition
or memorial, on a requisition to that effect being deposited in the
Private Bill Office, signed by him or by the agent who deposited
such petition or memorial; and where any such petition or
memorial is signed by more than one person, any person signing
such petition or memorial may withdraw his opposition by a
similar requisition, signed and deposited as aforesaid.

When second
or third read-
ing opposed, to
be postponed.

207. In cases where the second or third reading of a private
bill, or the consideration of a bill as amended by the committee, or
any proposed clause or amendment, or any motion relating to a
private bill, is opposed, the same shall be postponed until the day
on which the House shall next sit.

Certain private
bills to stand re-
ferred to Com-
mittees of Selec-
tion, General
Committee on
Railway and
Canal Bills, and
Divorce.

208. Every private bill, not being a railway, canal or divorce
bill, after having been read a second time and committed, shall
stand referred to the Committee of Selection; and if a railway or
canal bill, to the General Committee on Railway and Canal Bills;
and if a divorce bill, to the Select Committee on Divorce Bills.

Provisional
order bills to
stand referred
to Committee
of Selection,
or General
Committee on
Railway and
Canal Bills, &c.

208a. Every bill for confirming provisional orders or provisional certificates shall, after the second reading, stand referred
to the Committee of Selection, or to the General Committee on
Railway and Canal Bills, as the case may require, and be subject
to the Standing Orders regulating the proceedings upon private
bills, so far as they are applicable: providing that, when any order
or certificate contained in any such bill is opposed, the committee
to whom such opposed order or certificate is referred shall
consider all the orders or certificates comprised in such bill.

209. When the house shall have been informed by the Chairman of Ways and Means, that in his opinion any unopposed private bill should be treated as an opposed bill, such bill shall be again referred to the Committee of Selection ; or in the case of a railway or canal bill, to the General Committee on Railway and Canal Bills.

Practice of the House.

When unopposed bill is to be treated as opposed. to be again referred to Committee of Selection or General Committee.

210. Every petition against a private bill which shall have been deposited in the Private Bill Office not later than ten clear days after the first reading of such bill, and every petition against any bill to confirm any provisional order or provisional certificate, which shall have been deposited in the Private Bill Office not later than seven clear days after the Examiner shall have given notice of the day on which the bill will be examined, or which shall have been otherwise deposited in accordance with the Standing Orders of the House, and in which the petitioners shall have prayed to be heard, by themselves, their counsel or agents, shall stand referred to the committee on such bill, and such petitioners, subject to the rules and orders of the House, shall be heard upon their petition accordingly, if they think fit, and counsel heard, in favour of the bill, against such petition.

Petition against bill, if duly deposited in Private Bill Office, to stand referred to committee on bill, &c.

211. There shall be six clear days between the second reading of every private bill, and of every bill to confirm any provisional order or provisional certificate, and the sitting of the committee thereupon, except in the case of name bills, naturalization bills, and estate bills (not being bills relating to crown, church, or corporation property, or property held in trust for public or charitable purposes), in respect of which there shall be three clear days between the second reading and the committee.

Time between second reading and committee.

212. All reports made under the authority of any public department upon a private bill, or the objects thereof, laid before the House, shall stand referred to the committee on the bill.

Reports of departments to stand referred to committee on bill.

213. The report upon every private bill shall lie upon the table ; and every such bill, if amended in committee, or a railway or a tramway bill, shall be ordered to lie upon the table : but if not amended in committee, and not a railway or a tramway bill, it shall be ordered to be read a third time.

Report of bills.

214. Every private bill, as amended in committee, shall be printed at the expense of the parties applying for the same, and delivered to the Vote Office for the use of the members, three clear days at least before the consideration of such bill.

Bill to be printed after report.

215. In the case of private bills ordered to lie upon the table, three clear days shall intervene between the report and the consi-

Time between report and consideration of bill, &c.

Practice of the House.

deration of the bill; and no consideration of any such bill shall take place, unless the Chairman of the Committee of Ways and Means shall have informed the House, or signified in writing to Mr. Speaker, whether the bill contain the several provisions required by the Standing Orders.

No clause or amendment on consideration of bill, or on third reading, to be offered, unless Chairman of Ways and Means shall have informed the House, &c.

216. No clause or amendment shall be offered in the House on the consideration of any private bill ordered to lie upon the table, nor any verbal amendment on the third reading of any private bill, unless the Chairman of the Committee of Ways and Means shall have informed the House, or signified in writing to Mr. Speaker, whether, in his opinion, such clause or amendment be such as ought or ought not to be entertained by the House, without referring the same to the Select Committee on Standing Orders.

Clauses and amendments offered on consideration of bill, or verbal amendments on third reading, to be printed.

217. When any clause or amendment is offered on the consideration of any private bill ordered to lie upon the table, or any verbal amendment on the third reading of any private bill, such clause or amendment shall be printed; and when any clause is proposed to be amended, it shall be printed *in extenso*, with every addition or substitution in different type, and the omissions therefrom included in brackets and underlined, unless the Chairman of the Committee of Ways and Means shall consider such printing to be unnecessary. The expense of printing such clauses or amendments, when offered by a party promoting or opposing a bill, shall be paid by such party.

When referred, no further proceeding to be had until report of Select Committee on Standing Orders.

218. When any clause or amendment on the consideration of any private bill ordered to lie upon the table, or any verbal amendment on the third reading of any private bill, shall have been referred to the Select Committee on Standing Orders, no further proceeding shall be had until the report of the said Select Committee shall have been brought up.

No amendments, except verbal, on third reading.

219. No amendments, not being merely verbal, shall be made to any private bill on the third reading.

Lords' amendments to be printed and circulated with the votes prior to consideration, &c.

220. All amendments made by the House of Lords to any private bill shall be printed at the expense of the parties, and circulated with the votes, prior to such amendments being taken into consideration; and where any clause has been amended, it shall be printed *in extenso*, with every addition or substitution in different type, and the omissions therefrom included in brackets and underlined, unless the Chairman of the Committee of Ways and Means shall consider such printing to be unnecessary; and when any amendments are intended to be proposed to the Lords' amend-

ments, such proposed amendments shall also be printed in like manner.

221. Every private bill, after it has been read a third time, shall be printed fair, at the expense of the parties applying for the same.

222. In all cases where it is intended to appoint a committee to inspect the journals of the House of Lords with relation to any proceedings upon any private bill, previous notice thereof in writing shall be given by the agent to the clerks in the Committee Office.

223. No private bill shall pass through two stages on one and the same day without the special leave of the House.

224. Except in cases of urgent and pressing necessity, no motion shall be made to dispense with any sessional or Standing Order of the House without due notice thereof.

225. Each day, so soon as the House shall be ready to proceed to private business, the clerk at the table shall read from the private business list, and from the list of bills presented for first reading (*see* Order 196), the titles of the several bills set down therein, according to their precedence, as arranged under the following heads :—

    1. Consideration of Lords' amendments ;

    2. Third reading ;

    3. Consideration of bills ordered to lie upon the table ;

    4. Second reading ;

    5. First reading ;

and if upon the reading of each such title as aforesaid, no motion shall be made with respect to such private bill, the further proceedings thereon shall be adjourned until the next sitting of the House.

225a. All bills for confirming provisional orders or certificates shall be set down for consideration, each day, in a separate list, after the private business, and arranged in the same order as that prescribed by the Standing Orders for private bills.

226. This House will not insist on its privileges with regard to any clauses in private bills, or in bills to confirm any provisional orders or provisional certificates sent down from the House of Lords which refer to tolls and charges for services performed, and are not in the nature of a tax, or which refer to rates assessed and levied by local authorities for local purposes.

Side notes:

Practice of the House.

Bill to be printed fair after third reading.

Notice of committee to inspect Lords' Journals to be given to committee clerks.

Bill not to proceed two stages on same day.

Notice to be given of motion for dispensation.

Order of proceedings in House on private business.

Provisional order bills.

Tolls and charges not in the nature of a tax.

V.—THE ORDERS REGULATING THE PRACTICE IN THE PRIVATE BILL OFFICE.

Private Bill Office and registers.

227. Registers shall be kept in " The Private Bill Office," in which shall be entered by the clerks appointed for the business of that office, the name and place of residence of the parliamentary agent in town, and of the agent in the country (if any) soliciting the bill ; and all the proceedings, from the petition to the passing of the bill :—Such entries to specify, briefly, each day's proceeding before the Examiners of Petitions respectively, or in the House, or in any committee to which the bill may be referred : the day and hour on which the Examiner or the committee is appointed to sit ; the day and hour to which the proceedings before such Examiners or committee may be adjourned, and the name of the clerk attending the same.   Such registers to be open to public inspection daily in the said office.

Receipt of document to be acknowledged.

228. The receipt of all documents required by the Standing Orders of the House to be deposited in the Private Bill Office, shall be acknowledged by one of the clerks of the said office, upon the said documents, when deposited.

List of petitions to be kept.

229. A list of all petitions for private bills shall be kept in the Private Bill Office in the order of their deposit, according to such regulations as shall have been made by Mr. Speaker, which shall be called the " General List of Petitions," and each petition therein shall be numbered.

Memorials, when to be deposited.

230. All memorials complaining of non-compliance with the Standing Orders, in reference to petitions for bills deposited in the Private Bill Office on or before the 21st December, shall be deposited as follows :

If the same relate to petitions for bills numbered in the general list of petitions;

From

1 to 100	They shall be deposited	January 9th.
101 to 200	on or before - -	„ 16th.
201 and upwards		„ 23rd.

And in the case of any petitions for bills which may be deposited by leave of the House after the 21st December, such memorials shall be deposited three clear days before the day first appointed for the examination of the petition.

Deposit of memorials and copies

231. All memorials shall be deposited in the Private Bill Office before six of the clock in the evening of any day on which the

House shall sit, and between eleven and one of the clock on any day on which the House shall not sit ; and two copies of every such memorial shall be deposited for the use of the Examiners before twelve of the clock on the following day.

232. Every memorial complaining of non-compliance with the Standing Orders of the House in reference to petitions for additional provision in private bills, to bills brought from the House of Lords and to bills introduced by leave of this House in lieu of other bills which shall have been withdrawn, and to bills for confirming any provisional order or provisional certificate, shall be deposited in the Private Bill Office, together with two copies thereof, before twelve o'clock on the day preceding that appointed for the examination of any such petition or bill by the Examiner ; and the Examiner shall be at liberty to entertain such memorial, although the party (if any) who may be specially affected by the non-compliance with the Standing Orders shall not have signed the same.

233. Every private bill, after it has been read the first time shall be in the custody of the clerks of the Private Bill Office, until laid upon the table for the second reading ; and when committed, shall be taken by the proper committee clerk into his charge, till reported.

234. Between the first and second reading of every private bill, the bill shall be examined, with all practical despatch, by the clerks of the Private Bill Office, as to its conformity with the rules and Standing Orders of the House.

235. Three clear days' notice in writing shall be given by the agent for the bill, to the clerks in the Private Bill Office, of the day proposed for the second reading of every private bill ; and no such notice shall be given until the day after that on which the bill has been ordered to be read a second time.

236. Four clear days' notice in the case of opposed bills, and one clear day's notice in the case of unopposed and re-committed bills, shall be given to the clerks in the Private Bill Office by the clerk to the Committee of Selection, or by the clerk to the General Committee on Railway and Canal Bills, with regard to all bills referred to either of the said committees, and with regard to bills not referred to either of the said committees, by the clerk to the committee to which any such bill is either referred or re-committed, of the day and hour appointed for the first meeting of the committee on every private bill, and notice shall be given in like manner of the postponement of the first meeting of the committee

Practice in the
Private Bill
Office.

on every private bill on the day on which such postponement is made.

Filled-up bill
to be deposited
in Private Bill
Office.

237. A filled-up bill is signed by the agent for the bill, as proposed to be submitted to the committee on the bill, and in the case of a re-committed bill, a filled-up bill, as proposed to be submitted to the committee on re-committal, shall be deposited in the Private Bill Office two clear days before the meeting of the committee on every private bill; and a copy of the proposed amendments shall be furnished by the promoters to such parties petitioning against the bill as shall apply for it one clear day before the meeting of the committee.

Notice of
adjournment.

238. Notice, in writing, shall be given by the committee clerk to the clerks in the Private Bill Office, of the day and hour to which each committee is adjourned.

Notice of
consideration
of bill.

239. One clear day's notice, in writing, shall be given by the agent for the bill to the clerks in the Private Bill Office, of the day proposed for the consideration of every private bill ordered to lie upon the table.

Bill as amended
in committee
to be delivered
in.

240. The committee clerk, after the report is made out, shall deliver in to the Private Bill Office a printed copy of the bill, with the written amendments made in the committee; in which bill all the clauses added by the committee shall be regularly marked in those parts of the bill wherein they are to be inserted.

Bill printed as
amended to be
examined.

241. Every private bill printed as amended in committee shall be examined by the clerks in the Private Bill Office, with the bill delivered in by the committee clerk, and the examining clerks shall indorse thereon a certificate of such examination.

Notice to be
given of
clauses, &c.
on considera-
tion of bill, or
verbal amend-
ment on third
reading.

242. When it is intended to bring up any clause or to propose any amendment on the consideration of any private bill ordered to lie upon the table, or any verbal amendment on the third reading of any private bill, notice shall be given thereof, in the Private Bill Office, one clear day previous to such consideration or third reading.

Notice of third
reading.

243. One clear day's notice, in writing, shall be given by the agent for the bill, to the clerks in the Private Bill Office, of the day proposed for the third reading of every private bill; and no such notice shall be given until the day after that on which the bill shall have been ordered to be read a third time.

Amendments
on considera-
tion of bill and
third reading.

244. The amendments (if any) which are made on the consideration of any private bill ordered to lie upon the table, and on the third reading of any private bill, and also such amendments made by the House of Lords as shall have been agreed to by this

House, shall be entered by one of the clerks in the Private Bill Office, upon the printed copy of the bill as amended in committee ; which clerk shall sign the said copy so amended, in order to its being deposited and preserved in the said office.

245. Every private bill, after it has been printed fair, shall, before the same is sent to the Lords, be examined by the clerks in the Private Bill Office with the bill as read a third time ; and the examining clerks shall indorse thereon a certificate of such examination.

246. When amendments made by the House of Lords to any private bill are to be taken into consideration, one clear day's notice shall be given thereof in the Private Bill Office, and if any amendments be intended to be proposed thereto, a copy of such amendments shall also be deposited, and notice given thereof one clear day previous to the same being proposed to be taken into consideration ; and no such notice shall be given until the day after that on which such bill shall have been returned from the House of Lords.

247. All notices required to be given or deposits to be made in the Private Bill Office shall be delivered in the said office before six of the clock in the evening of any day on which the House shall sit, and between eleven and one of the clock on any day on which the House shall not sit ; and after any day on which the House shall have adjourned beyond the following day, no notice shall be given for the first day on which it shall again sit.

248. The clerks in the Private Bill Office shall prepare, daily, lists of all private bills, and petitions for private bills upon which any committee or Examiner is appointed to sit ; specifying the hour of meeting, and the room where the committee or Examiner shall sit; and the same shall be hung up in the lobby of the House.

249. Every plan, and book of reference thereto, which shall be certified by the Speaker of the House of Commons, in pursuance of any Act of Parliament, shall previously be ascertained, and verified in such manner as shall be deemed most advisable by the Speaker, to be exactly conformable in all respects to the plan and book of reference which shall have been signed by the chairman of the committee upon the bill.

APPENDIX (A.)

No. ————————

SIR,—We beg to inform you that application is intended to be made to Parliament in the ensuing session for " An Act " [here insert the title of the Act], and that the property mentioned in the annexed schedule, Part I., or some part thereof, in which we understand you are interested as therein stated, will be liable to be taken compulsorily for the purposes of the said undertaking [and that the property mentioned in the annexed schedule, Part II., in which we understand you are interested as therein stated, will be liable to have an improvement charge imposed upon it].

We also beg to inform you that a plan and section of the said undertaking, with a book of reference thereto, have been or will be deposited with the [several clerks of the peace, or principal sheriff clerks, as the case may be] of the counties of [specify the counties in which the property is situate], on or before the 30th of November, and that copies of so much of the said plan and section as relates to the [parish or other area in accordance with the terms of Standing Order 29, as the case may be], in which your property is situate, with a book of reference thereto, have been or will be deposited for public inspection with the [clerk, or other officer in the said Order respectively mentioned, as the case may be], on or before the 30th day of November, on which plan your property is designated by the numbers set forth in the annexed schedule.

As we are required to report to Parliament whether you assent to or dissent from the proposed undertaking, or whether you are neuter in respect thereto, you will oblige us by writing your answer of assent, dissent or neutrality in the form left herewith, and returning the same to us with your signature on or before the   day of   next; and if there should be any error or misdescription in the annexed schedule, we shall feel obliged by your informing us thereof, at your earliest convenience, that we may correct the same without delay.

We also beg to inform you that it is intended that the Act shall provide to the effect that, notwithstanding section 92 of the Lands Clauses Consolidation Act, 1845 [*or* section 90 of the Lands

Clauses Consolidation (Scotland) Act, 1845], you may be required
to sell and convey a part only of your property, numbered
on the deposited plans.

We are, Sir,

Your most obedient servants,

To

Note.—If the application be forwarded by post, the words " Parliamentary
Notice" are to be written or printed on the cover.

SCHEDULE referred to in the foregoing notice, describing the
property therein alluded to.

	Parish, or other area as the case may be.	Number on Plans.	Description.	Owner.	Lessee.	Occupier.
Property which may be taken compulsorily.		PART I.				
Property on which an improvement charge may be imposed.		PART II.				

APPENDIX (B.)

ANNO PRIMO VICTORIÆ REGINÆ.
CAP. LXXXIII.

An Act to compel clerks of the peace for counties and other
persons to take the custody of such documents as shall be
directed to be deposited with them under the Standing
Orders of either House of Parliament.

Whereas the Houses of Parliament are in the habit of requiring
that, previous to the introduction of any bill into Parliament for
making certain bridges, turnpike-roads, cuts, canals, reservoirs,

aqueducts, waterworks, navigations, tunnels, archways, railways, piers, ports, harbours, ferries, docks and other works, to be made under the authority of Parliament, certain maps or plans and sections, and books and writings, or extracts or copies of or from certain maps, plans or sections, books and writings, shall be deposited in the office of the clerk of the peace for every county, riding or division in England or Ireland, or in the office of the sheriff clerk of every county in Scotland, in which such work is proposed to be made, and also with the parish clerk in every parish in England, the schoolmaster of every parish of Scotland, or in Royal Burghs with the town clerk, and the postmaster of the post town in or nearest to every parish in Ireland, in which such work is intended to be made, and with other persons: and whereas it is expedient that such maps, plans, sections, books, writings and copies or extracts of and from the same, should be received by the said clerks of the peace, sheriff clerks, parish clerks, schoolmasters, town clerks, postmasters and other persons, and should remain in their custody for the purposes hereinafter mentioned ; be it therefore enacted by the Queen's most Excellent Majesty, by and with the advice and consent of the Lords Spiritual and Temporal, and Commons, in this present Parliament assembled, and by the authority of the same, that whenever either of the Houses of Parliament shall by its Standing Orders, already made or hereafter to be made, require that any such maps, plans, sections, books or writings, or extracts or copies of the same, or any of them, shall be deposited as aforesaid, such maps, plans, sections, books, writings, copies and extracts shall be received by and shall remain with the clerks of the peace, sheriff clerks, parish clerks, schoolmasters, town clerks, postmasters and other persons with whom the same shall be directed by such Standing Orders to be deposited, and they are hereby respectively directed to receive and to retain the custody of all such documents and writings so directed to be deposited with them respectively, in the manner and for the purposes and under the rules and regulations concerning the same respectively directed by such Standing Orders, and shall make such memorials and endorsements on and give such acknowledgments and receipts in respect of the same respectively as shall be thereby directed.(1)

II. And be it further enacted, that all persons interested shall have liberty to, and the said clerks of the peace, sheriff clerks, parish clerks, schoolmasters, town clerks and postmasters, and every of them, are and is hereby required, at all reasonable hours of the day, to permit all persons interested to inspect during a reasonable time and make extracts from or copies of the said maps, plans, sections, books, writings, extracts and copies of or from the same, so deposited with them respectively, on payment by each person to the clerk of the peace, sheriff clerk, clerk of the parish, schoolmaster, town clerk or postmaster having the custody of any such map, plan, section, book, writing, extract or copy, one shilling for every such inspection, and the further sum of one shilling for every hour during which such inspection shall continue after the first hour, and after the rate of sixpence for every one hundred words copied therefrom.(¹)

III. And be it further enacted, that in case any clerk of the peace, sheriff clerk, parish clerk, schoolmaster, town clerk, postmaster or other person shall in any matter or thing refuse or neglect to comply with any of the provisions hereinbefore contained, every clerk of the peace, sheriff clerk, parish clerk, schoolmaster, town clerk, postmaster or other person shall for every such offence forfeit and pay any sum not exceeding the sum of five pounds; and every such penalty shall, upon proof of the offence before any justice of the peace for the county within which such offence shall be committed, or by the confession of the party offending, or by th · oath of any credible witness, be levied and recovered, together with the costs of the proceedings for the recovery thereof, by distress and sale of the goods and effects of the party offending, by warrant under the hand of such justice, which warrant such justice is hereby empowered to grant, and shall be paid to the person or persons making such complaint; and it shall be lawful for any such justice of the peace to whom any complaint shall be made of any offence committed against this Act to summon the party complained of before him, and on such summons to hear and determine the matter of such complaint in a summary way, and on proof of the offence to convict the offender, and to adjudge him to pay the penalty or forfeiture incurred, and to proceed to recover the same, although no information in writing or in print shall have been exhibited or taken by or before such justice; and all such proceedings by summons without information shall be as good, valid and effectual to all intents and purposes as if an information in writing had been exhibited.(¹)

(¹) In parishes in England and Wales having a Parish Council the Clerk, if there is one, of such Council, or, if there is not one, then the Chairman, now receives the documents deposited (Local Government Act, 1894, s. 17; S. O. 29, *ante*.)

APPENDIX (C.)

ANNO NONO VICTORIÆ REGINÆ.(¹)

CAP. XX.

An Act to amend an Act of the second year of Her present Majesty, for providing for the custody of certain monies paid in pursuance of the Standing Orders of either House of Parliament by subscribers to works or undertakings to be effected under the authority of Parliament."

Whereas an Act was passed in the second year of the reign of Her present Majesty Queen Victoria, intituled, " An Act to provide for the custody of certain monies paid in pursuance of the Standing Orders of either House of Parliament, by subscribers to works or undertakings to be effected under the authority of Parliament :" and whereas it is expedient that the said Act should be repealed and should be re-enacted, with such modifications, extensions and alterations as after mentioned : Be it therefore enacted, by the Queen's most excellent Majesty, by and with the advice and consent of the Lords Spiritual and Temporal, and Commons, in this present Parliament assembled, and by the authority of the same, that the said Act shall be and is hereby repealed : provided always, that all acts done under the provisions of the said Act shall be good, valid and effectual to all intents and purposes, and that all sums of money paid under the provisions of the said Act shall be dealt with in all respects as if this Act had not been passed.

II. And be it enacted, that in all cases in which any sum of money is required by any Standing Order of either House of Parliament, either now in force or hereafter to be in force, to be deposited by the subscribers to any work or undertaking which is to be executed under the authority of an Act of Parliament, if the director or person or directors or persons having the management of the affairs of such work or undertaking, not exceeding five in number, shall apply to one of the clerks in the office of the Clerk of the Parliaments with respect to any such money required by any Standing Order of the Lords Spiritual and Temporal in Parliament assembled, or to one of the clerks of the Private Bill Office of the House of Commons with respect to any such money required by any Standing Order of the Commons in Parliament assembled, to be deposited, it shall be lawful for the clerk so applied to, by

marginal notes:
1 & 2 Vict. c. 117.

Recited Act repealed. Monies already paid in to be dealt with as directed by former Act.

Authority to deposit.

(¹) See as to repayment of deposit 55 & 56 Vict. c. 27.

warrant or order under his hand, to direct that such sum of money shall be paid in manner hereinafter mentioned; (that is to say) into the Bank of England in the name and with the privity of the accountant-general of the Court of Chancery in England, if the work or undertaking in respect of which the sum of money is required to be deposited is intended to be executed in that part of the United Kingdom called England; or into any of the banks in Scotland established by Act of Parliament or royal charter in the name and with the privity of the Queen's remembrancer of the Court of Exchequer in Scotland, at the option of the person or persons making such application as aforesaid, in case such work or undertaking is intended to be executed in that part of the United Kingdom called Scotland; or into the Bank of Ireland in the name and with the privity of the accountant-general of the Court of Chancery in Ireland, in case such work or undertaking is intended to be made or executed in that part of the United Kingdom called Ireland; and such warrant or order shall be a sufficient authority for the accecountant-general of the Court of Chancery in England, the Queen's remembrancer of the Court of Exchequer in Scotland, and the accountant-general of the Court of Chancery in Ireland, respectively, to permit the sum of money directed to be paid by such warrant or order to be placed to an account opened or to be opened in his name in the bank mentioned in such warrant or order.

III. And be it enacted, that it shall be lawful for the person or persons named in such warrant or order, or the survivors or survivor of them, to pay the sum mentioned in such warrant or order into the bank mentioned in such warrant or order in the name and with the privity of the officer or person in whose name such sum shall be directed to be paid by such warrant or order, to be placed to his account there ex-parte the work or undertaking mentioned in such warrant or order, pursuant to the method prescribed by any Act or Acts for the time being in force for regulating monies paid into the said courts, and pursuant to the general orders of the said court respectively, and without fee or reward; and every such sum so paid in, or the securities in or upon which the same may be invested as hereinafter mentioned, or the stocks, funds or securities authorized to be transferred or deposited in lieu thereof as hereinafter mentioned, shall there remain until the same, with all interest and dividends (if any) accrued thereon, shall be paid out of such bank, in pursuance of the provisions of this Act: provided always, that in case any such director or person, directors or persons, having the management of any such proposed work or undertaking as aforesaid, shall have previously invested in the Three per Centum Consolidated or the Three per Centum Reduced Bank Annuities, Exchequer Bills, or other government securities, the sum or sums of money required by any such Standing Order by either House of Parliament as aforesaid to be deposited by the subscribers to any work or undertaking which is to be executed under the authority of an Act of Parliament, it shall be lawful for the person or persons named in such warrant or order, or the survivors or survivor of them, to deposit such Exchequer Bills or other Government securities in the bank mentioned in such warrant or order in the name and with the privity of the officer or person in whose name such sum shall by such a warrant or order be directed to be paid, or to transfer such Government stocks or funds into the name of the officer or person; and such transfer or deposit shall be directed by such clerk of the office of the Clerk of the Parliaments, or such clerk of the Private Bill Office of the House of Commons, as the case may be, in lieu of payment of so much of the sum of money required to be deposited as aforesaid as the same Exchequer Bills or other the Government stocks or funds, will extend to satisfy at the price at which the same were originally purchased by the said person or persons, director or directors, as aforesaid, such price to be proved by production of the broker's certificate of such original purchase.

IV. And be it enacted, that if the person or persons named in such warrant or order, or the survivors or survivor of them, desire to have invested any sum so paid into the Bank of England or the Bank of Ireland, or any interest or dividend which may have accrued on any stocks or securities so transferred or deposited as aforesaid, the court in the name of whose accountant-general the same may have been paid may, on a petition presented to such court, in a summary way by him or them, order that such sum or such interest or dividends shall, until the same be paid out to the parties entitled to the same in pursuance of this Act, be laid out in the Three per Centum Consolidated or Three per Centum Reduced Bank Annuities, or any Government security or securities, at the option of the aforesaid person or persons, or the survivor or survivors of them.

V. And be it enacted, that on the termination of the session of Parliament in which the petition or bill for the purpose of making or sanctioning any such work or undertaking shall have been introduced into Parliament, or if such petition or Bill shall be rejected or finally withdrawn by some proceeding in either

House of Parliament, or shall not be allowed to proceed, or if the person or persons by whom the said money was paid or security deposited, shall have failed to present a petition, or if an Act be passed authorizing the making of such work or undertaking, and if in any of the foregoing cases the person or persons named in such warrant or order, or the survivors or survivor of them, or the majority of such persons, apply by petition to the court in the name of whose accountant-general the sum of money mentioned in such warrant or order shall have been paid, or such Exchequer Bills, stocks, or funds shall have been deposited or transferred as aforesaid, or to the Court of Exchequer in Scotland, in case such sum of money shall have been paid in the name of the said Queen's remembrancer, the court in the name of whose accountant-general or Queen's remembrancer such sum of money shall have been paid, or such Exchequer Bills, stocks or funds shall have been deposited or transferred, shall by order direct the sum of money paid in pursuance of such warrant or order, or the stocks, funds or securities in or upon which the same may have been invested, and the interest or dividends thereof, or the Exchequer Bills, stocks or funds so deposited or transferred as aforesaid, and the interest and dividends thereof, to be paid or transferred to the party or parties so applying, or to any other person or persons whom they may appoint in that behalf; but no such order shall be made in the case of any such petition or Bill being rejected or not being allowed to proceed, or being withdrawn or not being presented, or of an Act being passed authorizing the making of such work or undertaking, unless upon the production of the certificate of the Chairman of Committees of the House of Lords, with reference to any proceeding in the House of Lords, or of the Speaker of the House of Commons, with reference to any proceeding in the House of Commons, that the said petition or bill was rejected or not allowed to proceed, or was withdrawn during its passage through one of the Houses of Parliament, or was not presented, or that such Act was passed, which certificate the said Chairman or Speaker shall grant on the application in writing of the person or persons, or the majority of the persons named in such warrant, or the survivor or survivors of them : Provided always that the granting of any such certificate, or any mistake or error therein or in relation thereto, shall not make the Chairman or Speaker signing the same liable in respect of any monies, stocks, funds and securities which may be paid, deposited, invested or transferred in pursuance of the provisions of this Act, or the interest or dividends thereof.

INDEX TO STANDING ORDERS OF HOUSE OF COMMONS.

Note.—The Figures, 127, 238, &c., refer to the Number of each Standing Order relating to Private Bills; *App.* (A.), &c., to the Appendices (A.), (B.) & (C.).

A

Additional Provision. See *Petitions for Additional Provision.*

Adjournment of Committees:

Causes of adjournment of committee on opposed bill to be specially reported, 127.

The committee clerk to give notice of adjournment in the Private Bill Office, 238.

See also *Committee Clerk. Postponement of Consideration of Bills in Committee.*

Advertisements. See *Notices by Advertisement.*

Affidavits:

To be admitted by the Examiner in proof of compliance with the Standing Orders, 76.

To be admitted by committees on private bills in proof of compliance with such Standing Orders as are directed to be proved before them, 142.

And in proof of consents to bills, 143.

And in proof of notices and allegations of bills for inclosing lands, 176.

How such affidavits shall be sworn, 142.

Agents:

Declaration by the agent to be annexed to the petition and bill deposited in the Private Bill Office, 32.

Particulars required to be stated in the agent's declaration, *ib.*

Copies of the estimate or declaration of expense of the undertaking to be delivered at the Private Bill Office, for the use of any agent who may apply for the same, 35, 36.

Declaration or estimate, signed by the party or agent soliciting the bill, may be deposited in certain cases, and no deposit of money required, 59.

B

C

N

Course to be pursued in case of opposed bills in which no parties shall appear upon their petitions against bills, 136.

Four clear days' notice to be given of meeting of committee, 236.

2. Committees on unopposed bills:

Quorum of committee, 137.

Chairman of Committee of Ways and Means may report special circumstances, or that a bill ought to be treated as opposed, 83.

Local member not to vote in committee on unopposed bills, 139.

3. Committees on bills, whether opposed or unopposed:

The Committee of Selection to fix the time for the first sitting of every committee on a private bill, subject to the order in regard to the interval between the second reading and the sitting of the committee, 105, 211.

All reports from public departments to stand referred to committee, 212.

Filled-up copies of bill to be laid before each member of the committee, 138.

Names of members attending to be entered on the minutes of the committee, 140.

Committee not to inquire into compliance with any Standing Orders which are directed to be proved before the Examiner, 141.

The committee may admit affidavits in proof of compliance with such Standing Orders as are required to be proved before them, 142.

Consents, how to be proved before them, 143.

Petitioner who has discussed clauses of a bill in House of Lords not precluded from opposing preamble of bill in this House, 143a.

Clause compelling payment of subscriptions, 144.

Allegations of bills to be reported, 148.

And preamble and clauses and any alteration of preamble to be specially reported, 149.

Chairman to report where parties have stated that they do not intend to proceed with the bill, 149.

The committee to notice in their report any recommendation from any Government department upon the bill, 150.

Minutes of committee to be laid on the table with the report, 152.

Committee to consider clauses of bill in reference to matters affecting local government or rating, and report of committee to be printed and circulated with votes, 173a.

In case of bill providing for compensation for water impounded, committee to inquire into expediency of making the flow continuous, and to report accordingly, 184.

The report on every private bill to lie upon the table; and the bill, if amended in committee, or a railway bill, when reported, to be ordered to lie upon the table, 213.

Every other bill, when reported, to be ordered to be read a third time, *ib.*

Bill to be printed after the report, 214.

Committee clerk, after report is made out, to deliver in Private Bill Office a printed copy of bill, with written amendments made by committee, 240.

Re-committed Bill.—One clear day's notice to be given of meeting, 236.

Railways.—Orders regulating proceedings of committees on railway bills, 153—169.

Letters Patent.—The like as to committees on letters patent bills, 175.

Inclosure and Drainage Bills.—The like as to committees on inclosure and drainage bills, 176—182.

Inclosures.—The like as to committees on private bills containing provisions relating to the inclosure of land, 183.

Public Carriage Road Bills.—The like as to committees on road bills, 110.

Turnpike Roads (Ireland).—The like as to committees on turnpike road bills (Ireland), 187.

Divorce Bills, Select Committee on.—The like as to committees on divorce bills, 189–192.

Opposed Private Bills.—Four clear days' notice of the day and hour appointed for the meeting of the committee, to be given by the clerk to the Committee of Selection to the clerks in the Private Bill Office, 236.

III. *Notices in the Private Bill Office, and Lists of Committees:*

Notice to be given of sitting of committee on the bill, 236.

Notice of adjournment, 238.

Time for delivering notices, 247.

Daily lists of committees sitting to be prepared and hung up in the lobby, 248.

Committee of Selection.   See *Selection, Committee of.*

Committee to inspect Lords' Journals:

Notice of intention to appoint committee to be given to committee clerks, 222.

Companies:

Bills for incorporating, regulating, or giving powers to, included in the 1st class of private bills, 1.

See also *Private Bills.*

Compensation Water.   See *Water.*

Competition:

The committee on a bill may admit petitioners to be heard against a bill on the ground of competition, 130.

Completion of Line:

Clause imposing penalty unless line be opened, 158.

Deposit to be impounded as security for completion of line, *ib.*

Deposit or penalty in compensation to parties injured, *ib.*

Time limited for, *ib.*

Consents:

Bills originating in the Commons, or brought from the Lords, empowering certain companies to do any act not authorized by the instruments constituting or regulating the same, to be approved in certain cases by a special resolution of the company, and in other cases consented to by a majority of the shareholders, 63–65.

Requirements as to consent of proprietors in respect of sums to be raised in aid of undertaking of another company, 66.

In cases of bills brought from the Lords, for the purpose of establishing a company for carrying on any work or undertaking, the consent of directors, &c., named in bill to be proved, 68.

How the consents of parties concerned in any interest in any private bill may be proved, 143.

Consent Bill and Statement to be delivered in to committee on any inclosure bill, 177.

The like in regard to any drainage bill, 178.

Corporation Property.   See *Crown, &c., Property.*

Corporations.   See *Charters and Corporations.*

Correction, Houses of.   See *Gaols, &c.*

Counsel:

Petitioners depositing a petition against a bill in the Private Bill Office, praying to be heard by themselves, their counsel or agents, to be heard before the committee on the bill accordingly, 210.

Counsel to Mr. Speaker:

To assist the Chairman of Ways and Means in the examination of all private bills, whether opposed or unopposed, 80.

See also *Ways and Means, Chairman of Committee of.*

County Rates:

Bills relative to, included in the first class of private bills, 1.

County or Shire Hall, Court House:

Bills relative to, included in the first class of private bills, 1.

Cross Sections. See *Railway Bills, 3. Sections.*

Crossings (Railways). See *Level Crossings.*

Crown, Church, or Corporation Property:

Bills respecting, included in the first class of private bills, 1.

Notices to be served, in bills relating thereto, upon owners, lessees, trustees, &c., 17.

Curves (Railways):

A memorandum of the radius of every curve not exceeding one mile in length, to be noted on the plan of every railway in furlongs and chains, 42.

Committees on Railway Bills to direct their attention especially thereto, and to take evidence thereon, 157.

Custody of Documents:

Act to compel Clerks of the Peace and others to take the custody of documents required to be deposited by the Standing Orders of either House of Parliament, *App.* (B).

Custody of Monies:

Act providing for custody of monies paid in pursuance of Standing Orders, *App.* (C.).

Custody of Private Bills:

In whose custody private bills are to be kept, 233.

Cuts, Cuttings, &c.:

Bills for making, maintaining, or varying, to be included in second class of Private Bills, 1.

The depth of every cutting to be exhibited on the section, 47.

Extreme depth of every cutting exceeding five feet to be marked on the section of every railway, and on each side of any intervening tunnel, 53.

See also *Canals, Cuts, &c.*

D

Datum Horizontal Line :

To be the same throughout the whole length of the work, and to be referred to some fixed point (stated in writing on the section) near some portion of the work, or of the termini, 47.

In the case of railways, the distances on Datum line to be marked in miles and furlongs, to correspond with those on the plan, and a vertical measure from the Datum line to the line of railway to be marked at each change of gradient, &c., 50.

December :

Applications to be made to owners, lessees, and occupiers on or before 15th December, 11–16.

If sent by post, to be posted on or before 12th December, 19.

Notices to be given to owners and occupiers of houses on or before 15th December in the cases of any bill for a burial ground or cemetery, or for gas works, 15.

Deposits to be made on or before the 21st December, 32–34*a*.

Deposits to be made on or before 31st December, 35, 35*a*, 36.

Deposit in the Private Bill Office to be made on or before 31st December, of statement of houses occupied by the labouring classes to be displaced by the promoters, 38.

Declaration of Promoters or Party soliciting Bill :

Printed copies to be deposited in the Vote Office and Private Bill Office, 35, 35*a*, 36.

Cases wherein a declaration may be deposited and wherein deposits of money are not to be required, 58, 59.

Declaration of Agents. See Agents.

Declaration of Members :

Blank form of declaration to be transmitted to every member when appointed to serve on a committee on a private bill, 112.

The name of every member to be reported to the House if he return no answer, 113.

Declaration to be signed by members, 118.

And no committee to proceed to business until declaration be signed, *ib.*

Definition of Improvement, &c. :

Definition of improvement and limits of improvement area, 45*b*.

Deposit of Documents :

Documents required to be deposited, and times and places of deposit, viz.:

Deposits on or before 30th November, 24–31.

Deposits on or before 21st December, 32–34*a*.

Deposits on or before 31st December, 35, 35*a*, 36.

Deposits on or before 31st December, in the Private Bill Office, of statement of houses occupied by the labouring classes to be displaced by the promoters, 38.

No deposit to be valid if made on Sunday, Christmas Day, Good Friday, or Easter Monday, or before eight in the forenoon or after eight in the afternoon, 23.

Time for making deposits in Private Bill Office, 247.

See also *Memorials. Petitions against Private Bills. Petitions relating to Private Bills.*

Deposit of Money :

Five per cent. on the amount of the estimate of expense in the case of railway bills, and four per cent. in the case of all other bills, to be deposited with Court of Chancery in England, Court of Exchequer in Scotland, or Court of Chancery in Ireland, before 15th January, 57.

Clause to be inserted in every railway bill, providing for application of deposit or penalty in compensation to parties injured, 158.

In case of abandonment of railway or tramway bill, and release of deposit money, committee on bill to report to House how recommendations of Board of Trade on the bill have been dealt with by committee, 158*a*.

Clause to be inserted in every railway bill prohibiting payment of deposits required by the Standing Orders out of capital raised under existing Acts, 168.

Act to provide for the custody of monies paid in pursuance of the Standing Orders, *App.* (C).

Deviation, Limits of :

To be defined upon the plan, and all lands included within the same to be marked thereon, 40.

Book of reference to contain the names of owners, lessees and occupiers of lands and houses within the limits of deviation, 46.

Dispensing with Standing Orders. See *Petitions for Dispensation, &c.*

E

Easter Monday :

No notice to be given or application made on Easter Monday, 21.

Except in the case of delivery of letters by post, *ib.*

No deposit of documents on Easter Monday to be deemed valid, 23.

Edinburgh Gazette. See Gazette.

Education Office :

Printed copy of every bill affecting the boundaries of any school district, or the jurisdiction of any school board, to be deposited at the Education Office, 33.

Embankments :

Bills for making and maintaining, included in the 2nd class of private bills, 1.

The section to exhibit the height of every embankment, 47.

Extreme height thereof, when exceeding five feet, to be marked in figures on the section of every railway, and on each side of any intervening bridge or viaduct, 53.

Enlarged Plans :

To be added of any building, yard, courtyard, or land within the curtilage of any building, or of any ground cultivated as a garden, 40.

Estate Bills :

Three clear days between the second reading of estate bills (not being bills relating to crown, church, or corporation property) and the sitting of the committee thereupon, 211.

Committee on bill to report specially in certain cases, and report to be printed and circulated with the votes, 188*b.*

Estimate of Application of Money :

Estimates of proposed application of money borrowed by local authorities to be recited in bill, and proved before Select Committee thereon, 172.

Estimate of Expense :

Form of estimate for works proposed to be authorized by any railway, dock, or harbour bill, 37.

Estimate of the expense of the undertaking under each bill of the 2nd class to be made, and signed by the person making the same, 56.

Printed copies to be delivered at the Vote Office and Private Bill Office on or before the 31st December, 36.

In certain cases to make a special report, 78.

All petitions for additional provision in bills from the Lords, and bills introduced by leave in lieu of other bills withdrawn and bills to confirm any provisional order, to be referred to the Examiners, 72.

All reports in which he shall report that the Standing Orders have not been complied with, and all special reports of the Examiner, to be referred to Standing Orders Committee, 199.

Daily lists of petitions for private bills on which the examiners are appointed to sit, to be prepared and hung up in the lobby, 248.

F

Fences. See *Bridges.*

Ferries :

Bills relative to, included in the 1st class of private bills, 1.

And in the 2nd class where any work is to be executed, *ib.*

No railway company to acquire any ferry, unless the committee on the bill report that such restriction ought not to be enforced, 156.

Filled-up Bill :

To be deposited in Private Bill Office, 237.

Fisheries :

Bills relating to, included in the 1st class of private bills, 1.

Frontagers. See *Tramways.*

G

Gaols and Houses of Correction :

Bills relative to, included in the 1st class of private bills, 1.

Gardens :

Enlarged plan, on a scale of not less than a quarter of an inch to every 100 feet, required in the case of any ground cultivated as a garden, 40.

Gas or Water Companies :

Provision for raising additional capital, 188*a*.

Gas Works :

Bills relating to, included in the 1st class of private bills, 1.

Notices of bills to specify limits of, 5.

Notice to be given on or before 15th December to the owner and occupier of every dwelling-house within 300 yards, 15.

Clause to define limits of works, 188.

Examiner of petitions to report as to compliance with the Standing Orders in respect of bills originating in the House, 72, 77.

Two days' notice to be given in the Private Bill Office of the day on which Examiner will examine bills brought from the Lords, 73.

Requirements in respect of amendments made in the House to any private bill, 86.

See also *Private Bills. Ways and Means, Chairman of Committee of.*

Lords' Journals :

Notice of intention to appoint committee to inspect Lords' Journals, with relation to proceedings upon a private bill, to be given to the committee clerks, 222.

M

Magistrates. See *Stipendiary Magistrates.*
Maps :

In the case of railway bills, the Ordnance Map, or a published map, to a scale of not less than half an inch to a mile, with the line of railway delineated thereon, to be deposited with the clerk of the peace, &c., 24, 25, 27.

In Ireland to be to a scale of not less than a quarter of an inch to a mile, 24.

In case of proposed alteration or extension of municipal boundaries, map and duplicate to be deposited with town clerk, &c., *ib.*

Markets and Market Places :

Bills for erecting, improving, maintaining, or regulating, included in the 1st class of private bills, 1.

Meetings of Proprietors :

Bill to be submitted to a meeting of proprietors in certain cases, 62–65.

How such meetings are to be called, *ib.*

Requirements as to consents, or approval of bill, at meetings of proprietors or shareholders, 63–66.

Proof to be required before Examiner of consent of proprietors of any company to sum authorized to be raised in aid of undertaking of another company, 66.

Cases in which, on petition for additional provision, it shall not be necessary to submit bill to the approval of a meeting of proprietors, *ib.*

Dissentient proprietors, on compliance with certain conditions, to be allowed to be heard against proposed bills, 75, 132.

See also *Consents.*

Members :

Printed copies of private bills to be delivered at the **Private Bill Office** for the use of members, 32.

Copies of estimate, declaration, &c., in private bills, to be deposited in the Vote Office for the use of members, 36.

To receive notice of the week in which their attendance will be required for serving on committees, 111.

To receive sufficient notice of appointment, with a blank form of declaration in those cases where required, 112.

Members to be reported to the House, if they do not return the declaration filled up and signed, 113.

Any member or members may be discharged, and other members substituted, 114.

Orders as to the appointment, attendance, and voting of members of committees on opposed private bills, 116–125.

Form of declaration to be signed by members, 118.

No member to absent himself, except in case of sickness, or by order of the House, 120,

See also *Committees on Private Bills. Declaration of Members. Local Interest.*

Memorials :

Parties to be entitled to appear and to be heard before the Examiners on memorials complaining of non-compliance with Standing Orders, 74, 232.

When such memorials are to be deposited, and copies to be furnished, 230–232.

Memorials may be withdrawn on depositing requisition to that effect in the Private Bill Office, 206.

Minutes of Committees on Private Bills :

To be brought up and laid on the table with the report of the bill, 152.

Monies, Custody of. See Custody.

Money, Deposit of. See Deposit.

Money Bills (London County Council). See London County Council.

Mortgage :

No railway company to raise by loan or mortgage more than one-third of their capital, and none to be so raised until 50 per cent. of capital has been paid up, 153.

Municipal Authorities :

To be admitted to be heard before the Committee on any railway or canal bill on their petition against such bill, 134.

Also, to be heard against lighting and water bills, 134*a*.

N

Name Bills :

Not to be printed, 203.

Three clear days between the second reading of name bills and the sitting of the committee thereupon, 211.

One clear day's notice of the day and hour appointed for the meeting of the committee, to be given by the Clerk to the Committee of Selection to the clerks in the Private Bill Office, 236.

To be charged one-half only of the usual fees, *p*. 107.

Narrowing of Roads, &c. See Public Carriage Roads.

Naturalization Bills :

Three clear days between the second reading of naturalization bills and the sitting of the committee thereupon, 211.

One clear day's notice of the day and hour appointed for the meeting of the committee, to be given by the clerk to the Committee of Selection to the clerks in the Private Bill Office, 236.

To be charged one-half only of the usual fees, *p*. 107.

Navigations. See Canals, &c. Docks, Harbours, &c.

Newspapers :

Publication of notices therein, directed, 9.

See also *Gazette.*

Notices by Advertisement :

Notices by advertisement to state objects of bill, and powers to be sought thereby, 3.

Also to contain the names of the parishes through which the work is intended to be made, and to state the time and place of deposit of plans, 4.

In cases of burial grounds or gas works, notices to specify limits thereof, 5.

eight in the forenoon, or after eight in the afternoon, except by post, 21.

Form of application to owners, lessees, and occupiers, *App.* (A.)

Book of reference to contain names of all owners, lessees and occupiers, within limits of deviation, 46.

Owners, lessees, or occupiers of houses, &c., affected by proposed tramways, entitled to be heard before select committees, 135.

See also *Drainage Bills. Inclosure Bills.*

P

Parish Clerks :

Parish plan, section, and book of reference to be deposited with, on or before 30th November, 29.

Patents. See *Letters Patent Bills.*

Parliamentary Agents. See *Agents.*

Paving, Lighting, Watching, Cleansing, or Improving Towns :

Bills for, included in the 1st class of private bills, 1.

Petitions, General List of. See *General List.*

Petitions for Private Bills :

Petition for bill, with agent's declaration and printed copy of bill annexed, to be deposited in the Private Bill Office on or before 21st December, 32.

Such petition, bill, and declaration, to be open to the inspection of all parties, *ib.*

Printed copies of the bill to be delivered therewith for the use of members or agents applying for the same, *ib.*

Each petition to be certified or indorsed by one of the Examiners, 71.

Petitions for re-insertion of petitions in the general list to be presented to the House by deposit of the same in the Private Bill Office, 200.

When any petition struck off the general list of petitions, the committee on Standing Orders to report whether it ought to be re-inserted, 96.

Petition to be signed by the parties, and to be indorsed by one of the Examiners, 193.

To be presented not later than three clear days after the same have been indorsed by the Examiner, 195.

A list of, to be kept in the Private Bill Office, to be called the " General List of Petitions," 229.

See also *Examiners of Petitions for Private Bills.*

Petitions against Private Bills :

Not to be considered by the committee on the bill unless the grounds of objection be distinctly specified, 128.

To be presented, by being deposited in the Private Bill Office not later than ten clear days after first reading, &c., 129.

To stand referred to the committee on the bill, if deposited not later than ten clear days after the first reading of such bill, 210.

Petitioners against bill not to be heard unless petition be prepared in strict conformity to the rules of the House, 129.

Committee may admit petitioners to be heard against a bill on the ground of competition, 130.

In what cases shareholders are to be heard, 75, 131, 132.

In what cases railway companies are to be heard, 133.

Also municipal authorities and inhabitants of towns, &c., 134.

Also proprietors in incorporated companies in certain cases, 66.

Petitions relating to Private Bills :

To be presented to the House by being deposited in the Private Bill Office, 205.

Name of bill to be written on every petition, with statement whether the same be in favour of or against the bill, or otherwise, *ib.*

Any petitioner may withdraw his petition, on depositing a requisition to that effect in the Private Bill Office, 206.

Petitions for additional Provision :

Requirements as to consent of proprietors in cases of proposed amendment of any bill, on petition for additional provision, 66.

Petitions for additional provision in private bill, with the proposed clauses annexed, to be referred to the Examiners of petitions, who shall report thereon, 72.

Examiner to give two days' notice, and to report whether Standing Orders have been complied with or not, 73.

Not to be received, unless a copy of the proposed clauses be annexed, 198.

All such petitions to be referred to the Examiner of petitions for private bills, 72.

Regulation as to memorials being deposited and entertained in respect of non-compliance with the Standing Orders in reference to petitions for additional provision, 232.

Duplicates of plans, &c., in cases of application for Provisional Orders or certificates to be deposited in Private Bill Office, 39.

Receipt of, to be acknowledged by one of the clerks in the Private Bill Office, 228.

Form in which plans are to be prepared.—To describe the lands intended to be taken; the line or situation of the whole of the work, and the lands in or through which it is to be made; the limits of deviation, and all lands within the same to be shown, 40.

To be on a scale of not less than four inches to a mile; and in certain cases buildings, yards, courtyards, and gardens to be on an enlarged scale of not less than a quarter of an inch to every 100 feet, *ib.*

To describe brooks and streams proposed to be diverted in the case of canal, &c., bills, 41.

In the case of railway bills, to set forth certain particulars in connection with extensions, curves, tunnelling, &c., 42.

To specify the intended widening or narrowing of any road, canal, railway, &c., 43.

In the case of railway junctions to show course of existing line, 44.

Every plan and book of reference thereto, produced in evidence before committee, to be signed at length by Chairman of Committee, and every alteration with his initials, 146.

Plan and book of reference certified by the Speaker, in pursuance of any Act of Parliament, to be verified as the Speaker shall direct, 249.

See also *Canals, &c. Railway Bills. Sections. Tramways.*

Police:

Bills relative to, included in 1st class of private bills, 1.

Poor and Poor Rate:

Bills relative to, included in the 1st class of private bills, 1.

Ports. See Docks, Harbours, &c.

Post Office:

Service of applications and notices by post, and evidence thereof, 12, 19–21.

Printed copy of every private bill to be deposited at the General Post Office on or before 21st December, 33.

Postponement of Consideration of Bills in Committee:

The committee clerk to give notice of postponement in the Private Bill Office, 126.

See also *Adjournment of Committees. Committee Clerk.*

Preamble of Private Bills :

Petitioner who has discussed clauses of a bill in House of Lords not precluded from opposing preamble of bill in this House, 143*a*.

When any alteration has been made in the preamble of any bill, such alteration, together with the ground of making it, to be specially reported, 149.

Preference Shares :

In railway bills granting preference in payment of interest, &c., provision to be made that the same shall not prejudice former grants of preference, 160.

And no such company to be authorized to alter the terms of any preference except under special circumstances, 161.

Presentation of Private Bills :

Form in which private bills are to be presented to the House, 196, 201, 202.

No bill to be read a first time unless presented not later than one clear day after the presentation of the petition for leave to bring in the same, 197.

Principal Sheriff Clerk (Scotland) :

Deposit of documents in his office, 24, 27, 31.

Private Bill Office :

Notices of intended application for private bill to specify time when copies of the bill will be deposited in the Private Bill Office, 3.

No deposit to be valid if made on a Sunday or Christmas-day, or before eight o'clock in the forenoon, or after eight o'clock in the afternoon, 23.

Documents required to be deposited in the Private Bill Office on or before 30th November : viz., plans, sections, and books of reference, and in the case of railways, published map, 25.

Also, copy of *Gazette* notices, 31.

Duplicates of plans, &c., in cases of applications for provisional orders or certificates, 39.

Sundry other documents to be deposited in the Private Bill Office, 39, 63, 67, 200, 230–232.

Documents required to be deposited in the Private Bill Office on or before 21st December ; viz., petition for bill, with agent's declaration, and printed copy of bill annexed, 32.

Also printed copies of the bill for the use of members and agents applying for the same, *ib.*

Duplicates of plans, &c., in cases of application for provisional orders or certificates, to be deposited in Private Bill Office, 39.

No bill for confirming provisional order or certificate to be read first time after first day of June, 193*a*.

See also *Petitions against Provisional Order Confirmation Bills.*

Public Carriage Roads:

Bills relative to, included in the 2nd class of private bills, 1.

In the case of bills for, a section and duplicate to be deposited, together with plan and book of reference, with clerks of the peace, &c., 24.

And in the Private Bill Office, 25.

And so much thereof as relates to each area, with the clerk, &c., 29.

Printed copy of bill to be deposited at office of Local Government Board, 33.

All road bills to be referred to a committee, consisting of a chairman and three other members not interested therein, 110.

If any public carriage road is to be diverted, widened, or narrowed, the course of such diversion, and extent of such widening or narrowing, shall be marked on the plan, 43.

Where line of railway crosses any public carriage road, &c., the height over or depth under, and the height and span of every arch by which the railway will be carried over the same, to be marked in figures, 51.

And level crossings to be shown, *ib.*

Where rate of inclination of any road crossed by a railway will be altered, such alteration to be shown by cross sections, 52.

Level of roads when altered by any public work, 145.

Ascent of roads, where the level is altered, limited, in the case of railways, unless a report from an officer of the Railway Department recommending the same be laid before the committee, 154.

The like in regard to roads crossed on a level, 155.

Fence of 4 ft. high to be made on each side of every bridge erected, 154.

See also *Level Crossings.*

Public Departments. See Board of Trade. Home Office. Reports from Public Departments.

Copy of all plans, sections, and books of reference, and published map, with the Board of Trade, 27.

And in the Private Bill Office, 25.

A copy of so much of the plan, section, and book of reference as relates to each area to be deposited with the clerk, &c., 29.

And a copy of the *Gazette* notice, wherever plans, sections, and books of reference are required to be deposited, 31.

Printed copy of every railway bill to be deposited at the Board of Trade on or before 21st December, 33.

3. *Form in which Plans and Sections are to be prepared :*

Scale for plan to be not less than 4 in. to a mile ; and in certain cases, buildings, courtyards, and gardens, to be on an enlarged scale of not less than a quarter of an inch to every 100 ft., 40.

Plan to exhibit the distances in miles and furlongs from one of the termini, a memorandum of the radius of every curve not exceeding a mile, and tunnelling by a dotted line, 42.

Diversion, widening or narrowing of railways to be shown, 43.

The course of a junction railway to be shown on plan for a distance of 800 yards on either side of proposed junction, 44.

Section to be drawn to the same horizontal scale as the plan, and to show the surface of the ground, the datum line, &c., 47.

The line of railway marked thereon to correspond with the upper surface of the rails, 49.

Distances to be marked on datum line, and the vertical heights and gradients to be marked, 50.

Height of railway over or depth under surface of roads, &c., to be marked ; height and span of arches, and level crossings, 51.

And the height and span of every arch of all bridges and viaducts by which a railway is to cross any road, &c., to be marked in figures on the section, *ib.*

And when rates of inclination will be altered, such alterations to be explained by cross sections, 52.

Embankments and cuttings, 53.

Tunnelling or viaduct to be shown, 54.

4. *Estimate, and Deposit of Money :*

An estimate of the expense of the undertaking under each bill of the second class to be made, 56.

S

Service of Notices:

Sessional and Standing Orders:

Committee are to report whether they ought or ought not to
be dispensed with, 95.

No motion to dispense with any sessional or Standing Order
to be made without notice, 224.

Sewage Works :

Notices of bills to specify limits of, 5.

Notice to be served upon owners and occupiers within
300 yds. of the limits of construction of, 15.

Sewers :

Bills relating to, included in the 2nd class of private bills, 1.

Shareholders :

Power of individual shareholders, in certain cases, and unde
certain conditions, to be heard before the committee on the bil
75, 131, 132.

See also *Committees on Private Bills. Consents. Meetings of Proprietors.*

Shares (Railways), Calls on. See *Calls on.*

Sheriff Clerk (Scotland). See *Principal Sheriff Clerk.*

Shire Hall Court House. See *County.*

Sittings of Committees :

The Committee of Selection and general committee on railway
bills to appoint first sitting of all committees on private bill
referred to them respectively, 105, 126.

See also *Committees on Private Bills.*

Speaker :

To appoint Examiners of Petitions for private bills, 2.

The examination of such bills to commence on the 18th January, in such order and according to such regulations as shall
have been made by Mr. Speaker, 69.

Plans and books of reference to be verified as Mr. Speaker
shall direct, 249.

Speaker's Counsel. See *Counsel to Mr. Speaker.*

Special Circumstances. See *Examiners of Petitions for Private
Bills. Ways and Means, Chairman of Committee of.*

Special Reports. See *Examiners of Petitions for Private
Bills.*

T

The committee to report specially to the House on railway, &c., bills seeking powers to levy tolls, &c., in excess of those already authorised, 145a.

This House not to insist on its privileges with regard to clauses in private bills sent down from the Lords which refer to tolls and charges for services performed, 226.

Town Clerk :

Plan, section, and book of reference to be deposited with, in Royal burghs in Scotland in certain cases, 29.

Trade :

Documents to be deposited in the Private Bill Office in regard to bills for trading companies, 35a.

Trade, Board of. See *Board of Trade.*

Tramroads :

Notice in the case of tramroad bills to specify gauge to be adopted and motive power to be employed, 6b.

Application of Standing Orders 145a and Nos. 158 to 168 to subways, tramroads, &c., bills, 168a.

Application of Railway and Canal Traffic Act, &c., to tramroads, 168b.

Length of tramroad along street or road to be stated, 168c.

Tramways :

Bills relative to, included in the 2nd class of private bills, 1.

Notices and plans relative to street tramways, and particulars to be specified therein, 6, 10, 45.

And applicable in the case of a tramroad, wherever carried along a street or road, 45.

Notice to frontagers in case of tramway bills, 13.

Notice to owners and lessees of railways, tramways, or canals crossed, &c., by proposed tramway, *ib.*

Consents in case of tramway bills, 22.

Deposit of tramway map at the office of Board of Trade, 25a.

Deposit of plans, &c., at the Board of Trade, 27.

Sums to be deposited, 57.

Owners, lessees, or occupiers of houses, &c., affected by proposed tramways, entitled to be heard before Select Committees, 135.

Clause providing for application of deposit or penalty in compensation to parties injured, 158.

Provisions as to penalty unless line completed and opened; time limited for completion, *ib.*

Length of tramway to be specified in clause describing the works, 170.

No powers for construction, &c., of tramways to be given to local authorities beyond limits of district, except under special local circumstances, 170*a*.

Where a local authority are empowered to work tramways, power may be given to enter into agreements for running powers over connected tramways, 171.

Treasury, The :

Printed copy of every private bill to be deposited at Her Majesty's Treasury on or before 21st December, 33.

Trust Property (Charitable Purposes) :

Bills relating to, included in the 1st class of private bills, 1.

Tunnels :

Bills relating to, included in the 2nd class of private bills, 1.

Tunnelling to be marked by a dotted line on the plan of every railway, 42.

Where tunnelling is intended as a substitute for open cutting, to be marked on the section, 54.

Ventilation of tunnels to be specially reported by committees on railway bills, 157.

Turnpike Roads (Ireland) :

What roads in Ireland to be considered turnpike roads, 145. 154.

Clause to be inserted in every turnpike road (Ireland) bill, for qualification of commissioners, 187.

U

Union, Clerk of. See *Clerk of Union.*

Unopposed Private Bills. See *Committees on Private Bills,* 2.

Private Bills. Ways and Means, Chairman of Committee of.

V

W

Copies of bill as proposed to be submitted to the committee on any private bill, to be laid before the Chairman of the Committee of Ways and Means and the Counsel to Mr. Speaker two days before the meeting of the committee, 82.

To report special circumstances relative to any bill, or opinion that an unopposed should be treated as an opposed bill, 83.

Copy of bill as amended in committee to be laid before Chairman of Ways and Means and the Counsel to Mr. Speaker three days before consideration of any private bill ordered to lie upon the table, 84.

Clauses and amendments offered on consideration of any bill ordered to lie upon the table, or on third reading of any private bill, to be submitted to the Chairman of the Committee of Ways and Means and the Counsel to Mr. Speaker, and the said Chairman is to report whether the same should be entertained without being referred to Standing Orders Committee, 85, 216.

Copy of amendments made in the House of Lords to a Bill, and of proposed amendments thereto, to be laid before the Chairman of the Committee of Ways and Means and Mr. Speaker on the day previous to the consideration of the same by the House, 86.

On the chairman's report that any unopposed bill ought to be treated as opposed, it is to be again referred to the Committee of Selection, or general committee on railway and canal bills, who are so to treat it, 209.

On consideration of report of bill, to acquaint House if the Standing Orders have been observed, 215.

Widening of roads, &c. See Diversion, &c., of roads, &c.

Withdrawal of Petitions and Memorials :

Course to be pursued in cases of opposed private bills where opponents do not appear or withdraw their opposition, 136.

Any petitioner or memorialist may withdraw his petition or memorial on depositing requisition to that effect in the Private Bill Office, 206.

See also *Memorials. Petitions.*

Works. See Relinquishment of works.

STANDING ORDERS OF THE HOUSE OF LORDS.

The Bills in the two classes are termed Local Bills.

———————

1 to 68 of these Orders are practically identical with S. O.'s 1 to 68 of the Commons, with the exception of—

(1) A few trifling verbal differences ;

(2) The substitution of the Office of the Clerk of the Parliaments for the Private Bill Office, and Commons for Lords, and *vice versâ* where appropriate ;

(3) Order 32 of the Lords, which is much shorter than Order 32 of the Commons, and runs thus :

A printed copy of every local bill proposed to be introduced into either House of Parliament shall be deposited in the Office of the Clerk of the Parliaments on or before the seventeenth day of December.

The remaining Orders are set out in full where they vary from the Commons' Orders, but where they are the same the number of the corresponding Commons' Order merely is given.

Lords.						Commons.
69	is	-	-	-	-	S. O. 194
69(*a*)	,,	-	-	-	-	,, 194A
69(*b*)	,,	-	-	-	-	,, 194B
69(*c*)	,,	-	-	-	-	,, 194C
69(*d*)	,,	-	-	-	-	,, 194E

REFERENCE OF BILLS, &C., TO AND DUTIES OF AND PRACTICE BEFORE EXAMINERS.

When examination of bills to commence.

70. The examination of the local bills proposed to be introduced into either House of Parliament and duly deposited in the Office of the Clerk of the Parliaments, in pursuance of Order 32, shall commence on the eighteenth day of January.

70*a*. Every provisional order confirmation bill and every local bill brought from the House of Commons shall, after the first reading, be referred to the Examiners, but in respect of such Standing Orders only as have not been previously inquired into.

71. All petitions for additional provision in local bills originating in this House shall, on the presentation thereof, be referred to the Examiners, who shall examine the same and report thereon in respect of all orders which would have been applicable in the case of a bill.

72. One of the Examiners shall give at least two clear days' notice of the day on which any bill referred to them after the first reading, or any petition for additional provision shall be examined ; but, in the case of a bill for confirming any provisional order or certificate, he shall not give such notice until after the bill has been printed by order of this House.

73 is S. O. 74, Commons.

74 is S. O. 75. Commons.

75. Every memorial complaining of non-compliance with the Standing Orders in respect of any bill referred to the Examiners after first reading. or in respect of any petition for additional provision, shall, together with two copies thereof, be deposited in the Office of the Clerk of the Parliaments before twelve o'clock on the day preceding that appointed for the examination.

76 is S. O. 71. Commons.

77 is S. O. 76. Commons.

78 is S. O. 78. Commons.

79. All certificates from the Examiners shall be laid upon the table not later than the first sitting day after the deposit of the certificates in the Office of the Clerk of the Parliaments.

APPOINTMENT AND DUTIES OF THE STANDING ORDERS COMMITTEE.

80. At the commencement of every session of Parliament a Standing Orders Committee shall be appointed, consisting of forty Lords, besides the Chairman of Committees, who shall be always Chairman of such Standing Orders Committee.

Quorum.

Notice of
meeting of
Standing
Orders Com-
mittee.

To report
whether Stand-
ing Orders
ought or ought
not to be dis-
pensed with.

Proceedings in
case of special
report.

81. Three of the Lords so appointed, including the chairman, shall be a quorum in all opposed cases.

82. Three clear days' notice shall be given of the meeting of the Standing Orders Committee.

83. All certificates from the Examiners in respect of bills in which they shall certify that the Standing Orders have not been complied with shall be referred to the Standing Orders Committee, and the committee shall report to the House whether the Standing Orders ought or ought not to be dispensed with, and in the former case, upon what terms and conditions, if any.

84. All special reports from the Examiners as to the construction of a Standing Order shall be referred to the Standing Orders Committee, and the committee shall determine, according to their construction of the Standing Order, and on the facts stated in the report, whether the Standing Orders have or have not been complied with, and they shall report accordingly to the House, and if the committee report that a Standing Order has not been complied with, they shall also report whether such Order ought to be dispensed with, and upon what terms and conditions, if any.

Proceedings be-
fore Standing
Orders Com-
mittee upon
Examiner's
certificate or
special report.

85. When an Examiner's certificate, or special report shall be referred to the Standing Orders Committee, the committee, if they think fit, shall hear the parties affected by any Standing Order referred to in such certificate or special report, provided such parties have deposited in the Office of the Clerk of Parliaments, not later than three o'clock on the second day after the order for the meeting of the committee is made, a statement (to be printed in all opposed cases) of the facts to be submitted to the committee. Such statement shall be confined strictly to the points reported upon by the examiner, and no party on the consideration thereof by the committee shall be allowed to travel into any matter not referred to in his statement.

FIRST AND SECOND READINGS OF BILLS.

Bill presented
on petition.

86. No local bill for which a petition has not been presented in the House of Commons shall be brought into this House except on petition for leave to bring in such bill, and a printed copy of the proposed bill shall be annexed to such petition and shall be deemed to form part thereof.

86*a*. No local bill shall be read a first time until the Examiner has certified whether the Standing Orders have or have not been complied with, and no local bill originating in this House shall be read later than three clear days after the certificate in respect of such bill has been laid on the table.

87. No local bill brought from the House of Commons shall be read a second time until the examiner has certified whether any further Standing Orders are applicable, and if so, whether such Orders have or have not been complied with.

88. No provisional order confirmation bill shall be read a second time until the Examiner has certified whether the Standing Orders have or have not been complied with.

89. Notice in writing of any bill relating to England or Ireland, and containing provisions whereby any application of the property of any charity not authorised by the Lands Clauses Consolidation Acts, shall be directed, or the patronage or the constitution of any charity, or the right of any charity to any property, shall be affected, shall be given to the Attorney General for England or Ireland, as the case may be, and no such bill shall be read a second time until the House has received a report from the Attorney General on such bill, and such report shall stand referred to the committee on the bill.

90. No bill by or under the powers of which the maximum rates authorised for the conveyance of passengers, goods, or animals on any railway shall or may be increased shall be read a second time until a report thereon from the Board of Trade has been laid upon the table of the House.

91. No local bill originating in this House shall be read a second time earlier than the fourth day or later than the seventh day after the first reading thereof, except bills, in the case of which the Examiner has certified that the Standing Orders have not been complied with, in which case the second reading shall not be later than the second day on which the House shall sit after the report from the Standing Orders Committee recommending that the bill be allowed to proceed, and except bills referred after the first reading to the Examiners under Order 62, 63, 66, or 67, which bills may be read a second time not later than the fourteenth day after the first reading thereof; and in the case of a certificate of non-compliance, the time for second reading of such last-mentioned bills shall be extended as in the former case.

PETITIONS.

Time for presenting petitions praying to be heard against H.L. bills.

92. No petition praying to be heard upon the merits against any local bill or provisional order confirmation bill originating in this House shall be received by this House unless the same is presented by being deposited in the Private Bill Office before three o'clock in the afternoon on or before the seventh day after the day on which such bill has been read a second time.

Time for presenting petitions praying to be heard against H.C. bills.

93. No petition praying to be heard upon the merits against any local bill or any provisional order confirmation bill brought from the House of Commons shall be received by this House, unless the same be presented by being deposited in the Private Bill Office before three o'clock in the afternoon on or before the seventh day after the day on which such bill has been read a first time.

Petition for additional provision.

94. No petition for additional provision shall be presented to this House without the sanction of the chairman of committees, and no petition for additional provision shall be received in the case of a bill brought from the House of Commons.

THE CHAIRMAN OF COMMITTEES—COMMITTEES ON BILLS— COMMITTEE OF SELECTION.

An unopposed bill may be treated as opposed.

95. The chairman of committees may, if he think fit, report to the House his opinion that any unopposed bill on which he shall sit as chairman should be proceeded with as an opposed bill.

Committees on opposed bills.

96. Every local bill or provisional order confirmation bill which is opposed shall be referred to a Select Committee of five.

Committee of Selection.

97. The chairman of committees and four other lords to be named by the House shall be appointed a committee to select and propose to the House the names of the five lords to form a Select Committee for the consideration of each opposed local bill or provisional order confirmation bill, and shall appoint the chairman of such committee, and shall name the bill or bills which shall be taken into consideration on the first day of meeting of such committee. If a vacancy occur in any such Select Committee in the interval between any two sittings of the House, the chairman of committees may appoint a lord to fill such vacancy, and in such case shall report the same to the House at the next sitting.

Lords interested exempted from serving.

98. Lords shall be exempted from serving on the committee on any local bill or provisional order confirmation bill wherein

they have an interest, and lords shall be excused from serving for any special reasons to be approved of in each case by the House.

99. Every Select Committee shall meet not later than eleven o'clock every morning, and shall sit till four, and shall not meet at a later hour nor adjourn at an earlier hour without leave of the House or without reporting to the House the cause of such later meeting or earlier adjournment. No committee shall adjourn over any day except Saturday, Sunday, Christmas Day, and Good Friday, without leave of the House, or without reporting to the House the cause of such adjournment, but should a committee meet on a Saturday the sitting is to be in conformity with this order.

Hour of meeting, &c., of committees on opposed bills.

99a. Every Select Committee shall take the bill or bills first into consideration which shall have been named by the Committee of Selection, and may from time to time appoint the day on which they will enter upon the consideration of each of the remaining bills without reporting to the House any adjournment of the committee caused thereby.

Order in which bills are to be considered.

100. Every member of a Select Committee shall attend the proceedings of the committee during the whole continuance thereof, and no lord who is not a member of the committee shall take any part in the proceedings thereof.

All the members to attend.

101. If any member of a Select Committee is prevented from continuing his attendance, the committee shall adjourn, and shall not resume its sittings, in the absence of such member, without leave of the House; but if the House is not then sitting, the committee may, with the consent of all parties, continue its sittings in the absence of any member, provided that the number of the committee be not less than four, and that the committee report accordingly to the House at its next meeting.

Absence of any member.

102. In all cases of opposed local bills, in which no parties have appeared on the petitions against such bills, or having appeared have withdrawn their opposition before their case has been fully opened or whose locus standi has been disallowed, the committees on such bills shall report accordingly to the House, and such bills shall thereupon be referred to the chairman of committees, to be dealt with by him as if originally unopposed.

Withdrawal of opposition.

Provided that nothing in this order contained shall prevent a committee from requiring the preamble of a bill to be proved in any case in which an application for costs has been made.

Costs.

Q

Discussion of
clauses in H.C.
not to preclude
opposition to
preamble in
H.L.

Provisional
order con-
firmation bills
may be re-
ferred to the
chairman of
committees.

102*a.* A petitioner against a bill originating in the House of Commons, who has discussed clauses in that House, shall not on that account be precluded from opposing the preamble of the bill in this House.

102*b.* Any provisional order confirmation bill may, before being committed to a committee of the whole House, be referred to the chairman of committees, with respect to all or any of the Orders scheduled thereto, to be dealt with in the same manner as an unopposed local bill.

Proceedings by and in Relation to Committees on Local Bills.

General Provisions.

No committee
on any bill to
inquire into the
standing
Orders proved
before the Ex-
aminers.

Scheduled
agreements to
be subject to
alteration by
Parliament.

Committees on
local bills
may admit
affidavits as
evidence.

103. No committee on any local bill shall examine into the compliance with any Standing Orders required to be proved before the Examiners.

104. Any agreement intended to be scheduled to any bill shall contain a clause declaring the same to be made subject to such alterations as Parliament may think fit to make therein; but if the committee on the bill make any material alteration in any such agreement it shall be competent to any party thereto to withdraw the same.

104*a.* The committee on any local bill may, if they think fit, admit affidavits in proof of any deed or document mentioned or set forth in the bill or in any schedule thereto, or may require further evidence. Such affidavits shall be intitled " In the matter of a bill now pending in the House of Lords, of which the short title is [insert the short title]," and shall be sworn, if in England, before a justice of the peace or a commissioner to administer oaths in the Supreme Court of Judicature; if in Scotland, before any sheriff depute or his substitute, or a justice of the peace; and if in Ireland, before any judge or assistant barrister of that part of the United Kingdom, or before a justice of the peace. Such affidavits shall be filed in the office of the Clerk of the Parliaments.

105 is S. O. 132. Commons.

105*a* is S. O. 133*a*. Commons.

105*b* is S. O. 133*b*. Commons.

County Council
alleged to be
injuriously

105*c.* Where the council of any administrative county or county borough petition against a bill, alleging that such county or county borough or some part thereof will be injuriously affected by the bill, it shall be competent for the Select Committee to whom the bill is referred, if they think fit, to hear such petitioners or their counsel or agents and witnesses on such allegation against the bill or any part thereof.

affected by bill may be heard.

106. Is S. O. 212. Commons.

107. In every local bill by which any second-class work is authorized, a clause shall be inserted to the effect that in case such work be not completed, within a period to be limited, all the powers and authorities given by the bill shall thenceforth cease and determine, save only as to so much of such work as has been completed within such time, with such provisions and qualifications as the nature of the case shall require. Such period shall not exceed in the case of a new railway five years, of a new tramroad three years, and of a new tramway two years, and in the case of extension of time for the completion of a railway three years, of a tramroad two years, and of a tramway one year, unless the committee on the bill think fit, in the special circumstances of the case, to allow a longer period. In the case of extension of time the additional period shall be computed from the expiration of the period sought to be extended.

If work not completed within time limited power to cease.

Periods for completion.

108 is S. O. 145, 154. Commons.

109. In any bill by which the profits of any company are limited, provision shall be made that the company shall not have power to raise the money by the bill authorized to be borrowed on mortgage or any part thereof by the creation of shares or stock instead of borrowing or to convert into capital the amount borrowed under the provisions of the bill, or any part thereof, unless in either case all dividends upon the shares or stock, whether ordinary or preferential, are limited to a rate not exceeding five pounds per centum per annum.

As to conversion of borrowed money into capital in certain cases.

110. Where a public navigable tidal river or channel is included within the limits of deviation of any work, other than a railway, a clause shall be inserted in the bill that no deviation of such work shall be made from the lines thereof, as marked on the deposited plan, even within the limits of deviation shown on such plan, in such manner as to diminish the navigable space, without the previous consent of the Board of Trade, or otherwise than in such manner as is expressly authorized by the Board of Trade.

Consent of Board of Trade to be given to variation of work, other than a railway, affecting tidal waters.

110a is S. O. 184. Commons.

111 is S. O. 183a. Commons.

Lords.						Commons.	
112 is	-	-	-	-	-	S. O.	153
113 ,,	-	-	-	-	-	,,	155
114 ,,	-	-	-	-	-	,,	158
115 ,,	-	-	-	-	-	,,	,,
116 ,,	-	-	-	-	-	,,	,,

Clause prohibiting use of compulsory powers may be inserted in railway and tramway bills promoted merely to serve private interests.

Proviso that penalty for non-completion shall not accrue.

Proviso for return of deposit to promoters.

117. If the committee on any railway bill or tramway bill decide that general compulsory powers to enter upon, take, or use lands for the purposes of any railway or tramway ought not to be given on the ground that the direct object of such railway or tramway is to serve private interests in any lands, mines, manufactories, or other property, the committee may insert a clause or proviso to that effect :

If the bill contains a penalty clause,

That no penalty shall accrue in respect of such railway or tramway if it shall appear by a certificate to be obtained from the Board of Trade that the company was prevented by the want of such compulsory powers from making such railway or tramway without incurring unreasonable delay, inconvenience, or expense :

If a deposit has been made,

That the High Court [Court of Exchequer in Scotland] may and shall at any time on the application of the persons named in the warrant or order issued in pursuance of the said Parliamentary Deposits Act, 1846, or of the survivors or survivor of them, or of the majority of such persons or survivors, or the legal personal representatives of the last survivor, and on the production of a certificate to be obtained from the Board of Trade that the company was prevented by want of such compulsory powers from making such railway or tramway without incurring unreasonable delay, inconvenience, or expense, order that the cash, or exchequer bills, stocks, or funds, as the case may be, deposited or transferred in respect of such railway or tramway, and the interest or dividends thereon, may be paid or transferred to the person or persons so applying, or to any other person or persons whom they or he may appoint in that behalf.

Lords.						Commons.	
118 is	-	-	-	-	-	S. O.	158
119 ,,	-	-	-	-	-	,,	159
120 ,,	-	-	-	-	-	,,	160
121 ,,	-	-	-	-	-	,,	162
122 ,,	-	-	-	-	-	,,	163

123. No bill by which a railway company is incorporated shall contain any powers of purchase, sale, lease, or amalgamation, or any working agreement not made unconditionally determinable by the company at the expiration of a period not exceeding ten years from the passing of the Act, or any power of entering into working agreements, except under the provisions of Part III. (working agreements) of the Railways Clauses Act, 1863, as amended by the Railway and Canal Traffic Acts, 1873 and 1888.

Restriction on powers of purchase, &c. in bills for incorporation of a railway company.

123a is S.O. 166a. Commons.

124. When by any bill powers are applied for to amalgamate with any other company, or to sell or lease the undertaking, or any part thereof, or to purchase or take on lease the undertaking of any other company, public body, or private undertakers, or any part thereof, or to enter into a working agreement, otherwise than under the provisions of Part III. (working agreements) of the Railways Clauses Act, 1863, as amended by the Railway and Canal Traffic Acts, 1873 and 1888, the company, person or persons, with, to, from, or by whom, and the terms and conditions on which it is proposed that such amalgamation, sale, purchase, lease, or working agreement shall be made, shall be specified in the bill as introduced into Parliament.

Terms of proposed amalgamation, &c., to be specified.

Lords.		Commons.
125 is	- - - - -	S. O. 164
126 ,,	- - - - -	,, 165
127 ,,	- - - - -	,, 166
128 ,,	- - - - -	,, 167
129 ,,	- - - - -	,, 168

130. The following clause shall be inserted in every railway bill by which a new company is proposed to be incorporated:

Election of directors in railway companies.

The directors appointed by this Act shall continue in office until the first ordinary meeting to be held after the passing of the Act, and at such meeting the shareholders present, personally or by proxy, may either continue in office the directors appointed by this Act, or any number of them, or may elect a new body of directors, or directors to supply the places of those not continued in office, the directors appointed by this Act being, if they continue qualified, eligible as members of such new body.

Lords.		Commons.
131 is	- - - - -	S. O. 170
132 ,,	- - - - -	,, 169
133 ,,	- - - - -	,, 170a

Lords.						Commons.	
133*a* is	-	-	-	-	-	S. O.	171
133*b* „	-	-	-	-	-	„	168*a*
133*c* „	-	-	-	-	-	„	168*b*
133*d* „	-	-	-	-	-	„	168*c*
134 „	-	-	-	-	-	„	172
135 „	-	-	-	-	-	„	173
136 „	-	-	-	-	-	„	175

Clauses for protection of persons who may have availed themselves of subject-matter of patent after it has been declared void.

137. In any case in which a bill to restore a patent is entertained, the following clauses shall be inserted for the protection of persons who may have availed themselves of the subject-matter of the patent after it has been announced as void in the official journal of the Patent Office, with such alterations as the circumstances of each case may require :

" No action or other proceeding shall be commenced or prosecuted, nor any damage recovered :—

" (1.) In respect of any infringement of the said patent which shall have taken place after the   day of   (the day on which the patent was announced to be void in the official journal), and before the passing of this Act.

" (2.) In respect of the use or employment at any time hereafter of any machine, machinery, process, or operation actually made or carried on within the British Islands, or of the use or sale of any article manufactured or made in infringement of the said patent, after the said   day of   and before the passing of this Act. Provided that such use, sale, or employment is by the person or corporation by or for whom such machine or machinery or article was *bonâ fide* manufactured or made, or such process or operation was *bonâ fide* carried on, his or their executors, administrators, successors, or vendees, or his or their assigns.

" (3.) In respect of the use, employment, or sale at any time hereafter by any person or corporation entitled for the time being under the preceding sub-section to use or employ any machine, machinery, process, or operation, or any improved or additional machine or machinery, or any improved, extended, or developed process or operation, or of any article manufactured or made by any of the means aforesaid, in infringement of the said patent. Provided that the use or employment of any such improved or additional machine or machinery, or of any such improved, extended, or developed process or operation, shall be limited to the buildings, works, or premises of the person or corporation by or for whom such machine or machinery was manufactured, or such process or operation was carried on within the meaning of the preceding sub-section, his or their executors, administrators, successors, or assigns.

" If any person shall, within one year after the passing of this Act, make an application to the Board of Trade for compensation in respect of money, time, or labour expended by the applicant upon the subject-matter of the said patent, in the *bonâ fide* belief that such patent had become and continued to be void, it shall be lawful for the said Board, after hearing the parties concerned, or their agents, to assess the amount of such compensation, if in their opinion the application ought to be granted, and to specify the party by whom and the day on which such compensation shall be paid, and if default shall be made in payment of the sum awarded, then the said patent shall, by virtue of this Act, become void, but the sum awarded shall not in that case be recoverable as a debt or damages."

138 is S.O. 179. Commons.

139 is S.O. 188. Commons.

Cemeteries—Gasworks, &c.

140. In every bill for making, altering, or enlarging any cemetery or burial ground a clause shall be inserted prohibiting the making, altering, or enlarging of such cemetery or burial ground, within 300 yards of any house of the annual value of 50*l*., or of any garden or pleasure ground occupied therewith, except with the consent of the owner, lessee, and occupier thereof in writing. *Cemeteries and burial grounds.*

140*a* is S.O. 188*a*. Commons.

RE-COMMITMENT AND MISCELLANEOUS MATTERS.

141. No local bill which has been reported from a Select Committee shall be recommitted to the same or another Select Committee before the third day on which the House shall sit after the day on which notice has been given of the motion to recommit the bill. *Recommitment.*

142. The chairman of committees may, if he think fit, propose to the House that any local bill shall, after it has been reported, be committed to a committee of the whole House. But no local bill committed to a committee of the whole House under this Order shall by reason of such commitment be allowed to proceed as a public bill.

143. A copy of every railway bill, tramroad bill, tramway bill, and subway bill, if amended in committee, shall, as so amended, be deposited at the office of the Board of Trade three days before the bill is read a third time, and proof of compliance with this order shall be given by depositing a certificate from that board in the office of the Clerk of the Parliaments.

143a. A copy of every local bill, if amended in committee, shall, as so amended, be deposited at the office of Her Majesty's Treasury and at the General Post Office three days before the bill is read a third time.

144. No amendment shall be moved to any local bill on report or third reading, unless the same has been submitted to the chairman of committees, and copies of such amendment (to be printed unless the chairman of committees shall consider printing to be unnecessary) deposited in the office of the Clerk of the Parliaments one clear day at least prior to the report or third reading of the bill.

145. All local bills in which any amendments have been made in committee shall be reprinted, as amended, previously to the third reading, unless the chairman of committees shall consider the reprinting to be unnecessary.

147. Clerks of the peace, sheriff clerks, and their respective deputies, shall make a memorial in writing upon the plans, sections, and books of reference deposited with them under these Orders, denoting the time at which the same were lodged in their respective offices, and shall at all reasonable hours of the day permit any person to view and examine one of the same, and to make copies or extracts therefrom; and one of the two plans and sections so deposited shall be sealed up and retained in the possession of the clerk of the peace or sheriff clerk until called for by order of one of the two Houses of Parliament. (See Act, 1 Vict. c. 83.)

147a. Petitions for additional provision, and petitions praying to be heard upon the merits, against any local or personal bill or provisional order confirmation bill, and petitions praying to be heard against alterations, shall be printed by the agent concerned for the same as soon as he may consider it necessary that copies should be made and printed copies shall be supplied on payment to all parties interested.

APPLICATION OF ESTATE BILL ORDERS.

148. The Orders, 162 to 174 inclusive, relating to estate bills, shall apply to any part of any local bill which may be of the nature of an estate bill.

Certain Orders respecting estate bills to apply to certain local bills.

PROCEEDINGS IN RELATION TO PERSONAL BILLS.

149. All estate, divorce, naturalization, and name bills, and all other private bills not specified in Order 1 as local bills, are in these Orders termed personal bills.

Personal bills defined.

150. No personal bill shall be brought into this House except on petition for leave to bring in such bill, and a printed copy of the proposed bill shall be annexed to such petition, and shall be deemed to form part thereof.

Personal bills to be brought in on petition.

151. One or more of the parties principally concerned in the consequences of any personal bill shall sign the petition that desires leave to bring such bill into this House.

Petitions for personal bills to be signed by parties concerned.

152. A copy of every personal bill introduced into this House shall be delivered to every person concerned in the bill before the second reading; and in case of infancy, such copy shall be delivered to the guardian, or next relation of full age, not concerned in the consequences of the bill.

Personal bills to be delivered to all persons concerned.

Estate Bills.

153. Every petition for an estate bill not approved by the High Court of Justice concerning estates in land in England shall, on presentation to this House, be referred to two of the judges of the said Court, who shall report to the House under their hands, whether, presuming the allegations contained in the preamble to be proved to the satisfaction of the lords spiritual and temporal in Parliament assembled, it is reasonable that the bill do pass into law, and whether the provisions thereof are proper for carrying its purposes into effect, and what amendments, if any, are required therein : And in the event of their approving the bill, they are to sign a copy of the same containing the required amendments (if any).

Petitions for estate bills to be referred to two of the judges for their opinion. (English bills.)

154. Every petition for an estate bill concerning estates in land or heritable subjects in Scotland shall, on presentation to this House, be referred to two of the judges of the Court of Session in Scotland, who shall forthwith summon all parties before them who

(Scotch bills.)

may be concerned in the consequences of the bill, and after hearing all the parties, and perusing the bill, and taking such proof of
the allegations therein contained, and such consents of the parties
interested, and such acceptances of trusts as may be tendered to
them, shall report to the House the state of the case, and their
opinion thereon, under their hands, and what amendments (if any)
are required in the bill, and in the event of their approving the
bill, they are to sign a copy of the same containing the required
amendments (if any).

155. When a petition for an estate bill concerning estates in
land in Ireland is offered to this House, it shall be referred, if the
petitioners for the bill desire it, and the chairman of committees so
determine, to two judges of the High Court of Justice, who shall
forthwith summon all parties before them who may be concerned
in the consequences of the bill, and after hearing all the parties,
and perusing the bill, and taking such proof of the allegations
therein contained and such consents of the parties interested, and
such acceptances of trusts as may be tendered to them, shall report
to the House the state of the case, and their opinion thereon, under
their hands, and what amendments (if any) are required in the bill,
and in the event of their approving the bill they are to sign a copy
of the same containing the required amendments (if any).

156. No estate bill shall be read a first time until a copy of the
petition, and of the report of the judges thereon, has been delivered
by the party or parties concerned to the chairman of committees.

157. Notice of an estate bill shall be given to every mortgagee
upon the estate affected by the bill before the second reading.

158. No committee shall sit upon an estate bill until ten days
after the second reading.

159. Petitions against estate bills shall be presented at such
times and such proceedings shall be had thereon as the chairman of
committees shall in each case, having regard to all the circumstances
thereof, direct.

Proceedings by and in relation to Committees on Estate Bills.

160. When any of the parties interested in any estate bill
have power by such bill to name trustees in the room of trustees
dying, resigning, or refusing to exercise the trust, provision shall be
made by the committee on the bill that the approbation of the High
Court shall be required to every such appointment of new trustees.

161. There shall be annexed to every estate bill for exchanging an
estate in settlement, and substituting another estate in lieu thereof, a

schedule or schedules of the respective estates, showing the annual rent and the annual value thereof, and also the value of the timber growing thereupon; and to all bills for selling a settled estate, and purchasing another estate, to be settled to the same uses, there shall be annexed a schedule or schedules of such estates, specifying the annual rent thereof; and every such schedule shall be signed and proved upon oath by a surveyor or other competent person, before the committee on the bill. *estates to have schedules of the estates and their values, &c. annexed.*

Consents and Acceptance of Trusts.

162. Where the petitioners for and consenting parties to an estate bill relating to an entailed estate are together competent to bar the entail, the consent of any persons entitled in remainder after the estates of the petitioners and consenting parties shall not be required. *Respecting consents to bills where petitioner and consenting parties can bar entail.*

163. Except as aforesaid, all parties concerned in the consequences of an estate bill shall consent thereto before the committee, unless the committee shall, on account of remoteness of interest, or for any other reason, dispense with such consent. *In other cases all persons interested to consent.*

163*a*. In any case in which an infant is or may be interested in the consequences of an estate bill, the chairman of committees may, if he think fit, require that such infant shall be represented before the committee on the bill by a person to be appointed as or in the nature of a guardian or protector of such infant by the Lord Chancellor, or the Lord Keeper of the Great Seal by writing under his hand. *Appointment of guardian or protector of an infant interested in an estate bill.*

164. Where a tenant in tail, under age, is a promoter of an estate bill, or a consenting party thereto by his guardian, and any person entitled in remainder after such estate tail, whose consent is required, withholds his consent to such bill, the consent of a person appointed as or in the nature of a guardian or protector of such minor, and of the settlement or will under which he claims, by the Lord Chancellor or the Lord Keeper of the Great Seal, by writing under his hand, for the special purpose of assenting to or dissenting from such bill shall be sufficient, without the consent of such remainderman as aforesaid. *Consent on behalf of a tenant in tail under age when the consent of a remainder-man is withheld.*

165. The consent of all trustees shall be required in person before the committee, where any money is to pass through their hands, whether for jointure, pin money, the fortunes of younger children, or any other interest whatsoever; but the consent of trustees to preserve contingent remainders only shall not be necessary. *Trustees to consent in person.*

166. No notice shall be taken by the committee of the consent of any person, except trustees for a charity, to any estate bill, unless such person appear before the committee, or proof be given to the committee, by two credible witnesses, that such person is not able to attend, and has in their presence signed a printed copy of the bill in testimony of consent thereto.

167. In the case of a trustee for a charity proof may be given by one credible witness that such trustee has in his presence signed a printed copy of the bill in testimony of consent thereto.

168. Any person appointed trustee by any estate bill shall appear personally before the committee and accept the trusts proposed to be vested in him by the bill, except in cases otherwise provided for by these orders.

169. When a petition for an estate bill concerning estates in land situate in Ireland has been referred, under Order 155, to two judges in Ireland, any person resident in Ireland concerned in the consequences of the bill may give his consent thereto before the two judges to whom the bill is referred; and such judges shall certify that such person appeared personally before them, and, being aware of his interest in the bill, gave his consent for himself and for those for whom he might be entitled to consent, and if any trustee is appointed by the bill, that such trustee appeared personally before them, and accepted the trust proposed to be vested in him by the bill, and that the person so consenting or accepting the trust in their presence signed a printed copy of the bill, and such bill, together with the certificate, shall be produced to the committee.

170. It shall be a general instruction to the judges who shall meet to take the consent of any person concerned in the consequences of an estate bill relating to estates in Ireland, that they take no notice of the consent of any person to such bill unless such person appear before them, or proof be given to them by two credible witnesses that such person is not able to attend, and has in the presence of the witnesses signed a printed copy of the bill in testimony of consent thereto.

171. It shall be sufficient to have the consent of the following persons only concerned in the consequence of estate bills regarding entailed estates in land or heritable subjects in Scotland; that is to say,

1. Where the deed of entail is dated on or after the first day of August 1848, and the heir of entail in possession of the entailed estate is of lawful age, and born before the date of

such deed of entail, the consent of such heir, and of the heir
next in succession, being heir apparent under the entail of
the heir in possession, and of the age of twenty-five years
complete, and not subject to any legal incapacity, and born
after the date of such deed of entail.

2. Where the deed of entail is dated prior to the first day
of August 1848, and the heir of entail in possession of the
entailed estate is of full age, and born before the said first
day of August, the consent of such heir, and of the heir next
in succession, being heir apparent under the entail of the heir
in possession, and born on or after the said first day of
August, and of the age of twenty-five years complete, and
not subject to any legal incapacity.

3. Where the deed of entail is dated prior to the first day
of August 1848, and the heir of entail in possession of the
entailed estate is of full age, the consent of such heir alone,
if he shall be the only heir of entail in existence for the time,
and unmarried :

Or otherwise, the consent of such heir, and of all the
heirs of entail, if there are less than three in being at the
date of such consents :

Or otherwise, the consent of such heir, and of the three
next heirs who at the date of such consent are for the time
entitled to succeed to such estate in their order successively,
immediately after such heir in possession :

Or otherwise, the consent of such heir, and of the heir
apparent under the entail, and of the heir or heirs in number
not less than two, including such heir apparent, who in their
order successively would be heir apparent.

4. In any case not provided for by the aforesaid Orders,
whatever be the date of the deed of entail, the consent of the
heir in possession, and of all the heirs entitled to succeed to
the entailed estate, if less than three, or if not less than
three, then of the three heirs next entitled to succeed to the
entailed estate.

Provided, that if, in any of the cases aforesaid, the heir
next entitled to succeed to the entailed estate after the heir
in possession shall be under the age of twenty-five years, or
if any of the heirs of entail descended of the heirs of entail
in possession whose consents are required in the several
cases aforesaid shall be under the age of twenty-one years,
then the consents also of so many heirs next entitled to

succeed to such estate, not being descendants of the heir in possession, as are equal to the number of the said heirs of entail respectively under the ages before mentioned, without prejudice nevertheless as heretofore for any person concerned to petition against the bill, and to be heard for his interest therein.

Consent to bills relative to estates in Scotland.

172. When a petition for an estate bill concerning estates in land or heritable subjects in Scotland has been referred under Order 154 to two judges in Scotland, any person resident in Scotland concerned in the consequences of the bill may give his consent thereto before the two judges to whom the bill is referred; and such judges shall certify that such person appeared personally before them, and, being aware of his interest in the bill, gave his consent for himself, and for those for whom he might be entitled to consent, and if any trustee is appointed by the bill, that such trustee appeared personally before them, and accepted the trust proposed to be vested in him by the bill, and that the person so consenting or accepting the trust in their presence signed a printed copy of the bill, and such bill, together with the certificate, shall be produced to the committee.

Such consent to be personal or disability to attend proved.

173. It shall be a general instruction to the judges who shall meet to take the consent of heirs of entail or other persons concerned in the consequences of any estate bill relating to estates in land or heritable subjects in Scotland, that they take no notice of the consent of any person to such bill unless such person appear before them, or proof be given to them by two credible witnesses that such person is not able to attend, and has in the presence of the witnesses signed a printed copy of the bill in testimony of consent thereto.

Evidence.

Committees on estate bills may admit affidavits as evidence.

174. The committee on any estate bill may admit affidavits in proof of the allegations made in the preamble of the bill in all cases not otherwise provided for by these Orders or may require further evidence. Such affidavits shall be intitled " In the matter " of a bill now pending in the House of Lords of which the short " title is [insert the short title]," and shall be sworn, if in England, before a justice of the peace or a commissioner to administer oaths in the Supreme Court of Judicature; if in Scotland, before any sheriff depute or his substitute, or a justice of the peace; and if in Ireland, before any judge or assistant barrister of that part of the United Kingdom, or before a justice of the peace. Such affidavits shall be filed in the office of the Clerk of the Parliaments.

Divorce Bills.

175. No petition for any bill of divorce shall be presented to this House unless an official copy of the proceedings taken or had in the court having jurisdiction over matrimonial causes at the place of his domicile or residence, or in some other court having jurisdiction in that behalf, at the suit of the party desirous to present such petition, be delivered upon oath at the bar of this House at the same time.

No petition for a divorce bill to be presented without a copy of the previous proceedings.

176. No bill grounded on a petition to this House to dissolve a marriage for the cause of adultery, and to enable the petitioner to marry again, shall be received by this House unless a provision be inserted in such bill that it shall not be lawful for the person whose marriage with the petitioner shall be dissolved to intermarry with any offending party on account of whose adultery with such person it shall be therein enacted that such marriage shall be so dissolved; provided that if at the time of exhibiting the said bill such offending party or parties be dead, such provision as aforesaid shall not be inserted in the bill.

No divorce bill to be received without a clause prohibiting the offending parties from marrying.

177. When any petition for any Bill of Divorce has been presented to this House in any case in which any trial at nisi prius has been had, or any writ of inquiry executed within the United Kingdom, wherein the petitioner has been party, the judge or under sheriff before whom such trial has been had, or such writ of inquiry executed, shall transmit to the Clerk of the Parliaments, to be laid upon the table of this House, a report of the proceedings upon such trial or writ of inquiry; and no such bill of divorce shall be read a second time until such report has been so laid upon the table of this House.

In case of divorce bills report of previous proceedings to be laid before the House.

178. Upon the second reading of any bill of divorce, the petitioner praying for the same shall attend this House, in order to his being examined at the bar, if the House think fit, whether there has or has not been any collusion, directly or indirectly, on his part, relative to any act of adultery that may have been committed by his wife, or whether there be any collusion, directly or indirectly, between him and his wife, or any other person or persons, touching the said bill of divorce, or touching any proceedings or sentence of divorce had in any court for matrimonial causes at his suit, or touching any action at law which may have been brought by such petitioner against any person for criminal conversation with the petitioner's wife; and also whether, at the time of the adultery of which such petitioner complains, his wife was, by deed, or otherwise by his consent,

Petitioner to attend on the second reading of the bill.

living separate and apart from him, and released by him, as far as
in him lies, from her conjugal duty, or whether she was at the
time of such adultery cohabiting with him, and under the protection and authority of him as her husband.

Naturalization Bills.

No naturaliza-
tion bill to be
read a second
time without a
certificate being
produced touch-
ing the peti-
tioner's conduct.

179. No bill for naturalizing any person shall be read a second
time until the petitioner shall produce a certificate from one of
Her Majesty's Principal Secretaries of State respecting his conduct,
and shall take the oath of allegiance at the bar of the House.

Consent of the
crown.

180. No Naturalization bill shall be read a second time unless
the consent of the Crown has been previously signified.

Application of Local Bill Orders.

Certain Orders
respecting
local bills
to apply to
personal bills.

181. The Orders 95 to 102 inclusive, 141, 142, 144, and 145,
with reference to local bills, shall, so far as applicable, be observed
in reference to personal bills also.

TAXATION OF COSTS.

COSTS TAXABLE BY THE TAXING OFFICER OF THE HOUSE OF LORDS, AND MODE OF PROCEEDING.

The costs taxable by the Taxing Officer of the House of Lords
are—

Private bill
provisional
orders, &c.

All costs, charges, and expenses, including the expenses of witnesses, of and incidental to the preparation, bringing in, and
carrying through Parliament any railway or other local and personal bill, and any estate or other private bill, or any provisional
order or provisional certificate, and the costs, charges, and expenses
incurred in opposing any such bill, provisional order, or provisional
certificate. Such costs are taxed either under the provisions of
the 12 & 13 Vict. c. 78, and the 28 and 29 Vict. c. 27, or upon a
requisition of one of Her Majesty's Principal Secretaries of State,
or of a Government department, or of any court in England,
Ireland, or Scotland, or in the discretion of the Taxing Officer at
the request of the parties interested in the same.

The Mode of Proceeding.

When the costs are to be taxed under the provisions of 12 & 13
Vict. c. 78, a copy of such costs, with an indorsement thereon
stating that a copy of such costs has been duly served upon A. and
B., who are the parties liable to pay the same, and requesting an
appointment to tax, must be deposited in the Taxing Office of the

House of Lords. Due notice of an appointment to tax will be sent from the Taxing Office to each party.

When costs are to be taxed under the provisions of 28 & 29 Vict. c. 27, a copy of such costs (with an endorsement thereon stating that the provisions of Section 3 of the above Act, so far as the same relate to the delivery of the Bill of Costs to the party chargeable with the same, have been complied with, and requesting an appointment to examine and tax the same), must be deposited in the Taxing Office; and such application must be made to the Taxing Officer within the time limited by the said Section of the said Act.

The bills of costs which are referred by either of the courts are usually exhibits in the court by which they are referred, in which case there is endorsed on the back of the original bill a requisition in the following words :—

The Master of the Rolls, Chief Clerk, Taxing Master of the Chancery Division of the High Court of Justice (or as the case may be) requests the Taxing Officer of the House of Lords to tax the within bill of costs, and to report to him the amount at which he has allowed the same.

(Signed)   A. B.

NOTICE.

Any Parliamentary agent, attorney, solicitor, or other person applying for the taxation of any bill of costs, charges, and expenses incurred by him in promoting or opposing any private bill, provisional order, or provisional certificate, in Parliament, is desired to deposit in the office of the Taxing Officer, at the time of making such application, a copy of such bill of costs, charges, and expenses with the several items added up and the amount ascertained and set out, together with a declaration signed by him stating that such bill of costs, charges, and expenses has been duly delivered to the parties charged therewith (naming the parties), in conformity with the Taxation of Costs Acts, 1847 and 1849, or the Act for Awarding Costs, 1865, as the case may be.

Taxing Office, House of Lords,   R. W. MONRO,
2nd August 1897.   Taxing Officer.

NOTE.—The Taxing Office is open throughout the Session, and from the second Monday in the month of November in each year.

Printed lists of charges for Parliamentary agents, attornies, solicitors, and others, prepared by the Clerk of the Parliaments, may be obtained at the Office for the Sale of Printed Papers, House of Lords.

R

FORM OF PETITION FOR LEAVE TO BRING IN A BILL.

[See S. O. 32, 193, *ante*, pp. 98, 153; and see *ante*, pp. 8–10.]

In Parliament.

Session 18 .

[A & B RAILWAY, *or as the short title may be.*]

[*Here insert the abstract of the bill as given in the advertisement, e.g.*, Incorporation of Company; Railway between A & B, and works ancillary thereto; Running Powers over portions of Great Western Railway Company's Railway; Working Agreements with Great Western Railway Company and with South Eastern Railway Company; Payment of Interest out of Capital; Compulsory Purchase of Lands and Houses; Power to levy Tolls.]

PETITION FOR LEAVE TO BRING IN BILL.

To the Honourable the Commons of the United Kingdom of Great Britain and Ireland in Parliament assembled.

The humble Petition of [*state names of petitioners who sign, or, in the case of a body corporate petitioning under its seal, the style or title thereof.*]

Sheweth as follows :—

[*Here insert the particular circumstances, as for instance—*

1. That it is for the public and local advantage of the towns of A and B, in the counties of   and   respectively, and of the districts between those towns, and of the country surrounding those towns that a railway should be made from A to B, and the necessary works ancillary thereto constructed.

2. That your petitioners are ready and willing to make a railway between those towns, and to construct the necessary works ancillary thereto ; and that for that purpose it is expedient that your petitioners should be incorporated and become a body corporate, and should be empowered to enter into working agreements with the Great Western Railway Company and with the South Eastern Railway Company, and entitled to have running powers over portions of the Great Western Railway Company's railway, and to levy rates and tolls.

3. That for the purpose aforesaid it is also expedient that your petitioners should be enabled to purchase compulsorily land and houses required for the purposes of their undertaking, and be empowered during the construction of the railway and the said works ancillary thereto to pay interest out of the capital monies to be raised for the purposes of the undertaking.

4. That notices by advertisement as required by the Standing Orders of your Honourable House have been published, and plans, sections, books of reference made out and deposited as by the said Standing Orders required, and all matters and things required by the said Orders preliminary to this petition have been duly done and performed.

5. That the purposes aforesaid cannot be effected without the aid and authority of Parliament.

> Your Petitioners therefore humbly pray your Honourable House that leave may be given to bring in a Bill (a printed copy of which is hereunto annexed) for effecting the purposes aforesaid in such manner and under such rules, regulations, and restrictions as to your Honourable House may seem meet.

INDORSEMENT OF PETITION.

The indorsement may be as follows :—
    In Parliament.
        Session 18   .
            [A & B RAILWAY, *or as the short title*
                may be.]
                PETITION
            for leave to bring in Bill.
        [Name of Agents, *e.g.*, X & Y.]

FORM OF DECLARATION OF AGENT.

I, *A. B.*, of No.   ,   Street, Westminster, Agent
for the bill which is annexed to the petition deposited
herewith, do hereby declare that in my judgment such bill
belongs to [the second] of the two classes into which bills
to which the Standing Orders of your Honourable House
apply are, for the purposes of those Standing Orders,
divided, and I do hereby further declare that of the
objects enumerated in the Standing Order of your
Honourable House numbered 32, the proposed bill gives
power to effect the following, namely :—It gives,

> Power to take lands and houses compulsorily
> (Clauses, *state which*).
> Power to levy tolls, rates, or duties (Clauses, *state
> which*).
> Power to make a railway (Clauses, *state which*).

It does not give power to effect any other of the objects
in the said Standing Order numbered 32 enumerated.

It does not give any powers other than those included
in the notices for the bill.

                A. B., **Agent for the Bill.**

FORM OF MEMORIAL TO EXAMINERS OF STANDING ORDERS.

[See S. O. 74, 230–232, *ante*, pp. 120, 162 ; S. O., 73–75,
H. L. : and see *ante*, pp. 11–14].

In Parliament.

Session 18   .

[A AND B RAILWAYS AND HARBOURS,
or as the short title may be.]

A MEMORIAL complaining of non-compliance with the Standing Orders.

TO THE EXAMINERS of STANDING ORDERS for PRIVATE
BILLS in the HOUSE OF LORDS, and to the EXAMINERS
of PETITIONS for PRIVATE BILLS in the HOUSE OF
COMMONS.

THE MEMORIAL of the C and D RAIL
WAY COMPANY, under their Common
Seal.

Sheweth.—

A PETITION has been deposited in the Private Bill
Office of the House of Commons, praying for leave to bring
in a bill under the above short title, intituled [" A bill to
extend the time for completion of works authorized by the
X and Y Railway and Pier Act, 1895, and to authorize the
construction of new railways from A to B, and for other
purposes, *or as the case may be*], a copy of which bill is
annexed to the said petition, and a copy of which bill has
also been deposited in the office of the Clerk of the Parliaments. [The said bill is a bill of the second class of bills
referred to in the Standing Orders, being a bill authorizing
the construction of railways. It is promoted by the A B
Railways and Harbours Company, *or as the case may be*.]

In this Memorial the following expressions have
respectively the several meanings hereby attached to
them, unless otherwise stated, or unless there be anything

repugnant in the subject or context to such meanings respectively (that is to say): The expression "the Standing Orders," means the Orders of both Houses of Parliament; the expression "the bill," means the bill deposited as before mentioned; the expression "the notices," or "the notice," means the notices of the intended application to Parliament for the bill published [in the London *Gazette*, and in the local newspapers in the month of November last]: the expression "the promoters," or " the company," means the [A B Railways and Harbours Company, *or as the case may be*]: the expression "the plans," "the sections," "the books," or "the books of reference," means, as the case may be, the plans, sections, and books of reference, as deposited by the promoters in relation to the bill in the office of the Clerk of the Parliaments, and in the Private Bill Office of the House of Commons, and with the clerk of the peace for the counties of [*state which*], in November last; the expression "the limits of deviation," means the limits of lateral deviation defined upon the plans; the expression "the Memorialists," means the [C and D Railway Company, *or as the case may be*].

All lands, buildings, and properties, in respect of which any breach of the Standing Orders is in this Memorial alleged, are situate wholly or partially within the limits of deviation, and may be taken compulsorily under the powers of the Bill.

THE MEMORIALISTS respectfully represent that the Standing Orders have not been complied with in respect of the bill in the following particulars, that is to say :—

[*Here give the particulars of the non-compliance relied on, e.g., as follows*] :—

NOTICES.

1. The notices are misleading and defective, and are not copies of one another as required by the Standing Orders ; the following are the instances relied on :—

(*a*) Discrepancies occur between the notices published in the London *Gazette* and those published in the local newspaper, the ——— *Advertiser*. The following table shows these discrepancies :—

[*Set out Table of Discrepancies.*]

(*b*) The notices make no mention of the branch railway from the pier at Y to Z, which it is proposed under the bill to make.

(*c*) The notices do not contain a correct description of the termini of Railway No. 2 proposed to be authorized by the bill. It is described as commencing in the township of L ; there is no such township.

(*d*) The bill authorizes the taking of common land, but the notices contain no estimate of the quantity proposed to be taken.

2. The short title descriptive of the undertaking at the head of the notice is misleading and defective ; it does not give a fair or correct statement or summary of the objects proposed in the body of the notice, inasmuch as it does not specify the powers to acquire further land by agreement, or to raise additional capital, in regard to all which matters very extensive powers are contained in the bill.

3. Power is given by the bill to acquire compulsorily lands situate in the following extra-parochial places for the purposes of the undertaking authorized by the bill, viz., [the bed of the tidal river S, the W Harbour, *or as the case may be*], but the notices do not state the place of deposit of the plans and sections, or books of reference, or of the notices in respect of these extra-parochial lands.

Deposit of Documents.

4. Power is given by the bill to take compulsorily a part of the churchyard or burial ground attached to St. M's Church at ———, in the county of ———, for the purpose of Railway No. 3 in the bill, but no copy of so much of the plans, sections, and books of reference as relates to such churchyard or burial ground was on or

before the 30th of November last deposited at the office of
the Secretary of State for the Home Department, nor was
any copy of the notice published in the *Gazette* there
deposited therewith. No such copy or notice was there
deposited on or before the 30th of November last.

STATEMENT RELATING TO LABOURING CLASS HOUSES.

5. Power is given by the Bill to acquire compulsorily
[or by agreement] [ten or more] houses, occupied either
wholly or partially by persons belonging to the labouring
class, as defined by Standing Order 183A, as tenants or
lodgers, but the promoters have failed to comply with the
Standing Orders requiring them to deposit in the Private
Bill Office, and at the office of the central authority, as
defined in Standing Order 183A, on or before the 31st of
December last, a statement of the number, description, and
situation of such houses, the number (so far as can be
ascertained) of persons residing therein, and a copy of so
much of the plan (if any) as relates thereto. They have
failed in the following instances [*State same, as for
instance*—

In the Urban District of ——, in the county of
——, the bill authorizes the taking of one side of
—— street, from a point on the plan marked A
to a point thereon marked B, thus permitting the
taking of 50 houses occupied wholly or partially by
persons belonging to the labouring class, the statement only makes mention of 42 such houses, and
instead of giving the true number, which is about
1,100, of persons who may be there dispossessed by
the bill, the number is estimated or guessed at 250,
not "ascertained" so far as could be. A part of the
plan related to the said houses, but no copy thereof,
or of the plan, was on or before 31st December last
deposited either in the Private Bill Office or at the
office of the central authority.]

PLANS.

6. The plans are faulty and erroneous, and fail to comply with Standing Orders in the following particulars [*State same, as for instance*—

(*a*) Power is given by the bill to carry the railway No. 2 across the public carriage road No. 12 in the parish of R on the level, and to divert the said road so as to make the crossing square, but the course of such diversion is not marked upon the plans.

(*b*) Power is given by the bill to divert the public carriage road No. 5 in the parish of S (railway No. 3), but the course of such diversion is not marked upon the plans.

(*c*) All tidal waters have not been coloured blue on the plans.]

BOOKS OF REFERENCE.

7. The books of reference are faulty and erroneous; the instances relied on appear by the following table [*or, are as follows*]:—

[*State same in tabular form, or in detail.*]

APPLICATIONS to OWNERS, or REPUTED OWNERS, and LESSEES, or REPUTED LESSEES, and OCCUPIERS.

8. The applications made in writing to owners, or reputed owners, lessees, or reputed lessees, and occupiers, on or before the 15th December last, of lands or houses to be taken compulsorily by the promoters for the purposes of the railways authorized by the bill were not accompanied, as required by the Standing Orders of the House of Commons, by a copy of the Standing Orders of that House, which regulate the time and mode of presenting petitions in opposition to bills in that House, inasmuch as a copy of Standing Order 129 did not accompany such applications.

9. The applications in the previous paragraph did not [*State what is complained of*].

DEPOSIT OF MONEY.

10. The promoters are a company incorporated by Act of Parliament, and possessed of a railway opened for public traffic, but which has not during the year last past paid a dividend on its ordinary share capital. The promoters have not previously to the 15th of January 18 , as required by the Standing Orders, deposited a sum of not less than 5 per cent. on the amount of the estimate of expense of the undertaking authorized by the bill being railways situate [in England, with the Paymaster-General for and on behalf of the Supreme Court of Judicature in England].

THE MEMORIALISTS therefore request that they may be heard by their agents and witnesses in support of the allegations of this Memorial.

(Sealed, &c.)

INDORSEMENT OF MEMORIAL.

The indorsement may be as follows :—

In Parliament.

Session 18 .

[A AND B RAILWAYS AND HARBOURS BILL, or as the short title may be.]

MEMORIAL of the C and D Railway Company, complaining of non-compliance with the Standing Orders.

Z and Co., Agents for the Memorial.

A LIKE FORM OF MEMORIAL.

[*Heading as in preceding form.*]

THE MEMORIAL of the undersigned persons, and of the H and L Estate Company, Limited, under their common seal.

Sheweth as follow :—

1. A PETITION has been deposited in the Private Bill Office of the House of Commons praying leave to

bring in to that Honourable House a bill, a printed copy whereof is annexed to that petition, intituled, "A bill for incorporating and conferring powers on the H Harbour Company, and for other purposes" (hereinafter referred to as the bill), and a copy of the bill has also been deposited in the office of the Clerk of the Parliaments.

2. In this Memorial, unless otherwise stated, the following expressions have the following meanings (that is to say) :—

The expression "the Standing Orders," means the Standing Orders of both Houses of Parliament.

The expressions "the plans," "the deposited plans," "the sections," "the deposited sections," "the books of reference," mean (*as the case may be*) the plans, the sections, the books of reference, deposited on or before the 30th of November last, in respect of the bill at the office of the [Clerk of the Peace for the county of ———], and in the office of the Clerk of the Parliaments, and in the Private Bill Office.

The expression "the Parliament Office," means the office of the Clerk of the Parliaments of the House of Lords.

The expression "the Private Bill Office," means the Private Bill Office of the House of Commons.

The expression "the notices for the bill," means the notices of the intended application to Parliament for leave to bring in the bill published in the month of November last in the London *Gazette* and in the local newspapers, in which such notices were published in the months of October and November last, or in one of those months.

The word "marked," used in reference to any distance, means marked on the plans and sections.

The word "measured," means measured along the centre line of the railway in the direction proceeding from the commencement to the termination of the railway. on the plans and along the datum horizontal line in a similar direction on the sections, and according to the only horizontal scale to which the plans and sections purport to be drawn.

The expression "marked and measured," means (except when otherwise stated) marked as aforesaid on the plans and sections, and that the fraction of a furlong is measured from the distance so marked.

Every distance stated as being upon the plans or the sections means, as the case may be, the distance along the centre line of railway shown upon the plans, or, as the case may be, along the datum horizontal line of the sections.

The railways proposed to be authorized by the bill, and therein referred to as No. 1 and No. 2, are hereinafter referred to by the same respective numbers.

The expression "the limits of deviation," means the limits of lateral deviation defined upon the plans.

The expression "lands," and " buildings," and " properties," respectively means and includes any land, building, enclosure, or property of whatsoever description shown, or delineated upon the plans, or described in the books of reference, or which it is alleged in this memorial ought to have been shown or delineated upon the plans, or described in the books of reference.

All lands and buildings and properties in respect of which any breach of the Standing Orders is in this memorial alleged, are situate wholly or partially within the limits of deviation, and may be taken compulsorily under the bill.

Allegations in this memorial referring to the nature or condition of any land, building, or property mentioned or described in this memorial refer to the nature or condition thereof on and for some time before the 30th of November last.

And in this memorial words and expressions to

which meanings are assigned by the bill have those meanings, unless there be something in the subject or context repugnant to such construction.

3. The bill is a bill of the second class, namely, a bill for making railways, and the Standing Orders relating to the bill have not been complied with in the following respects :—

The plans, sections, and books of reference are erroneous and defective, and are not prepared in the manner required by the Standing Orders in the several instances hereinafter specified and set forth.

4. As regards railway No. 1 and railway No. 2, the datum horizontal line of the sections is not referred to any fixed point stated in writing on the sections.

5. Railway No. 2 is shown on the plans and sections as intended to be constructed in certain parts in tunnel, and one of such tunnels is shown on the plans as commencing at a point marked and measured 4 mls. 2 fur. 1·2 chs., and terminating at a point marked and measured 4 mls. 4 fur. 2·5 chs., whereas on the sections such tunnel is shown as commencing at a point 4 mls. 2 fur., and terminating at a point 4 mls. 4 fur. 2 chs., and in those regards the plans and sections are at variance with each other.

6. As regards railway No. 1 at and near the point marked and measured 3 mls. 1 fur. 2 chs., the deposited plans show a curve of a radius of 3 furlongs, whereas on the said plans it is noted as of a radius of 2 furlongs.

7. The deposited plans do not describe the several properties specified in the table next hereafter following, they are not shown thereon.

TABLE.

[Insert same.]

8. The books of reference omit all mention of the properties following [*State same, or give them in a tabular form*].

9. Your undersigned memorialists, L and M, are, and have for many years past, been owners of the property, consisting of house, garden, orchard, and premises, firstly mentioned and described in the table appended to paragraph 7 of this memorial, but no application in writing was on or before the 15th of December last made to your memorialists, L and M, or either of them, in respect of their said property by the promoters.

10. Between the points referred to in the next following table, cuttings exceeding 5 ft. in depth, or, as the case may be, embankments exceeding 5 ft. in height, are shown upon the sections, but the extreme depth of such cuttings under, or, as the case may be, the extreme height of such embankments over, the surface of the ground are not marked in figures on the sections.

11. The plans show that several public carriage roads will be crossed by railway No. 1, but in the instances specified in the table next following, no mention is made in the sections of the heights of the railway over, or the depths of the railway under, those roads.

TABLE.

[Insert same.]

12. The notices for the bill are not headed by a short title descriptive of the undertaking or bill, inasmuch as railway No. 2 is in no way indicated or described in or by such title or heading.

YOUR MEMORIALISTS therefore request that they may be heard by themselves, their agents and witnesses, in support of the allegations contained in this memorial.

(Signed)

(Sealed, &c.)

[From the above two forms it is thought the practitioner will readily be able to draft the memorial in the shape required to meet the particular breaches of Standing Orders he may discover in relation to the particular Bill he is opposing.]

FORM OF STATEMENT OF PROOFS.

[See *ante* pp. 12, 13. All these forms can be purchased from Messrs. Eyre and Spottiswoode.]

HOUSE OF COMMONS.

MEETING OF COMPANY INCORPORATED BY SPECIAL ACT OF PARLIAMENT.

Statement of Proofs before the Examiner for Standing Orders, after the First Reading of the Bill in the First House, or subsequently to the Introduction of the Bill in the Second House. (Under S. O. 62 or S. O. 64.)

Session 1898.

SHEFFIELD AND RETFORD RAILWAY BILL.

John Jones. Produced the *Times* newspaper (being a newspaper published in London) of the 20th and 27th Dec. 1897, being two consecutive weeks, containing notice calling a Special Meeting of the proprietors of the Sheffield and Retford Railway Company to consider the bill.

Also the *Sheffield Independent*, being a newspaper of the county of York (in which county the principal office of the said Company is situate) of the 20th and 27th days of Dec., 1897, being two consecutive weeks, containing the same notice.

Proved that a circular calling the said meeting, addressed to each proprietor at his last known or usual address, was sent by post or delivered at such address not less than ten days before the holding of such meeting, enclosing a blank form of proxy, with proper instructions for the use of the same.

Proved that the same form of proxy and the same instructions, and none other, were sent to every such proprietor, that no such form of proxy was stamped before it was sent out, nor have the funds of the company been used for the stamping of any proxies, nor was any intimation sent as to any person in whose favour the proxy might be granted; and no other circular or form of proxy relating to such meeting has been sent to any proprietor from the office of the company or by any director or officer of the company so describing himself (to the witness's best knowledge and belief).

Proved that such meeting was held on the 10th day of January, 1858, being a period not earlier than the seventh day after the last insertion of such advertisement.

Proved that at such meeting a print of the bill [as proposed to be introduced into the House of Commons] was submitted to the proprietors then present, and was approved of by proprietors present in person or by proxy, holding at least three-fourths of the paid-up capital of the company represented by the votes at such meeting, such proprietors being qualified to vote at all ordinary meetings of the company in right of such capital.

[Proved that the votes of proprietors of any paid-up shares or stock, other than debenture stock, not qualified to vote at ordinary meetings, whose interests may be affected by the bill, which were tendered at such meeting were duly recorded separately], or [That no votes of proprietors not qualified to vote at ordinary meetings of the company were tendered at such meeting].

[Proved that no poll was taken], or [That a poll was taken].

Proved that he deposited [in the Private Bill Office of the House of Commons] a statement of the number of votes, [and also of the number of votes recorded separately].

Proved that the names of the proprietors present in person at the said meeting were duly recorded.

Proof as to Amendments made in the First House.

[Proved that by the terms of the consent of the company already proved in the House of [Lords] [Commons], the bill as introduced, or proposed to be introduced, into that House, was approved of, or consented to, subject to such additions, alterations, and variations as Parliament might think fit to make therein.]

Stated that no Standing Orders are applicable to the amendments made in the bill further than those which were proved to have been complied with previously to its introduction into Parliament [except with reference to "Alteration of Work," with respect to which proof is tendered herewith].

Note.—" Separate Undertakings.

" *So far as any such bill relates to a separate under-*
" *taking in any company as distinct from the general*
" *undertaking, separate meetings shall be held of the pro-*
" *prietors of the company and of the separate under-*
" *takings, and the provisions of this Order applicable to*
" *meetings of proprietors of the company shall,* mutatis
" mutandis, *apply to meetings of proprietors of the separate*
" *undertakings."* [Consequently, proof of compliance
with this Order with reference to any such "Separate
" *Undertaking" must be given in accordance with the*
foregoing Form of Proof, which has reference to a com-
pany wholly.]

[This form is number 4 of the forms of Statements of Proofs published by Messrs. Eyre and Spottiswoode, the Queen's Printers; the titles of the others are—

(1.) Statement of Proofs, &c., previously to the introduction of the bill, in cases of bills of the 2nd class or bills of the 1st class, by which any lands or houses are intended to be taken compulsorily, or by which an extension of time granted by any former Act for that purpose is sought.

s

(2.) Statement of Proofs previously to the introduction of the bill in cases of 1st class bills, by which no lands or houses are intended to be taken compulsorily, nor by which any extension of time granted by any former Acts is sought.

(3.) Provisional orders confirmation bills:—Statement of Proofs, with respect to statements relating to houses inhabited by labouring classes, and places relating to such statements as required by S. O. 38 ; and also as to deposit of plans, &c., in the office of the Clerk of the Parliaments and Private Bill Office of the House of Commons as required by S. O. 39.

(5.) Meeting of company, society, association, or co-partnership (other than a company to which S. O. 62 or 64 is applicable). –Statement of Proofs under S. O. 63 or 65.

(6.) Statement of Proofs under S. O. 6 in case of subscription, &c., by any company incorporated by Act of Parliament, or by any class of holders of share or loan capital in any such company.

(7.) Statement of Proofs as to charging payments on grand jury cess or local rate in aid of railways in Ireland.

(8.) Statement of Proofs as to signatures of directors, &c., deposit of bill as introduced into the second House at the Home Office, Board of Trade, Local Government Board, General Register Office, Somerset House, or Board of Agriculture.

(9.) Statement of Proofs (to be made in the second House) as to alteration in the work since the introduction of the bill into Parliament.]

FORM OF AFFIDAVIT IN PROOF OF COMPLIANCE WITH STANDING ORDERS.

[See S. O. 76, *ante*, p. 120; S. O. H. L. 77, and see *ante*, p. 12.]

In Parliament.
Session 1898.

SHEFFIELD AND RETFORD RAILWAY BILL.

I, John Jones, of Snig Hill, Sheffield, in the county of York, clerk to Messrs. Smith and Brown, solicitors, Sheffield, make oath and say as follows :—

That in pursuance of the Standing Orders of Parliament a print of the Bill bearing the above name or short title was submitted to a meeting of the proprietors of the Sheffield and Retford Railway Company held especially for that purpose. That such meeting was called by advertisement inserted in the *Times* newspaper, being a London newspaper, of the 20th and 27th days of December 1897, being two consecutive weeks, and also in the *Sheffield Independent* newspaper, being a newspaper published in Sheffield, of the 20th and 27th days of December 1897, being two consecutive weeks.

That the principal office of the said company is situate in the county of York, in which county the said *Sheffield Independent* newspaper is published.

That a circular stating the object of such meeting was addressed to each proprietor at his last known or usual address, and sent by post or delivered at such address not less than ten days before the holding of such meeting, enclosing a blank form of proxy, with proper instructions, for the use of the same.

That the same form of proxy and the same instructions and none other were sent to every such proprietor, that no such form of proxy was stamped before it was sent out, nor have the funds of the company been used for the stamping of any proxies, nor was any intimation sent as to any person in whose favour the proxy might be granted, and no other circular or form of proxy relating to such meeting has been sent to any proprietor from the office of the company, or by any director or officer of the company so describing himself to the best of my knowledge and belief.

And I further say that such meeting was held on the 14th day of January 1898, being a period, not earlier than the seventh day after the last insertion of such advertisement, and that at such meeting a print of the Bill as proposed to be introduced into the House of Commons was submitted to the proprietors then present, and was approved of by proprietors present in person or by proxy, holding at least three-fourths of the paid-up capital of the company represented at such meeting, such proprietors being qualified to vote at all ordinary meetings of the company in right of such capital, and that no votes of proprietors not qualified to vote at ordinary meetings of the company were tendered at such meeting, and that no poll was taken.

And I further say that the names of the proprietors present in person at the said meeting have been recorded by the company.

> Sworn at Sheffield, in the
> county of York, this 12th
> day of January 1898 be-
> fore me,   JOHN JONES.
>   A B C,
>   A Commissioner
>   for Oaths.

FORM OF PETITION AGAINST A BILL.

[See S. O. 205, 89, 128, 129, *ante*, pp. 158, 123, 129 ; S. O. 92, 93, 147A, H.L., and see *ante*, pp. 22, 23, 35.]

In the House of Commons.

Session 18 .

R. & S. RAILWAY.

PETITION
AGAINST THE BILL,
Praying to be heard by Counsel.

To the HONOURABLE the COMMONS of the UNITED KING-
DOM of GREAT BRITAIN and IRELAND, in PARLIAMENT
ASSEMBLED.

The HUMBLE PETITION of A. B. and C. D.

Sheweth,—

1. That your petitioners have for more than ten years been and still are the lessees and occupiers of a field at   , in the county of   , and of large buildings and premises at   aforesaid, at a distance of a mile or thereabouts from the said field.

2. The said lease of the said field expires by effluxion of time on the   day of   , 19 , thus leaving an unexpired term of five years and two months; whilst there is of the said lease of the said buildings and premises an unexpired term of more than 60 years.

3. Your petitioners have occupied and used during the past ten years, and still occupy and use the said buildings and premises as a school for boys, and the said field as

a playground and cricket field for the said boys attending their said school.

4. A bill (in this petition referred to as "the bill") has been introduced and is now pending in your Honourable House intituled "A bill to authorize the construction of a Railway from R. to S., and railways and works in connection therewith, and for other purposes."

5. By the said bill the property of your petitioners is sought to be taken and interfered with, and the bill is in that respect and otherwise prejudicial to their property, rights, and interests.

6. By the said bill it is proposed to incorporate a company (clause　　) under the name of the "R. and S. Railway Company" (in the bill and hereinafter called "the company") for the purpose of making and maintaining, amongst other things, a railway from R., in the county of　　, to S,, in the county of　　, and (by clause　　) it is proposed to give power to the company to take compulsorily the said field, and to construct thereon the said railway or some part thereof, or to construct thereon a station or other works in connection with the said railway. The said field is within the limits of deviation, and is thus described in the deposited books of reference [*State description.*]

7. Your petitioners will be unable if the said field is thus taken to secure any field or playground for their said school in as convenient proximity to their school, or indeed, within any reasonable distance thereof, and their said school will be greatly injured thereby, or perhaps even destroyed.

8. There is already ample railway accommodation for all passenger and other traffic from R. to S. by the existing A. S. & R. Railway.

9. [The ·preamble of the said Bill is untrue and incapable of proof.]

> YOUR PETITIONERS therefore humbly pray your Honourable House that the said bill may not pass into law, and that they may be heard by themselves, their counsel, agents, and witnesses against [the preamble and] such of the clauses and provisions thereof as affect their property, rights, and interests, and in support of amendments and provisions for their protection.
>
> (*Signed*) A. B.
> C. D.

FORM OF INDORSEMENT OF PETITION AGAINST A BILL.

House of Commons,
Session 18 .

R. & S. RAILWAY.
PETITION
of
A. B. and C. D.
AGAINST—BY COUNSEL.
U. V.,
—, ——— Street,
Solicitor.

W & Co.,
—, ———— Street,
Westminster,
Parliamentary Agents.

FORM OF PETITION AGAINST A BILL.

KILPATRICK DOCK.

[Heading as in preceding Form of Petition.]

> The HUMBLE PETITION of the Trustees of the Port and Harbours of Greenock under their Corporate Seal.

Sheweth,—

1. That your petitioners were incorporated by [*stating Acts*], and the property, management, and control of the port and harbours of Greenock are vested in them.

2 & 3. [*Stating pecuniary position, and large in-indebtedness for money borrowed.*]

4. A bill (in this petition referred to as "the bill") has been introduced into and is now pending in your Honourable House intituled [*stating title of bill*].

5. Your petitioners object to the bill as prejudicially affecting the port and harbours of Greenock, and the rights and interests of your petitioners, in, amongst others, the respects hereinafter stated.

6. By the bill (clause 4) it is proposed to incorporate a company under the name of "The Kilpatrick Dock Company" (in the bill and hereinafter called "the company") for the purpose of making and maintaining the dock and railways thereinafter described; and (by clause 5) it is proposed to authorize the company, *inter alia*, to make and maintain a large tidal dock on the north side of the River Clyde and several railways in connection therewith.

7. By subsequent clauses of the bill the company also seek power to levy, &c., rates, not exceeding those specified in the schedules annexed to the said bill.

8. The company also seek power to act as warehouse keepers.

9. The bill is promoted substantially in the interests of the Caledonian Railway Company and the Lanarkshire, &c., Railway Company; and if the bill were to receive the sanction of Parliament the proposed dock would to all intents and purposes belong to and be worked by those companies.

10. Your petitioners submit that it is contrary to public policy that a railway company should be empowered to own or construct dock and harbour works such as those proposed by the bill. Irrespective of the great injury which the establishment of the proposed dock would do to the port and harbours of Greenock, and to the interests entrusted to your petitioners, even if the proposed undertaking were managed and conducted legitimately, the possession of such a dock in the hands of a railway company, and under their sole control, would enable them to charge such rates on vessels and goods within the maximum as they thought proper, or to remit them altogether, as they seek power under the bill to do, securing a return on the amount expended by fostering and encouraging their railway traffic, and so to compete with, and on terms most unfavourable to your petitioners, thereby seriously injuring their property and undertaking, by compelling your petitioners, with the view of retaining any portion of the trade of Greenock, to reduce their harbour and dock dues to an unremunerative rate, insufficient to enable them properly to maintain and extend their works and meet their obligations to their creditors.

11. There is no trade or traffic at Old Kilpatrick either to require or justify the construction of docks there. The extensive works, therefore, proposed to be executed under the bill cannot be required for local purposes or local convenience, and no necessity exists for their construction. So far as regards the Clyde, ample accommodation can be afforded at Glasgow, Greenock, Port Glasgow, and Bowling, and your petitioners and their predecessors have at all

times been anxious and willing, as the requirements of trade demanded it, to afford additional accommodation, and they are quite prepared to act in the future as in the past; and they submit that unless it can be shown that they have in this respect neglected their duties, or that a great public necessity exists for harbour and dock accommodation at Old Kilpatrick, the powers sought by the bill should not be granted.

12. Your petitioners are public trustees, and have no private interest in the matters above set forth. Parliament has entrusted to them the duty of providing harbour and dock accommodation at Greenock, and authorized them to raise the necessary funds for that purpose by mortgaging the rates and dues which Parliament has authorized them to levy at their harbours; and the public who have advanced the money have done so relying on the rates and dues thus mortgaged, and on the Parliamentary security thereby granted. The effect of authorizing the company to execute the works proposed by the bill would necessarily be to enable them to compete with the port and harbours of Greenock, and to divert therefrom traffic now coming to the same, and thus to affect most prejudicially the interest of your petitioners and of the creditors of the trust.

13. No case of public advantage to be derived from the construction of the proposed works can be substantiated, which would justify the great loss and injury thereby inflicted on your petitioners.

14. The dock scheme as proposed is badly devised; the proposed works are defective in many engineering respects; and the estimate of expense of the works, and the capital proposed to be raised by the bill, are insufficient for the purposes thereof.

15. The preamble of the bill is incapable of proof; but should your Honourable House deem the same proved

clauses and provisions at present stand in the bill which
are objectionable and ought to be removed, and other
clauses and provisions now absent ought to be inserted for
the protection of your petitioners.

> YOUR PETITIONERS therefore humbly
> pray your Honourable House that
> the bill may not be allowed to pass
> into law as it now stands, and that
> they may be heard by themselves,
> their Counsel, Agents, and Witnesses
> against the preamble of the bill, and
> such of the clauses and provisions
> thereof as affect their rights and
> interests, and that they may have
> such relief in the premises as to your
> Honourable House may seem meet.

And your Petitioners will ever pray.

Seal of the
Trustees of the
Port, &c., of
Greenock.

272 PRIVATE BILL PROCEDURE.

FORM OF PETITION AGAINST BILL.

KILPATRICK DOCK.

[Heading as before.]

The HUMBLE PETITION of the Corpora
tion of the City of Glasgow, under
their Corporate Seal.

𝕾𝖍𝖊𝖜𝖊𝖙𝖍,—

1. A bill (hereinafter called "the bill") has been introduced, &c. [*as in par.* 4 *of preceding form*].

2. Your petitioners are the municipal authority having the local management of the city of Glasgow (hereinafter called "the city"), and have the control of the public streets and thoroughfares of the city, and they are also the police, sanitary, and road authority of the city. Your petitioners as the water, gas, and electric lighting authorities, are charged with the supply of water and gas to the city and adjoining districts, and of electricity to the city. They also own and work an extensive system of tramways in and near Glasgow, and they own and manage the markets and slaughter-houses within the city, and are the local authority under the Contagious Diseases Acts, and own the only landing-places for foreign animals in the West of Scotland. In these several capacities your petitioners make extensive use of and are deeply interested in everything affecting the harbour of Glasgow and the river Clyde. They are also the official representatives of the citizens, and as such are entitled to speak for them regarding all interests affecting the general community, and to protect the same. Your petitioners possess by Royal Charter jurisdiction over the river and Firth of Clyde from Glasgow to the Cloch Stane below Gourock, including the area of the river over which jurisdiction is sought by the bill, and the site of the proposed dock is within their area of compulsory gas supply.

3. The preamble of the bill recites, *inter alia*, that the construction of a tidal dock or basin on the north side of the river Clyde, in the parish of Old Kilpatrick, in the county of Dumbarton, with railways and connections therewith, would be of local and public advantage, and that it is expedient, in order to facilitate the construction and working of such dock or basin, that a portion of the Lanarkshire and Dumbartonshire Railway at Old Kilpatrick should be deviated, and also that the persons named in the bill, with others, should be incorporated into a company for the purpose of executing the said works.

4. By the bill it is provided :—[*Setting out the material clauses of the bill.*]

5. Your petitioners allege that their interests and the interests of the inhabitants, traders, and merchants of the city, will be injuriously affected, and the rateable valuation of the city seriously depreciated by the provisions of the bill if passed into law, and specially by the several clauses before referred to.

6. The prosperity of the city of Glasgow, and of the burghs adjoining thereto, has depended in the past and must depend in the future upon the maintenance and development of the harbour accommodation of the city so as to meet the wants of the manufactures, trade, and commerce of which Glasgow is the centre. Consequently, everything which affects the harbour interests is of the greatest importance to the city and to your petitioners.

7. By virtue of ancient rights and charters, and in particular by virtue of a charter granted by King Charles I., dated at Newmarket, 16th October, 1636, your petitioners possess and enjoy jurisdiction and other rights over the river and firth of Clyde, extending from Glasgow Bridge to the Cloch Lighthouse, which comprehends the portion of the river over which powers are sought by the intended bill, and specially, your petitioners are empowered to elect annually a bailie and deputy-bailie of the river

and firth of Clyde, who, by virtue of the said charter and
of various local statutes, exercise jurisdiction from the
eastern termination of the harbour of Glasgow to the
southernmost point of the island of Little Cumbrae, in the
firth of Clyde. As acting in the execution of the Glasgow
Police Acts and other local statutes, your petitioners are also
vested with important functions connected with the police
of the river and firth within the said limits.

8. The said charter of King Charles I. so far as is
material, is as follows :—[*Setting out the same.*]

9. Having regard to the rights so conferred, and in the
interest of the trade of the city, the corporation have from
the earliest times been at considerable expense in deepening
and straightening the river, and removing rocks and other
obstructions. They also have expended large sums in providing quayage, warehouse and other accommodation for
ships. The result of that expenditure was to draw to
Glasgow an amount of trade which would otherwise have
been impracticable. This trade increased to such an extent
that it was deemed expedient to have the administration
of the navigation of the river and the construction of such
further works as might be found necessary to meet the
growing requirements of the navigation transferred to the
Clyde Trustees, in which body the corporation, along with
others, is represented. That body, by virtue of various Acts
of Parliament, has from to time further deepened the
river and extended the dock and quayage accommodation
till ships of the largest tonnage can now be brought up to
the city. In order to meet the cost and maintenance of
those works the trustees have, under the authority of
Parliament, expended nearly £9,000,000, and at the present time about £5,500,000 of that sum is due to bond-
holders and other lenders to the trustees. If the dock
were constructed as proposed in the bill, and other similar
docks in the interest of railway companies were authorized,
the position of those lenders might be seriously prejudiced.

10. By the incorporation in the bill of the Harbours, Docks and Piers Clauses Act, 1847, powers are sought to be conferred on the harbour-master to be appointed by the company to interfere with the navigation of vessels within the limits prescribed by the bill. By such incorporation new offences within the river are created, and powers are given to make bye-laws and to enforce the same by the imposition of penalties. The powers so sought are inconsistent, and will conflict with the powers and jurisdiction of your petitioners hereinbefore referred to, and your petitioners and the interests they represent will be injuriously affected thereby. The powers so sought to be conferred will affect every vessel passing up and down the river to and from the city.

11. Your petitioners are convinced that it is in the interest of the city, and of the districts adjoining thereto, that the supply and control of harbour accommodation on the river Clyde should continue in the hands of the Clyde Trustees, who have expended and are expending large sums of money in constructing additional accommodation, to meet not only the present but the future needs of the traffic of the river and district. Those trustees have no other interest than the interest of the public. Their surplus revenues, after meeting the annual charges for borrowed money, and of the maintenance, management, extension and improvement of their docks and quays, are applied to the reduction of debt or the lowering of the rates and charges exacted by the trustees.

12. Your petitioners view with alarm the formation of a dock on the Clyde by a company whose aim is to make a profit for themselves. It is believed that the dock is sought to be authorized chiefly for the benefit of and in the interest of the railway connecting with it, and with which the company seek wide powers of making working and other agreements by clause 64 of the bill.

13. Your petitioners submit that the powers sought in the bill to remit or return dues in whole or in part, and to confer facilities for which no fixed charge is provided, might be so used as to create an unfair and injurious preference to traders in certain districts of the country as against those represented by your petitioners.

14. Your petitioners, in connection with the departments administered by them, purchase and use large quantities of material which are brought to the city by ship. Your petitioners believe that the construction of the proposed dock might have the effect of so reducing the revenue of the Clyde Trustees that they might be unable to deepen the river and to maintain and extend their docks and quays so as to meet the requirements of the port, and in that event the whole trade and interests of the city would be injuriously affected.

15. The Clyde Trustees have hitherto at great cost provided in advance for the development of the trade of the city and neighbourhood, and your petitioners believe the trustees are both able and willing to provide such new docks as may be necessary to meet the requirements of the trade. Your petitioners believe that there is no necessity whatever for the proposed dock, and it will interfere with and take traffic already amply provided for.

16. It is in the public interest that docks and harbours should be under the control of an efficient public body. It is against public policy that they should be under the control of and conducted in the interests of any particular railway company.

17. Your petitioners, twenty years ago, at a cost of upwards of 100,000l., acquired lands near the site of the proposed dock, a portion of which lands, under the Glasgow Corporation Sewage Act, 1895, they have power to utilise as a site for the treatment of the sewage of the city, and for sewage works. In connection with those works, they have power on those lands, or on other lands to be

acquired by them by agreement, or in the bed of the Clyde, to construct landing piers, docks, or wharves. The powers proposed to be conferred by the bill may injuriously affect the use of such landing piers, docks, or wharves.

18. No case of public advantage to be derived from the construction of the proposed dock can be substantiated which would justify the loss and injury to be thereby inflicted on your petitioners, the inhabitants of Glasgow, and the other interests they represent.

19. The estimates for the works are quite inadequate.

20. The preamble is incapable of proof.

[Prayer as in preceding form.]

FORM OF PETITION AGAINST A BILL.

KILPATRICK DOCK.

[Heading as in previous forms.]

The HUMBLE PETITION of the North British Railway Company, under their common seal.

Sheweth —

1. A bill (hereinafter called " the bill ") has been introduced, &c. *[as in paragraph 1 of preceding form.]*

2. The bill prejudicially affects the rights and interests of your petitioners, and your petitioners object thereto.

3. By the bill it is proposed to incorporate a company (clause 4), and to authorize the company (clause 5) to construct a tidal dock and three railways in connection therewith, all as therein described.

4. Railway No. 1, 5 fur. 7·7 chs. in length, is a new railway, being a deviation of the main line of the Lanarkshire and Dumbartonshire Railway authorized by the Lanarkshire and Dumbartonshire Railway Act, 1891. The bill does not propose, however, to abandon the portion

of the authorized railway of the Lanarkshire and Dumbartonshire Company, to be superseded as such by Railway No. 1, but to transfer it to the promoters. Railway No. 2, 3 fur. 1·7 chs. in length, is a proposed new dock line; and Railway No. 3, 2 fur. 7 chs. in length, is also a dock line along the east side of the proposed dock.

5. By the bill, clause 9, Railway No. 1 is declared to vest in the Lanarkshire and Dumbartonshire Company as part of their undertaking under the Act of 1891; and, section 10, the portion of the railway of the Lanarkshire and Dumbartonshire Railway Company between the points of commencement and termination of Railway No. 1 shall vest in the company as part of their undertaking.

6. By clause 11 the capital of the company is fixed at 150,000l., and clause 16 gives the usual borrowing powers of one-third of the capital in addition.

7. By the bill, clause 64, the company take power to enter into working agreements with the Lanarkshire and Dumbartonshire Railway Company and the Caledonian Railway Company, and the Trustees of the Clyde Navigation.

8. Your petitioners believe that the bill is promoted in the interests, and with the approval and sanction of the Lanarkshire and Dumbartonshire Railway Company, and for the purpose of placing traffic on the railway of that company and withdrawing and diverting it from the railways of your petitioners, over which a large portion of the coal, ore, and other traffic now dealt with at Queen's Dock, belonging to the Trustees of the Clyde Navigation, is carried.

9. Your petitioners' Glasgow, Dumbarton, and Helensburgh Railway, is in direct competition with the authorized railway of the Lanarkshire and Dumbartonshire Railway Company between Glasgow and Dumbarton, and at Old Kilpatrick, the railway of your petitioners is close to the railway of the Lanarkshire and Dumbartonshire Company.

The construction of the proposed new dock and relative railways will form a new source of competition with the railways of your petitioners, and abstract and divert traffic from your petitioners' railways.

10. When the Lanarkshire and Dumbartonshire Railway was sanctioned by the Act of 1891, it was enacted for the protection of your petitioners, *inter alia*, section 6, sub-section (11), that the Lanarkshire and Dumbartonshire Company should not oppose any application to Parliament by your petitioners to authorize your petitioners to connect their railway with any works on the south side of the railway of the Lanarkshire and Dumbartonshire Company between Clydebank and Bowling. Such provision was a recognition of the right of your petitioners to connect with any works on the north bank of the Clyde, and if the proposed dock works are authorized, they should only be so subject to a right to connect their railways with the same being specially reserved to your petitioners.

11. The proposed dock and railways are wholly unnecessary, and are not required in the interests of the public or of traders or shippers on the Clyde, which already possesses ample dock accommodation at Glasgow, and to which docks the railways of your petitioners as well as of the Caledonian Company and Lanarkshire and Dumbartonshire Company have access. The transfer of the traffic to the new dock would entail an additional land carriage, which would go into the pockets of the Lanarkshire and Dumbartonshire Company, and doubtless this is the real object of the bill.

12. The dock and railways are badly and injudiciously laid out, and cannot be constructed for the amount stated in the deposited estimate of expense.

13. The capital proposed to be raised by the bill is altogether insufficient.

14. By clause 32 of the bill, it is proposed to cross on the level with four lines of rails the public road leading

from Erskine Ferry to the station of your petitioners at Kilpatrick, to the serious prejudice and inconvenience of your petitioners' traffic.

15. The preamble is untrue and incapable of proof.

[Prayer, see preceding form.]

FORM OF PETITION AGAINST A BILL.

[Heading and Prayer as in previous forms.]

> The HUMBLE PETITION of the MAYOR, ALDERMEN, and COMMONS of the CITY of LONDON, in COMMON COUNCIL assembled.

1. A bill has been introduced, &c. [*as in previous forms*].

2. By the bill it is proposed to incorporate a company for the purpose [*stating what*].

3. Your petitioners are the municipal authority for the City of London, and property, rights, and interests of your petitioners, and of the citizens of the City of London, whom they represent, will be prejudicially affected by the Bill in the manner hereinfter appearing.

4. Certain of the railways and works proposed by the bill, and described in clause 30 thereof, are intended to be made wholly or partly in the City of London, and for that purpose a large amount of valuable property, including property of your petitioners, is proposed to be taken.

5. By clause 31 of the bill the company seek powers to stop up and discontinue as public thoroughfares Brackley Street and part of Fann Street, in the parish of, &c., and appropriate the site and soil of those streets for the purposes of their undertaking.

6. By clause 67 of the bill the company seek power to acquire parts only of any lands, houses, buildings, or

manufactories, which they may require for the purposes of their undertaking, notwithstanding the provisions of the 92nd section of the "Lands Clauses Consolidation Act, 1845," and by clause 68 they seek exceptional powers with reference to their superfluous lands.

7. Your petitioners object to the compulsory purchase of their property for the purposes of the bill, and to the powers which the company seek by clauses 67 and 68. The taking of parts only of properties would be most unjust to your petitioners and other owners and occupiers of property, and inflict great loss and detriment upon them. Such powers are unusual, and, when granted by Parliament, have been limited to certain specified properties, or to those which could be divided without material or substantial injury or detriment.

8. The proposed stopping and discontinuance of streets will cause great loss and inconvenience to owners and occupiers of property near or adjoining such streets, and your petitioners humbly submit that clauses for the compensation of such persons should be inserted in the bill.

9. The exceptional powers of dealing with superfluous lands which the company seek by clause 68 are not legitimate for a railway undertaking, and if passed would enable the company to embark in land speculation, and if granted at all, will, your petitioners submit, require modification.

10. The times limited for compulsory purchase of lands and for completion of works are excessive, and should not, your petitioners humbly submit, exceed three years and five years respectively. The effect of the company having compulsory powers over property (which they may probably never exercise) will be to seriously depreciate its value, and to prevent any street or other improvements being carried out either by the owner or by your petitioners.

11. The powers of underpinning, which the company seek by clause 66 of the bill, would most seriously and prejudicially affect the value of property near the line of the proposed works, and should not, your petitioners submit, be sanctioned, but if Parliament should see fit to confer those powers on the company, then proper and efficient clauses should be inserted in the bill for the protection of the owners and occupiers of property so affected.

12. By clause 64 of the bill, the company seek powers to make and maintain openings in the streets for the purpose of ventilating their railway. Your petitioners most strongly object to these powers, as they would be dangerous to traffic in the narrow and crowded streets of the City of London, and injurious to the health of the inhabitants of houses near such openings. The proposed openings are unnecessary as there are other modes of ventilation which, if somewhat more expensive, would be more efficient.

13. The railways and works proposed by the bill are not necessary, and are not called for by any public want or requirement.

14. Many of the clauses and provisions of the bill are objectionable to and prejudicially affect the interests of your petitioners and of the citizens of London, and will require to be modified should the bill pass into law, and clauses and provisions not now in the bill will, in such case, require to be inserted for the protection of the interests of your petitioners and of the said citizens.

15. Your petitioners object to the bill for the reasons above set forth, and submit that the preamble thereof is untrue and incapable of proof.

Your petitioners, &c.,

Signed by order of the Court,
X. Y.,
Town Clerk.

FORM OF NOTICE OF OBJECTIONS TO *LOCUS STANDI.*

[See S. O. 128–135. *ante,* pp. 129–131 ; S. O. 105A, B, and C,
H. L., and see *ante,* pp. 23, 35.]

In the House of Commons.

Session 18 .

[A. & B. RAILWAY, *or as the short title may be.*]

To the Clerk to the Referees on Private Bills, and to the
Agents for the undermentioned Petitioners.

TAKE NOTICE that the promoters of the above-named
Bill intend to object to the right of [the X. Y. & Z. Railway
Company, *or as the case may be*] to be heard upon their
petition against the said Bill on the following grounds,
viz.:—

1. The petition does not allege nor is it the fact that any
land or property of which the petitioners are owners,
lessees, or occupiers will be taken or interfered with by
the bill.

2, 3, 4, 5 [*State other grounds applicable to the particular case, as in following forms*].

6. The petition does not disclose any facts or reasons
which, according to the practice of Parliament entitle the
petitioners to be heard against the bill or any of the
clauses or provisions thereof.

Dated the   , day of   18 .

W. & Co.,

Agents for the Bill.

FORM OF INDORSEMENT OF NOTICE OF OBJECTIONS TO *LOCUS STANDI.*

In the House of Commons.
Session 18

A. & B. RAILWAY.

NOTICE OF OBJECTIONS to the *locus standi* of [the X.,
Y. & Z. Railway Company, *or as the case may be.*]

Agents for the Petitioners,
Messrs. C. & D.,
—————— Street,
Westminster.

W. & Co.,
[Insert name of Agents for the Bill]
—————— Street,
Westminster.

[In framing petitions against particular bills or notices
of objections to *locus standi* in particular cases the
practitioners may frequently find assistance by referring to
the numerous reported cases in the *Locus Standi* Reports.
In those reports the notices of objections are usually to be
found set out or summarised. Thus, for instance, for a
form of notice of objections to the *locus standi* of the
inhabitants of a district upon the ground that those petitioning were not sufficiently representative of the district,
and that their interests were already sufficiently represented
by the local authorities who had petitioned against the
bill, see *Tottenham, &c., Railway Bill,* 1890. *Petition of
Inhabitants of Leyton, &c.,* 1 R. & S. 72. For a form of
objection to the *locus standi* of a Chamber of Commerce
on a Rivers Pollution Bill see *West Riding Conservancy
Bill,* 1894. *Petition of the Morley Chamber of Commerce,*
1 R. & S. 356.]

FORM OF NOTICE OF OBJECTIONS TO *LOCUS STANDI.*

[This and the two following forms are applicable to the Forms of Petition against a Bill, which are given at pp. 268, 272, 277, *ante.*]

In the House of Commons.
Session 1897.

KILPATRICK DOCK.

To the Clerk to the Referees on Private Bills and to the Agents for the undermentioned Petitioners.

TAKE NOTICE that the promoters of the above-named bill intend to object to the right of the trustees of the port and harbours of Greenock to be heard upon their petition against the said bill on the following grounds, *videlicet :—*

1. The petition does not allege nor is it the fact that any land or property of which the petitioners are owners, lessees, or occupiers will be taken or interfered with by the bill.

2. The proposed dock will be situate several miles higher up the River Clyde than the docks of the petitioners, and on the opposite side of the river, and will not interfere with any of the rights or jurisdiction of the petitioners in connection with the port and harbours of Greenock.

3. The trade of the port of Greenock largely consists of traffic which goes to other harbours on the West Coast of Scotland lower down the Firth of Clyde, and cannot be affected by the proposed dock, which would serve the purposes and the trades and industries of a different county and locality altogether and no such competition could arise with the port of Greenock as would entitle the petitioners to be heard against the bill.

4. The allegations contained in paragraph 10 of the petition as to the possible reduction or remission of rates are unfounded. The proposed dock is to be constructed by an independent company, and revenue will require to be raised from the trade of the dock to pay interest upon the capital to be raised.

5. The petition does not disclose any facts or reasons which, according to the practice of Parliament, would entitle the petitioners to be heard against the Bill.

Dated the   day of   , 18   .

A. & B.,

Agents for the Bill.

FORM OF NOTICE OF OBJECTIONS TO *LOCUS STANDI.*

KILPATRICK DOCK.

[Heading and Prayer as in preceding form.]

TAKE NOTICE that the promoters of the above-named bill intend to object to the right of the Corporation of the City of Glasgow to be heard upon their petition against the said bill on the following grounds, viz. :—

1. *[As in paragraph 1 of preceding form.]*

2. The bill will not interfere with any of the various duties and authorities of the petitioners referred to in paragraph 2 of the petition, nor will any of the existing rights or jurisdiction of the petitioners under the ancient charters or the Acts of Parliament referred to in paragraphs 7, 8, and 10 of the petition be affected by the bill, or if any interference therewith could arise, the same would be too remote and inconsiderable to entitle the petitioners to be heard in respect thereof.

3. The administration and control of the River Clyde, and the navigation thereof and conservancy of that river between Glasgow and Newark Castle, is at the present time vested in the Trustees of the Clyde Navigation, who were constituted in 1858, and are petitioning against the bill, and whose *locus standi* is admitted. The petitioners have a large representation on the Clyde Trust, but since the constitution of that trust they have had no separate jurisdiction or control over the navigation or conservancy of the said river. The petitioners are thus fully represented by the Clyde Trustees in all matters connected with the navigation of the Clyde, and the improvement and conservancy of the river, and the maintenance and provision of docks and other similar matters, and the petitioners are not entitled to be heard separately against the bill in regard to any alleged interference or competition with the undertaking of the Clyde Trustees, or in regard to the position of the creditors of the Clyde Trust the fixing of rates, the reduction of revenues or the other matters referred to in paragraphs 9, 10, 11, 12, 13, 14, 15, and 16 of the petition.

4. The allegations in the petition of possible interference with the petitioners' future landing piers, docks, or wharves at Dalmuir, and of injury to the City of Glasgow (which is about nine miles away from the proposed dock and situate in a different county, with the burgh of Patrick and the burgh of Clydebank intervening between the dock and Glasgow on the same side of the river), and the depreciation of the rateable value of the city (which the promoters deny) are too vague and remote to entitle the petitioners to be heard in respect thereto.

5. The petitioners, as traders using the River Clyde and the Glasgow Docks, are not entitled to be heard against the bill in addition to the duly constituted trustees of the navigation on the ground of anticipated injury to the undertaking of the trustees.

6. The petitioners are not entitled to be heard against the bill on grounds of public policy or public interest affecting the navigation of the Clyde, in addition to the trustees who are the proper parties to watch and protect the navigation interests of Glasgow.

7. [*As in paragraph 5 of preceding form.*]

—— ——————

FORM OF NOTICES OF OBJECTION TO *LOCUS STANDI.*

[*For Heading and Prayer see preceding forms.*]

KILPATRICK DOCK.

TAKE NOTICE that the promoters of the above-named bill intend to object to the right of the North British Railway Company to be heard, &c.

1. [*As in previous form.*]

2. The petitioners are not the owners of Queen's Dock or of any of the dock accommodation at Glasgow, and are not entitled to be heard in regard to any alleged diversion of traffic from their docks.

3. The proposed dock and railways will not interfere with the continued use of the Queen's Dock and other docks at Glasgow to the which the Petitioners' railways have access, and the bill will not withdraw or divert traffic from such railways in such manner or under such circumstances as to entitle the petitioners to be heard against the bill.

4. Even if the bill is promoted with the approval and sanction of the Lanarkshire, &c., Railway Company as alleged (which the promoters do not admit) the railways of that company which are worked by the Caledonian Railway Company are in connection with the Caledonian Railway already in competition with the railways of the petitioners for the traffic using the Glasgow docks and

other traffic which it is alleged might be diverted from the railways of the petitioners, and no new competition or competition of such a character will be created by the bill as would entitle the petitioners to be heard against the bill.

5. The provisions of section 6, sub-section 11, of the Lanarkshire and Dumbartonshire Railway Act 1891, will not be repealed or altered by the bill, nor will the rights (if any) of the petitioners thereunder in connection with the said dock be affected, and the petitioners are not entitled to be heard to seek an alteration or extension of such rights.

6. The petitioners do not represent the public or the traders or shippers of the Clyde, and are not entitled to be heard in respect of any alleged interference with their interests.

7. The petitioners are not the owners of the road from Erskine Ferry, referred to in paragraph 14 of the petition, or the authority in charge of such road. The road is a public highway under the charge of a duly constituted road authority, and the petitioners have no such special interest therein as to entitle them to be heard in reference to any alleged interference therewith.

8. The petition does not disclose any facts, &c. [*as in preceding forms.*]

A TABLE OF FEES TO BE CHARGED AT THE HOUSE OF COMMONS.

Fees to be Paid by the Promoters of a Private Bill.

	£	s.	d.
On the deposit of the petition, bill, plan, or any other document in the Private Bill Office - - -	5	0	0
For every day on which the Examiners shall inquire into the compliance with the Standing Orders	5	0	0

For Proceedings in the House.

	£	s.	d.
On the presentation of the petition for the bill - -	5	0	0
On the first reading of the bill - - - - -	15	0	0
On the second reading of the bill - - - -	15	0	0
On the report from the committee on the bill - -	15	0	0
On the third reading of the bill - - - -	15	0	0

Bills from the Lords, commonly called estate bills, divorce bills, naturalization bills and name bills, to be charged only one-half of the preceding fees.

The preceding fees on the petition, first, second, and third readings, and report, to be increased according to the money to be raised or expended under the authority of any bill for the execution of a work, in conformity with the following scale :—

If the sum be 100,000*l.* and under 500,000*l.*, twice the amount of such fees.

If the sum be 500,000*l.* and under 1,000,000*l.*, three times the amount of such fees.

If the sum be 1,000,000*l.* and above, four times the amount of such fees.

For Proceedings before any Committee or the Referees.

For every day on which the committee or referees shall sit,—

	£	s.	d.
If the promoters of the bill appear by counsel - -	10	0	0
If they appear without counsel - - - -	5	0	0

Fees to be Paid by the Opponents of a Private Bill.

	£	s.	d.
On the deposit of every memorial complaining that the Standing Orders have not been complied with -	1	0	0
On the presentation or deposit of every petition against a private bill - - - - -	2	0	0

For Proceedings before the Examiners or before any Committee or the Referees.

	£	s.	d.
For every day on which the Examiners shall inquire into any memorial complaining of a non-compliance with the Standing Orders - - - -	3	0	0
For every day on which the petitioners appear before any committee or the Referees - - - -	2	0	0

General Fees.

	£	s.	d.
On every motion, Order, or proceeding in the House upon a private bill, petition, or matter not otherwise charged - - - - - - - -	1	0	0
For copies of all papers and documents, at the rate of 72 words in every folio,—			
If five folios or under - - - - - -	0	2	6
If above five folios, per folio - - - - -	0	0	6
For the copy of a plan made by the parties - -	1	0	0
For the inspection of a plan, or of any document -	0	5	0
For every plan or document certified by the Speaker pursuant to any Act of Parliament - - -	10	0	0
For every day on which any parties shall be heard by counsel at the bar, from each side - - -	10	0	0
For every day on which a committee of the whole House shall sit on a private bill or matter - -	6	0	0
For serving any summons or Order on a private bill or matter - - - - - - - -	1	0	0
For every Order for the commitment or discharge of any person - - - - - - -	1	0	0
For taking any person into custody for a breach of privilege or contempt - - - - -	5	0	0
For taking any person into custody for any other cause	2	0	0
For every day on which any person shall be in custody	1	0	0
For riding charges, per mile - - - - -	0	0	6

Fees to be Paid on the Taxation of Costs on Private Bills.

	£	s.	d.
For every application or reference to "the Taxing Officer of the House of Commons," for the taxation of a bill of costs - - - - -	1	0	0

	£	s.	d.
For every 100*l.* of any bill which shall be allowed by the Taxing Officer - - - - - -	1	0	0
On the deposit of every memorial complaining of a report of the Taxing Officer - - - -	1	0	0
For every certificate which shall be signed by the Speaker - - - - - - - - -	1	0	0
For copies of any documents in the office of the Taxing Officer per folio of 72 words - - - -	0	1	0

That the same fees be paid in case the Speaker shall refer to the Taxing Officer any bill of costs, under the authority of an Act of the sixth year of his late Majesty King George the Fourth, " To establish a taxation of costs on private bills in the House of Commons."

That every bill for the particular interest or benefit of any person or persons, whether the same be brought in upon petition or motion, or report from a committee, or brought from the Lords, hath been and ought to be deemed a private bill within the meaning of the table of fees.

FEES TO BE TAKEN BY THE SHORT-HAND WRITER.

For every day he shall attend - - - - -	2	2	0
For the transcript of his notes, per folio of 72 words -	0	0	9

The preceding fees shall be charged, paid, and received at such times, in such manner and under such regulations, as the Speaker shall from time to time direct.

SCHEDULE OF FEES
TO BE CHARGED AT THE HOUSE OF LORDS.

LOCAL OR PERSONAL BILLS.

	£	s.	d.
Deposit of plan - - - - - - -	0	10	0
Notice or order for consideration of Standing Order in order to its being dispensed with - - -	1	0	0
Order thereon - - - - - - -	1	0	0
Certificates of Examiners in case of any one bill -	5	0	0
Order referring certificate to Standing Orders Committee - - - - - - -	1	0	0
Standing Orders Committee thereon - - -	5	0	0
Report of Standing Orders Committee - - -	2	0	0
First reading - - - - - -	5	0	0
Notice of second reading - - - - -	0	10	0

Second reading :

Personal bills :

Estate - - - - - - · ⎫			
Patent - - - - - - ⎭	81	0	0
Disabilities removal - - - - ⎫			
Divorce - - - - - - ⎪			
A. Naturalisation - - - - ⎬	27	0	0
Name - - - - - - ⎪			
Oath - - - - - - ⎭			

(No second reading fee is charged upon an ⸗indemnity or restoration bill.)

Local bills :

Bills where the capital or money to be raised does not exceed 50,000*l.* - -	81	0	0
exceeds 50,000*l.*, and does not exceed 200,000*l.* - - - - -	108	0	0
exceeds 200,000*l.*, or is not defined in amount - - - - -	135	0	0
Bills relating to charitable, literary, or scientific purposes whereby no private profit or advantage is derived - -	27	0	0
Other bills - - - - - -	81	0	0

U

	£	s.	d.
Order referring petition for estate bill to judges -	1	0	0
Every petition in favour of or against a bill not praying to be heard - - -	1	0	0

„   praying to be heard against a bill -
     „   in favour of a bill and praying to
     be heard against alteration
     therein - . - - -
	2	0	0

For the first or first and second days on which an agent only appears in support of a petition - -	3	0	0
For every subsequent day - - - - -	1	0	0
For the first day on which counsel appear in support of a petition - - - - - -	10	0	0
For every subsequent day - - - - -	4	0	0
Order for attendance of witnesses, each witness -	1	0	0
Every witness to whom an oath or affirmation is administered at the bar of the House - - -	1	0	0
Every witness to whom an oath or affirmation is administered before a committee - - - -	0	2	0
Petition for additional provision - - - -	5	0	0
Certificate of Examiner thereon - - - -	5	0	0
Report of judges on petition for estate bill - -	1	0	0
Commitment of an unopposed bill - - - -	1	0	0
„ „ opposed bill, committee to be proposed by Committee of Selection	2	0	0
Report of Committee of Selection - - - -	1	0	0
Order for committee on opposed bill to meet - -	1	0	0
Order giving leave for counsel to be heard before a committee - - - - - - -	1	0	0
For the first day on which counsel appear in support of bill - - - - - - - -	8	0	0
For every subsequent day - - - - -	4	0	0
Committee on any personal bill in division marked A.	2	0	0
„ on any other bill - - - - -	5	0	0
Report, estate bill - - - - - - -	5	0	0
Report, any other bill, with amendment - - -	4	0	0
„ „ without amendment - -	2	0	0
Report, bill not to proceed - - - - -	1	0	0
Order on report that promoters do not intend to proceed further with bill - - - - -	1	0	0
Notice of third reading - - - - -	0	10	0

Third reading :	£	s.	d.
Bill (H. L.) containing not more than 20 pages of print - - - - - - - -	10	0	0
Bill (H. L.) containing more than 20 pages - -	15	0	0
Amendments on third reading H. L. bills - -	3	0	0
„ „ H. C. bills - -	5	0	0
Producing before a committee of the House of Commons any document or proof - - - -	1	0	0

PROVISIONAL ORDER CONFIRMATION BILLS.

The same fees are charged to promoters and opponents at the committee stage in the case of opposed bills as in the case of local bills.

No other fees are charged.

GENERAL FEES.

For every certificate signed by the chairman of committees - - - - - - - - -	2	0	0
Inspection of a plan or other document - - -	0	5	0
Copy of document, per folio of 72 words - -	0	0	6
The inspection fee to be charged in addition when the document is two years old and upwards.			
Copies of documents earlier than George III. to be charged double the above fees.			
Copy certified by the Clerk of the Parliaments -	1	0	0
in addition to the above.			

FEES ON TAXATION.

For every application or reference to the Taxing Officer of the House of Lords, for the taxation of a bill of costs - - - - - - - -	1	0	0
£1 per cent. upon the amount of the bill as sent in for taxation, or added to on taxation			
On the deposit of every memorial complaining of a report of the Taxing Officer - - - -	1	0	0
For every certificate signed by the clerk of the Parliaments or Taxing Officer - - - -	1	0	0
For copies of any documents in the office of the Taxing Officer, per folio of 72 words - - - -	0	0	6

LIST OF CHARGES FOR PARLIAMENTARY AGENTS, ATTORNIES, SOLICITORS, AND OTHERS. PREPARED BY MR. SPEAKER, IN PURSUANCE OF "THE HOUSE OF COMMONS COSTS TAXATION ACT, 1847."

ANY charges included in a bill of costs for proceedings previously to those connected with the preparation of the bill, or the notice or plans for the same, or for other proceedings which are not strictly Parliamentary, must be made out according to the scale allowed in courts of law.

I.—ATTENDANCES.

For every attendance hereinafter specified, whenever the same shall be necessary and shall be actually had (but not otherwise), Parliamentary agents will be entitled to the charges set down in the first column, and solicitors to the charges set down in the second column of this list.

	Parliamentary Agent.			Attorney or Solicitor.		
	£	s.	d.	£	s.	d.
AT THE HOUSE OF COMMONS:						
At each of the following proceedings in the House upon the petition and bill, viz.—						
Promoters:						
Attending to obtain petition for bill from the Private Bill Office, and get the same presented and petition referred to Standing Orders Committee, or bill ordered, or other proceeding thereon	1	1	0	1	1	0
First reading of the bill	1	1	0	1	1	0
Second reading	1	1	0	1	1	0
Report	1	1	0	—		
Consideration of report	1	1	0	1	1	0
Third reading	1	1	0	1	1	0

	Parliamentary Agent.			Attorney or Solicitor.		
	£	s.	d.	£	s.	d.
Consideration of Lords' amendments - - -	1	1	0	1	1	0

Note.—The above charges will include the attendances upon members at the House, who are to present petitions, or to move any stage of the bill in the House, and the drawing the requisite motions, and also the attendances upon officers of the House in reference to matters connected with any stage of the bill or other proceeding; except under special circumstances.

All other special attendances in reference to other proceedings in the House may be charged according to the circumstances of each case, in conformity with such parts of this list as may be applicable thereto.

Attendances before the Examiners of petitions for private bills:

Unopposed Cases:

To prove compliance with the Standing Orders in the case of a petition for a bill, and obtaining indorsement by Examiner,						
In first class bills - - -	2	2	0	2	2	0
In second class bills - -	3	3	0	3	3	0
If adjourned for further proofs, each subsequent attendance when the Examiner shall inquire into the same, or attending to apply for postponement or adjournment -	1	1	0	1	1	0

Note.—Only one attendance is allowed to be charged for proofs before the Examiner in respect of the Standing Orders of both Houses, when the same are taken simultaneously.

	Parliamentary Agent.			Attorney or Solicitor.		
	£	s.	d.	£	s.	d.
To prove compliance with the Standing Orders in the case of bills from the House of Lords, petitions for additional provision, or bills introduced in lieu of other bills which shall have been withdrawn -	1	1	0	1	1	0

Opposed Cases :

For every day on which memorials complaining of non-compliance with the Standing Orders are inquired into by the Examiner (according to circumstances) - - -

<table>
<tr><td></td><td colspan="3">from
3 3 0
to
5 5 0</td><td colspan="3">from
3 3 0
to
5 5 0</td></tr>
</table>

For entering appearances upon memorials before the Examiner, and watching proceedings in case such memorials are not called on, each day -

<table>
<tr><td></td><td colspan="3">from
2 2 0
to
3 3 0</td><td colspan="3">from
2 2 0
to
3 3 0</td></tr>
</table>

> *Note.*—When an agent or solicitor appears and attends for two or more memorials, complaining of non-compliance with the Standing Orders, on behalf of the same clients, against the same bill, he will be entitled to charge one day's attendance only in respect of the same.

For every day on which a petition for a bill is on the Examiner's daily list, but is not called on - - • -   2   2   0   2   2   0

> *Note.*—When two or more petitions for bills, being promoted or opposed by or on behalf of the same clients, are appointed for consideration by the same Examiner on the same day, but are not called on, the agents and solicitors of such clients respectively will not be

	Parliamentary Agent.			Attorney or Solicitor.		
	£	s.	d.	£	s.	d.

entitled to such charge in respect of each petition for a bill
so promoted or opposed, but
may charge any sum, not exceeding 1*l*. 1*s*., for additional
trouble (if any) in respect of
each other petition for a bill
on the same list; provided that
in no case (except under special
circumstances) shall a charge
exceeding 5*l*. 5*s*. be made in
respect of one such day's attendance on behalf of the same
clients.

For every day on which memorials complaining of non-compliance with the Standing Orders in the case of bills from the House of Lords, petitions for additional provision, or bills introduced in lieu of other bills which shall have been withdrawn are inquired into by the Examiner -	from 2	2	0	from 2	2	0
	to 3	3	0	to 3	3	0

Attendances before the Referees
on locus standi :

Attending clerk to obtain appointment, provided that in no case shall more than three such attendances be charged -	0	7	6	0	7	6
For every day when the case is in the paper but not reached -	1	1	0	1	1	0
For every day in which the case is considered, when the parties appear by counsel -	2	2	0	2	2	0
When the parties appear without counsel - - -	from 3	3	0	2	2	0
	to 5	5	0			

Attendances before committees :
Attending the Standing Orders
Committee each day in which

	Parliamentary Agent.	Attorney or Solicitor.
	£ s. d.	£ s. d.
the case is on the list, and is heard, postponed, or adjourned - - -	2 2 0	2 2 0
Attending the Committee of Selection, or the General Committee on Railway and Canal Bills when required to attend with reference to the grouping of the bill, or the appointment of the committee, or on other special and necessary occasions, provided that in no case shall more than three such attendances be charged:		
Promoters - - -	1 1 0	1 1 0
Opponents - - -	0 10 6	0 10 6

Committee on the Bill:

Unopposed Bills:

	Parliamentary Agent.	Attorney or Solicitor.
Attending when the bill is considered by the committee -	from 2 2 0 to 3 3 0	3 3 0
Under special circumstances in railway and other bills - - - -		from 3 3 0 to 5 5 0
Attending the committee to apply for a postponement or adjournment - - -	1 1 0	1 1 0

Opposed Bills:

Attending the committee every day on which the bill is considered by the committee:

	Parliamentary Agent.	Attorney or Solicitor.
When the parties appear without counsel (according to circumstances) -	from 3 3 0 to 5 5 0	from 3 3 0 to 5 5 0

	Parliamentary Agent.			Attorney or Solicitor.		
	£	s.	d.	£	s.	d.
When the parties appear by counsel, and the preamble is considered by the committee - -	2	2	0	from 3 3 0 to 5 5 0		
When the clauses of the bill are considered by the committee	from 3 3 0 to 5 5 0			from 3 3 0 to 5 5 0		
Note.—When an agent or solicitor appears and attends for two or more petitions against a bill, on behalf of the same clients, he will be entitled to charge one day's attendance only in respect of the same.						
Attending to watch proceedings of a committee on a group of bills when the bill in respect of which the agent or solicitor is concerned stands for consideration, but is not considered by the committee, per day :						
Promoters - - - -	2	2	0	2	2	0
Opponents - - - -	1	1	0	1	1	0
Note.—In no case (except under special circumstances) must a charge exceeding 5*l.* 5*s.* be made in respect of attending to watch proceedings in the case of petitions against a bill, previously to such petitions being considered.						
Attending to withdraw a petition	from 1 1 0 to 2 2 0			from 1 1 0 to 2 2 0		
Note.—When two or more bills, being promoted or opposed by or on behalf of the same clients, are appointed for consideration by the committee on the same day, but are postponed or adjourned without being considered, or are not separately considered by the committee, the agents or solicitors of such clients respectively will not be entitled to such						

	Parliamentary Agent.	Attorney or Solicitor.
	£ s. d.	£ s. d.
charge in respect of each bill so promoted or opposed; but may charge any sum, not exceeding 1l. 1s., for additional trouble (if any) in respect of each other bill so postponed or adjourned, or not separately considered: provided that in no case (except under special circumstances) shall a charge exceeding 5l. 5s. be made in respect of one such day's attendance upon the committee on behalf of the same clients.		
No charge is allowed for attendance of a clerk to the solicitor on a committee, except for the purpose of being examined as a witness.		
Other Attendances, at the House, or elsewhere:		
Special attendances upon Mr. Speaker or the Chairman of the Committee of Ways and Means, in reference to any bill - - - - -	1 1 0	1 1 0
Attending members at the House on special and necessary occasions (other than moving the stages of the bill)	1 1 0	1 1 0
First attendance on Mr Speaker's Counsel to go through bill - - -	1 1 0	1 1 0
Subsequent attendances - -	0 10 6	0 13 4
Special attendances (not included in the sessional fee) upon Mr. Speaker's Secretary or other officer of the House - - - -	0 10 6	0 13 4
Note.—Where more than one of the above attendances at the House take place on the same occasion with reference to the same bill, not more than 1l. 1s. to be charged for all such attendances unless the time occupied shall exceed one hour.		

	Parliamentary Agent.	Attorney or Solicitor.
	£ s. d.	£ s. d.
At consultation with counsel -	{ 1 1 0 when required to attend.	1 1 0
On counsel, at Chambers, with retainer; brief; to fix consultation and pay fee; with and for draft bill; and other attendances when fees are paid to counsel - - - - - -		0 10 0
Attending at the Private Bill Office to deposit the petition for the bill, with agent's declaration and printed copy of the bill annexed, and other printed copies of the bill, and registering the petition in the general list of petitions - - -	1 1 0	—
Note.—The making up the petition, with declaration and bill annexed, is included in the above charge.		
Attending at the Private Bill Office to deposit plan, section, and book of reference - -	1 1 0	1 1 0
Other attendances at the House or offices thereof - - -	0 10 6	0 13 4
Attending to deposit documents at a Government Office - -	0 10 6	0 10 6
Attending to deposit other documents required by the Standing Orders to be deposited (except bills, amendments, &c., the deposit of which, in certain cases, is included in the sessional fee). See II. - - - - - -	0 10 6	0 13 4
If at a distance, and for deposits with parish clerks, &c. (if numerous), clerk's time and expenses are to be charged instead of the preceding.		
Note.—The charge for attending to deposit includes any charge for drawing a memorandum		

	Parliamentary Agent.			Attorney or Solicitor.		
	£	s.	d.	£	s.	d.

of documents deposited, and obtaining signature of the depositor thereto, and the requisite copies of the same, except the same shall exceed one folio, when 1s. 4d. per folio may be charged for drawing the same, and 6d. per folio for copies to hand in to Examiner or other requisite copies; it also includes the drawing and obtaining the certificate or receipt for such deposit.

Attendances for the purpose of deposit cannot be charged both by Parliamentary agent and solicitor.

Attending at the Private Bill Office to deposit petitions in favour of or against any private bill, and registering the same; viz. :—

	Parliamentary Agent.			Attorney or Solicitor.		
If one petition or less than three - - - -	0	10	6	0	13	4
If three petitions, and less than seven - - -	1	1	0	1	1	0
If seven petitions, and less than twelve - - -	1	11	6	1	11	6
For any number exceeding twelve - - - -	2	2	0	2	2	0

Note.—The endorsing petitions and preparing the same for deposit are included in the above fees except when the same are prepared by the solicitor, when from 3s. 4d. to 6s. 8d. is allowed for endorsing a petition or set of petitions, and transmitting the same to the Parliamentary agent for the purpose of deposit (except when included in the sessional fee).

	Parliamentary Agent.			Attorney or Solicitor.		
On taxing officer, for the purpose of taxation of a bill of costs - - - -	from 0 10 6 to 2 2 0			from 0 13 4 to 2 2 0		

Note.—No charge is allowed for copies of a bill of costs for

	Parliamentary Agent.	Attorney or Solicitor.
	£ s. d.	£ s. d.

taxation except when necessarily made for the purpose of depositing the same in the Taxing Office.

On a witness settling his proof (if necessary) - - -	0 6 8	0 6 8

Note.—If attendance requisite on many witnesses on the same occasion, a charge to be made according to time occupied.

The attendance on a witness for the purpose of settling an affidavit is included in the charge for drawing affidavit.

The attendance on the witness previously to drawing his proof is included in the charge for instructions for proof.

With a witness to be sworn -	0 6 8	0 6 8
At Post Office registering and posting applications and taking receipt - - - -	0 10 6	0 13 4

Note.—The applications to owners, lessees, and occupiers should be made by post, if practicable and more economical.

Where personal service is required, a clerk's time and expenses for the purpose of such service may be charged, except where such service can be more economically made through local agents.

Preparing and despatching telegraphic message - - -	0 5 0	0 5 0
At Private Bill Office to take out appearances - - -	0 7 6	—

Note.—Only one charge to be made for taking out appearances on any number of petitions from the said clients on the same day.

—	Parliamentary Agent.			Attorney or Solicitor.		
	£	s.	d.	£	s.	d.
On printer with instructions -	0	6	8	0	6	8

Note.—When attendance to order proofs is charged, no charge is allowed for subsequent attendance to obtain proofs.

No attendance to be charged for ordering further additional copies.

PROVISIONAL ORDERS:

—						
Attendances at any Government Department for the purpose of giving proofs - - - -	2	2	0	2	2	0
		from			from	
Other attendances at a Government Department - - -	0	10	6	0	10	6
		to			to	
	1	1	0	1	1	0

If a Provisional Order is opposed in Parliament, the same charges may be made for attendances in committee and other proceedings consequent on such opposition as in the case of opposed private bills.

ATTENDANCES of a CLERK:

—						
Before a committee or the Examiner to give evidence - -	0	10	6	0	10	6
If in favour of or against an opposed bill, or in support of or against allegations of a memorial - - - - -	1	1	0	1	1	0
To order and obtain copies of a petition or petitions in favour of or against a bill or other documents - - - -	0	7	6	0	6	8

Note.—Only one attendance is allowed to be charged for ordering and obtaining any number of petitions against the same bill at the same time.

—						
Attendance on members of Standing Orders Committee (12 in number), to deposit statement -	1	1	0	1	1	0
Other attendances of a clerk -	0	7	6	0	6	8

II.—SESSIONAL OR SOLICITATION FEE

FOR SOLICITING THE BILL FOR THE PROMOTERS BY THE
PARLIAMENTARY AGENT.

	£	s.	d.
When the bill has received the Royal Assent -	26	5	0

[In case the bill should not receive the Royal Assent, a
sessional fee of two guineas and upwards may be
charged, according to the class of bill and the progress
made through its several stages.]

The sessional fee will include all attendances not otherwise specially
mentioned in this list, at the following offices of the House
of Commons; viz.:—

At the House for the purpose of watching proceedings, and
Royal Assent.

Chairman of the Committee of Ways and Means:
To deposit bills, clauses and amendments, and afterwards
to obtain the same; and all other formal attendances.

Committee of Selection or General Committee on Railway
and Canal Bills:
To deposit bills, and on other occasions when not specially
required to attend.

Mr. Speaker's Counsel:
To deposit prints of bills, and afterwards to obtain the
same; and all other formal attendances.

Mr. Speaker's Secretary:
All formal attendances to leave amended bills and clauses,
and to obtain the same agreed to.

The Examiner:
To deposit bills, and apply for appointments; and all
formal attendances.

Private Bill Office:
To give notices.
To examine register with reference to deposit of petitions
or memorials against bill, and for other purposes, and
other books.
To deposit prints of bills, amended bills, and copies of
proposed amendments.

Fee Office :
>   To pay fees, and all other attendances in reference thereto, and with copies of bills when required.

Journal Office :
>   To order and obtain copies of reports, petitions, and other papers : except in the case of opposed bills, when 7s. 6d. may be charged for attending to bespeak and afterwards to obtain the same.

Committee Clerks' Office :
>   To deposit bills, and all ordinary attendances with reference to the progress of the bill.

Doorkeepers :
>   To deliver prints of bills, &c.

Offices for the sale of Parliamentary papers :
>   To obtain printed reports and other papers required for use in the progress of the bill.

The sessional fee will also cover all ordinary communications of the agent with the solicitor, with reference to the progress of the bill through its various stages, when no professional advice or instruction is given.

PROVISIONAL ORDERS :

	£	s.	d.
Sessional fee for soliciting the order and confirmation bill for the promoters by the Parliamentary agent, when the bill has received the Royal Assent -	15	15	0

The sessional fee will include all attendances at the House, or the offices thereof, or at any Government department as to the stages of the provisional order or confirmation bill, or for examining the register with reference to petitions or memorials against the bill ; the obtaining, perusing, and examining the bill to ascertain that the provisional order has been correctly inserted therein, and attendances at any Government department with reference to the correct insertion of the provisional order ; watching, and, if necessary, assisting at the various stages of the bill in the House, or before the examiner ; all letters to the solicitor or client with reference to the progress of the provisional order or confirmation bill.

If the same agent is concerned for more than one provisional order relating to the same locality, and included in the same confirmation bill, an additional sessional fee of 5*l.* 5*s.* may be charged for every such provisional order exceeding one.

II.—SESSIONAL OR SOLICITATION FEE

FOR SOLICITING THE BILL FOR THE PROMOTERS BY THE SOLICITOR, WHEN A PARLIAMENTARY AGENT IS ALSO EMPLOYED.

	£	s.	d.
When the bill has received the Royal Assent - -	10	10	0

[In case the bill should not receive the Royal Assent, a sessional fee of two guineas and upwards may be charged according to the class of bill, and the progress made through its several stages.]

The sessional fee of the solicitor will include all charges for his ordinary communications with the Parliamentary agent, with reference to the progress of the bill through its various stages, when no professional advice or instruction is given; delivering documents to Parliamentary agent for deposit; attendances at the offices of the House to ascertain the position of the bill; attendances at the office for sale of Parliamentary papers; attendances at the House to watch proceedings; and at the Royal Assent.

When no other Parliamentary agent is employed, the solicitor acting in that capacity will be entitled to the sessional fee of Parliamentary agent, in lieu of that of Solicitor. The solicitor is not entitled to charge any sessional fee in the case of a provisional order.

In cases of opposition to bills no sessional fee is allowed.

III.—TIME CHARGES.

	Parliamentary Agent.			Attorney or Solicitor.		
	£	s.	d.	£	s.	d.
For attendances, &c.—						
Ordinary - - - -	0	10	6	from 0 to 0	6 13	8 4
If upwards of an hour - -	1	1	0	1	1	0
Or per hour - - - -	0	13	4	0	13	4
If required to leave London—						
Time per day - - -	4	4	0	4	4	0
Hotel expenses - -	1	1	0	1	1	0
and fares actually paid.						
A solicitor from the country absent from home in London, or elsewhere, is allowed—						
Time per day - - -	-	-	-	4	4	0
Hotel expenses - -	-	-	-	1	1	0
and fares actually paid.						
Note.—The day charge includes all charges for work done during the day.						
Clerks : per day - - - - - -				from 1 to 2	1 2	0 0
Hotel expenses, and fares actually paid.						

Note.—In taking the reference, and in serving applications on owners, &c., and making deposits with parish clerks, a charge of 1*l.* 11*s.* 6*d.* per day is allowed for each clerk so employed.

IV.—DRAWING DOCUMENTS.

	£	s.	d.
Special instructions (if required), and letters therewith :			
Notice :			
As to contents and publication - - -	1	1	0
Plans :			
As to form and deposit of - - - -	1	1	0
Notice to owners, lessees, and occupiers :			
As to form and service thereof - - -	0	10	6
List of owners, &c. :			
As to form of - - - - - -	0	10	6

Note.—Any other instructions as to the above documents or other requirements of the Standing Orders to be charged as a letter.

	£	s.	d.
Notice in Gazette or newspaper :			
Instructions - - - - - - -	0	13	4
If less than 11 folios - - - - -	1	1	0
If more than 11 folios, per folio - - -	0	2	0
Book of reference :			
Per folio - - - - - - -	0	2	0
Index to book of reference and register therewith, containing the answers received to applications (including any necessary copies), per folio - - - - - - - -	0	1	4
Lists of owners, lessees, and occupiers :			
Per folio - - - - - - -	0	2	0

Note.—The above charges include the entering the replies received from time to time for the purpose of such drawing.

	£	s.	d.
Applications to owners, lessees, and occupiers of lands and houses :			
Drawing, and fair copy for service, each application (including the letter of assent, dissent, or neutrality, left or forwarded therewith) -	from 0	6	8
	to 0	10	0
Each notice of abandonment and other notice, not being in the form set forth in Appendix (A) to the Standing Orders - - -	0	5	0

	£	s.	d.
List of applications to be posted or to be served by a witness, and copy for signature, including the obtaining the signature of the witness thereto :			
Each list - - - - - - -	0	3	1
or, per folio - - - - -	0	1	4

Note.—No second charge allowed for drawing the above lists of applications for the purpose of handing in to the Examiner, or other purpose, but only the charge for copying.

	£	s.	d.
Estimates of expenses, and requisite copies - -	0	10	6
Declaration in lieu or in aid of deposit of money, and requisite copies - - - -	1	1	0
Declaration and estimate, and requisite copies -	1	11	6
Declaration under Standing Order 41, and requisite copies - - - - - -	1	1	0
Subscription contract :			
Instructions - - - - - - -	0	13	4
Per folio - - - - - - -	0	1	4
Petition for bill :			
If less than 11 folios - - - -	1	1	0
If more than 11 folios, per folio - - -	0	2	0
Agent's declaration, and copies for deposit :			
1st class bill - - - - - -	1	1	0
2nd class bill - - - - - -	2	2	0
Bill :			
Instructions - - - - - - -	2	2	0
Drawing bill, per folio - - - - -	0	2	0
Additional clauses, per folio - - - -	0	2	0
Statements of proofs on Standing Orders :]			
Proofs previously to the introduction of the bill :			

Parliamentary Agent :

	£	s.	d.
Drawing or perusing same, and fair copy, and forwarding same to solicitor, together with letter accompanying the same, and instructions :			
1st class bill - - - - -	1	1	0
Ditto, where lands and houses are taken	1	11	6
2nd class bill- - - - - -	2	2	0

Solicitor :

Drawing or perusing and filling up the same, and arranging lists referred to therein, and

	£	s.	d.
forwarding the same, with letter accompanying, to the Parliamentary agent :			
1st class bill - - - - -	1	1	0
Ditto, where lands and houses are taken -	2	2	0
2nd class bill - - - -	3	3	0

Parliamentary Agent :

	£	s.	d.
Perusing and finally arranging the same for proof before the Examiner :			
1st class bill - - - - -,	0	10	6
2nd class bill - - - - -	1	1	0
If the solicitor is also acting as Parliamentary agent, he may charge for statement of proofs, including final arrangement of the same :			
1st class - - - - - -	2	2	0
Ditto, when lands and houses are taken -	3	3	0
2nd class - - - - - -	4	4	0
Proofs subsequent to introduction of bill :			
Solicitor - - - - -	from 1 1 0 to 2 2 0		
Parliamentary agent - - - -	from 1 1 0 to 2 2 0		
Or, if the solicitor is also acting as Parliamentary agent - - - -	from 2 2 0 to 3 3 0		
No other or further charge is allowed to Parliamentary agent or solicitor with reference to the preparation of the statement of proofs.			
Memorials complaining of non-compliance with Standing Orders :			
Instructions - - - - -	0	13	4
If less than 11 folios - - - -	1	1	0
If more than 11 folios, per folio - - -	0	2	0
Statements for Standing Orders Committee (according to length and other circumstances) -	from 0 13 4 to 2 2 0		
or, per brief sheet of 10 folios - - -	0	13	4
Petition against bill, and praying to be heard before the Committee :			
Instructions - - - - -	0	13	4

	£	s.	d.
If less than 11 folios - - - - -	1	1	0
If more than 11 folios, per folio - - -	0	2	0
Petitions for additional provision, or for dispensing with Standing Orders:			
If less than 11 folios - - - - -	1	1	0
If more than 11 folios, per folio - - -	0	2	0
Other petitions with reference to bill:			
If less than 11 folios - - - - -	0	13	4
If less than 15 folios - - - - -	1	0	0
If more than 15 folios, per sheet - - -	0	13	4
or, per folio - - - - - -	0	1	4
Briefs:			
Instructions for brief (according to circumstances).			
Drawing same, per brief sheet of 10 folios -	0	13	4
Retainers to counsel:			
Drawing and copy - - - - -	0	10	0
Case for opinion of counsel:			
Instructions - - - - - -	0	13	4
Drawing, per sheet - - - - -	0	13	4
Proofs of witnesses, or notes for cross-examination:			
Instructions (including, in case of proofs of witnesses, any previous attendance on the witness) - - - - - - -	0	13	4
Drawing, per sheet - - - - -	0	13	4
Statements, reports, abstracts, or other documents prepared for use in proceedings of the House, or in preparing to comply with the Standing Orders, per folio - - - -	0	1	4
or, per brief sheet of 10 folios - - -	0	13	4
Affidavits (including attendance on the witness):			
Each affidavit, including lists attached thereto, and copy - - - - - - -	0	10	0
or, per folio - - - - - -	0	1	4
Requisition for warrant for deposit of money and copy for signature - - - -	0	10	0
Warrant, and attendance to get same signed -	0	10	0
Requisition for certificate of speaker - - -	0	10	0
Certificate, and attendance to get same signed -	0	10	0
Requisition for withdrawal of petitions or memorials - - - - - - -	0	10	0
Motions, special, for members:			
Drawing, and fair copy for member - -	0	10	0

Note.—Charges for drawing, and copies of all ordinary motions on the several stages of the bills and other proceedings in the House, to be included in the fees for attendance.

	£	s.	d.
Summons for witnesses :			
Drawing, and copy for service - - -	0	5	0
Other documents connected with the case, and			
not specified above, per folio - - - -	0	1	0

> *Note.*—In all cases the charge for drawing any document will include the fair copy to keep, or for counsel or agent to settle.

PROVISIONAL ORDER.

The charges for drawing the provisional order notices and other documents similar to those required in the case of private bills, and copies thereof (limited according to Table A.) may be made out according to the same scale.

V.—PARLIAMENTARY AGENTS' CHARGES.

FOR PERUSING AND SETTLING DOCUMENTS DRAWN BY A SOLICITOR (when required).

	£	s.	d.
Notices for *Gazette* and newspapers :			
If less than 11 folios - - - - -	1	1	0
If more than 11 folios (according to length and other circumstances) - - - - -	from 1 1 0 to 2 2 0		
Petition for bill :			
If less than 11 folios - - - - -	1	1	0
If more than 11 folios - - - - - (Or if the same shall exceed 50 folios. 1s. per folio upon the whole petition.)	from 1 1 0 to 2 2 0		

Petitions for additional provision, or for dispensing with the Standing Orders :

Petitions against bill, and praying to be heard before the committee, or memorial complaining of non-compliance with the Standing Orders :

The same charges as for a petition for a bill.

	£	s.	d.
Other petitions, against or in favour of bills, each petition - - - - - - - -	0	6	8
Statements for Standing Orders Committee, reports, and other documents (if required), when the same have been drawn by the solicitor (according to circumstances) - -	from 0 6 8 to 1 1 0		
or, per brief sheet of 10 folios - - -	0	6	8

	£	s.	d.
Perusing and settling bills and preparing the same in Parliamentary form, and for press :			
For any bill not exceeding 60 folios, according to the length of the bill, and the nature and extent of revision.	from 2 to 5	2 5	0 0
For any bill exceeding 60 folios and less than 150, according to the length of the bill, and the nature and extent of revision - - -	from 5 to 10	5 10	0 0
For any bill exceeding 150 folios, according to the length of the bill, and the nature and extent of revision; but if above 10*l.* 10*s.*, not exceeding (except under special circumstances) one-half the charge for drawing any such Bill - - - - - - -	5 and upwards	5	0

Perusing and settling clauses and amendments (according to length and other circumstances, but not exceeding 1*s.* per folio).

> *Note.*—The charges for perusing and settling include a copy as perused and settled for own use, if required, and no copy is to be charged for the purpose of returning the same as settled.
>
> No charge is allowed for perusal and settling by the party who charges for the drawing, but he may charge for a perusal (if necessary) of the document as settled, according to circumstances, but not in any case exceeding half the charge allowed for perusal and settling of the Draft.

VI.—PERUSALS.

	£	s.	d.
Perusals, generally, should be charged by the time occupied, but if per folio, not exceeding -	0	0	4
Obtaining and perusing report of Board of Trade on bill - - - - - - - -	0	10	6
Perusing a petition or memorial against bill :			
If under 20 folios - - - - - -	0	6	8
If above, per folio - - - - -	0	0	4

VII.—COPIES OF DOCUMENTS.

	£	s.	d.
Books of reference, lists of owners, lessees, and occupiers, and other similar documents required by the Standing Orders to be deposited :			
For the copies so deposited, when deposited in manuscript, per folio (of 72 words or figures) -	0	0	9

	£	s.	d.
For such copies of other documents as are included in Table (A) annexed, per folio -	0	0	6
For ingrossing petitions, memorials, and other Parliamentary documents :			
Per folio - - - - -	0	0	9
For copies of documents not included in Table (A) :			
Per folio - - - - -	0	0	4

> *Note.*—For the number of copies allowed to be charged at 9*d.* and 6*d.* per folio, *vide* Table (A).
> In cases where minutes of evidence are printed, copies of the same are not allowed to be charged, but only the cost of printing and the necessary attendances on the printer.

VIII.—EXAMINING PRINTED DOCUMENTS.

	£	s.	d.
Prints of bills :			
Proofs - - - - - - - -	0	13	4
or, per page of print - - - -	0	1	0
Revises - - - - - -	0	6	8
or, per page of print - - - -	0	0	6
Ordering proofs of estimate or declaration, examining same and all revises, and returning same to printer, with instructions to print	0	13	4

NOTICES IN GAZETTE AND NEWSPAPER :

	£	s.	d.
Each newspaper :			
Forwarding notice to printer, with instructions -	0	6	8
Examining proof, 3*s.* 4*d.* to - - -	0	10	0
Returning proof, and ordering insertion for three weeks, or otherwise - - - -	0	6	8
Examining notice on each insertion - -	0	3	4
If a revise is necessary, an addition for ordering revise and examining same, of each revise - - - - - - - -	0	10	0
No other or further charge is allowed with reference to printing the notice.			

IX.—MAKING UP COPIES OF BILLS AND FILLING UP AMENDMENTS.

	£	s.	d.
Blanking bill, drawing arrangement of sections, and finally settling bill for printer - - -	1	1	0
Making up bill in Parliamentary form for House, and deposit of the same - - - -	1	1	0

	£	s.	d.

Filling up bills with amendments:

For the first copy - } unless the amendments {　0　6　8

For each other copy } be very numerous - {　0　3　4

If new clauses or amendments be added, exceeding six folios, copies of the same may be charged at 6d. per folio.

Marking on print of bill the amendments made therein for Examiner - - - - - 　0　6　8

Note. - A manuscript copy of the amendments is not allowed to be charged.

Altering bill as an act, and attending printer with instructions to strike off copies - - 　0　10　6

X.—MAKING UP DOCUMENTS.

Examining and making up plans and books of reference for the purpose of deposit, each set - 　0　10　6

Ditto, lists of owners, &c., and other documents deposited therewith - - - - 　0　10　6

The examining and making up the deposits for the parish clerks to be charged according to the time occupied.

XI.—LETTERS.

Letters containing professional advice or instructions - - - - - - - 　0　5　0

If exceeding six folios in length - - - 　0　10　0

Other letters - - - - - - - 　0　3　6

Note.—The ordinary correspondence between Parliamentary agents and solicitors is not to be charged to their clients, but such letters only as contain professional advice and instructions.

Circulars - - - - - - - - 　0　1　0

In cases for which no specific charge is stated in the foregoing table, the charge is to be made out according to the time occupied.

Parliamentary agents are required to make the same charges in respect of Scotch business as of English or Irish.

TABLE (A).

Copies allowed to be charged besides the copy the charge for
which is included in that for drawing.

	Number of Copies.	
	At 9d. per folio.	At 6d. per folio.
PROMOTERS.		
Notices :		
For *each* gazette and newspaper - -	—	1
Book of reference :		
For *each* deposit of entire book of reference (when deposited in manuscript) - -	1	—
Amongst parish clerks - - - -	1	—
For marking section for applications - -	—	1
Lists of owners, lessees, and occupiers; for deposit in Parliament - - - -	2	—
Applications served by a witness; for use before Examiner - - - - -	—	2
Petition for bill; ingrossed copy for deposit -	1	—
Bill; for press - - - - - -	—	1
Statements of proofs; for use before Examiner :		
For agent - - - - - -	—	1
For solicitor - - - - - -	—	1
For Examiner - - - - - -	—	2
Memorials :		
For agent - - - - - -	—	1
For solicitor - - - - - -	—	1
For engineer (if necessary) - - -	—	1
Statement for Standing Orders Committee :		
For committee and use - - - -	—	3
Petition against bill :		
For agent - - - - - -	—	1
For solicitor - - - - - -	—	1
Briefs :		
For *each* counsel (not exceeding three) -	—	1
Proofs of witnesses :		
For *each* counsel (not exceeding three) -	—	1
For witness (if required) - - - -	—	1
Notes for cross-examination :		
For *each* counsel (not exceeding three) -	—	1

	Number of Copies	
	At 9d. per folio.	At 6d. per folio.

OPPONENTS.

Memorial :		
Ingrossed copy for deposit - - -	1	—
For agent - - - - - -	—	1
For solicitor - - - - - -	—	1
For Examiner - - - - -	—	2
Statement for Standing Orders Committee :		
For committee and use - - - -	—	3
Petition against :		
Ingrossed copy for deposit - - -	1	—
For agent - - - - - -	—	1
For solicitor - - - - - -	—	1
Brief :		
For *each* counsel (not exceeding three) -	—	1
Proofs of witnesses :		
For *each* counsel (not exceeding three) -	—	1
For witness (if required) - - - -	—	1
Notes for cross-examination :		
For *each* counsel (not exceeding three) -	—	1

The copies above enumerated are those ordinarily allowed to be charged. Any further copies of the documents named in the foregoing table, or any copies of documents not named therein, which may be necessary for the case, are to be charged at the rate of 4*d.*, or if the document is in print at the rate of 2*d.*, per folio.

House of Commons, }   ARTHUR W. PEEL,
7 August 1888.   }   Speaker.

A similar list of charges to be made in the House of Lords has been prepared by the Clerk of the Parliaments for that House. It can be procured from Messrs. Eyre & Spottiswoode, price 2½*d.*

RULES AS TO PETITIONS AGAINST PRIVATE BILLS, HOUSE OF COMMONS.

1. Every petition must be written and not printed or lithographed.

2. Every petition must contain a prayer.

3. Every petition must be signed by at least one person, or sealed on the skin or sheet on which the prayer is written.

4. No erasures or interlineations may be made in any petition.

Every petition to be addressed "To the Honourable The Commons of the United Kingdom of Great Britain and Ireland, in Parliament assembled."

RULES TO BE OBSERVED AS TO PROOF OF COMPLIANCE WITH THE STANDING ORDERS PREVIOUS TO THE INTRODUCTION OF PRIVATE BILLS.

The sittings of the Examiners for Standing Orders will commence on the 18th January.

The promoters of each bill will be required to prove compliance with the Standing Orders of both Houses of Parliament at the time appointed by the Examiners, which can be ascertained at the Private Bill Office of the House of Commons.

The printed statements of proofs can be obtained at the Queen's printers.

Where lists are annexed to affidavits, the name of the agent is to be entered in the statement of proofs as delivering in such lists followed by the names of the witnesses proving the service of notices or deposit of documents as the case may be.

Memorials complaining of non-compliance with the Standing Orders (of either House) applicable previously to the introduction

of private bills must be deposited in the Private Bill Office, House
of Commons, as follows :—

> If the same relate to bills numbered in the general list pub-
> lished by the Private Bill Office of the House of
> Commons—

From	1 to 100	⎫ They must be depo-	⎧ Jan.	9.
,,	101 to 200	⎬ sited before Two	⎨ ,,	16.
,,	201 and upwards	⎭ o'clock on - -	⎩ ,,	23.

REGULATIONS AS TO DEPOSIT OF PETITIONS IN THE PRIVATE BILL OFFICE.

1. In order to facilitate the arrangement of the Petitions, and
the subsequent hearing thereof by the Examiners, in such order as
may be most convenient to the parties and their agents, a register
will be kept in the Private Bill Office, with blank lines numbered
consecutively from one to five hundred; and every agent will be
allowed to cause the petitions produced by him to be entered, respectively on such of the lines, not then having any petition entered
thereon, as he shall think fit ; and if he shall not prescribe any
order for the entry of such petitions, they will be entered in the
order in which they are deposited, upon the earliest consecutive
lines then remaining unoccupied.

2. When two or more agents shall appear in the Private Bill
Office at the same time for the purpose of depositing petitions,
unless they shall otherwise agree, their names will be placed in
a ballot glass, and the agents will have priority respectively in the
order in which their names shall be drawn : each in his turn being
entitled to deposit all the petitions offered by him at that time,
and to select such numbers for them as he shall think proper.

3. On the 22nd day of December, between the hours of twelve
and three, agents will be allowed to exchange, by agreement, the
numbers originally assigned to their petitions.   They will at the
same time be at liberty to transfer to other numbers in the register,
being then unoccupied, any of the petitions which may have
been deposited by them ; and their priority in the exercise of this
right will be determined by ballot, if necessary, as in the original
deposit of petitions.

4. Whenever two or more petitions, in respect of which the same witnesses are intended to be examined, shall occupy adjoining numbers in the register, the agent or agents for the same may cause any of them, not exceeding five in number, to be marked with a bracket; and regard will be had thereto in determining the days on which such petitions shall be set down for hearing, and the Examiner by whom they will be heard.

5. On or after the 22nd December the "General List of Petitions" will be made out in the Private Bill Office, in which the petitions will be numbered consecutively from one to the highest number according to the order in which they shall have been finally entered in the register.

NOTICE AS TO HEARING OF PETITIONS BY THE EXAMINERS.

1. Not less than seven clear days' notice will be given in the Private Bill Office of the day appointed for the examination of each petition; and the day so appointed will be written against the several petitions upon a printed copy of the "General List of Petitions," which will be kept in the Private Bill Office for that purpose.

2. So soon as the time allowed for depositing memorials complaining of non-compliance with the Standing Orders in the case of any petitions shall have expired, the word "unopposed" will be written in such printed list against each petition in respect of which no such memorial shall have been deposited; and the petitions will be set down for hearing before the Examiners in the order in which they stand in the "General List of Petitions," precedence being given, whenever it may be necessary, to unopposed petitions.

3. Petitions will be heard in the order in which they stand in the daily lists, and in case any petitions shall not be disposed of on the days on which they may be first appointed to be heard, they will be entered in the list of the following day before the opposed petitions appointed for that day; unless the Examiners shall otherwise adjourn or postpone the same.

4. In order to expedite the business of each day, petitions appointed to be heard by one of the Examiners will be transferred to the other from time to time, whenever it may seem advisable to the Examiners to direct such transfer.

SELECT COMMITTEE ON STANDING ORDERS.
RESOLUTIONS.

1. That reports of the Examiners of petitions shall be held by the Select Committee on Standing Orders to be conclusive on the question of any non-compliance with the Standing Orders reported therein.

2. That special reports of the Examiners, setting forth a statement of facts, without deciding whether the Standing Order or Orders applying thereto have or have not been complied with, shall be held by the committee to be conclusive as to the facts so set forth.

3. That in the case of special reports, the party contending that the Standing Orders have been complied with, shall set forth his argument in a written or printed statement, and shall strictly confine himself thereto, without entering on the question of dispensation with the Standing Orders, and the opposing party or parties shall do the same, under the like limitation.

4. That when, on the consideration of a special report, the committee shall have decided that the Standing Orders have not been complied with, the further consideration of the case, with a view to the question of the dispensation with Standing Orders, shall be postponed to the next meeting of the committee, in order to give time for the preparation of statements relating to that question.

5. That in the case of petitions for additional provision, where the Examiner reports that the Standing Orders have not been complied with, the party praying for dispensation of the Standing Orders shall set forth in a written or printed statement the grounds on which he rests his prayer.

6. That at the meeting of the committee both parties shall deliver in their statements.

7. Parliamentary agents are required, in all cases where statements are to be delivered in to the committee, to leave copies of the same, and of the proposed new clauses in the case of petitions for additional provision, with each member of the committee, at his residence, not later than three o'clock, and at the Committee Office

not later than one o'clock in the afternoon of the day preceding that fixed for the meeting of the committee.

8. That if the committee desire to hear argument in addition to such statements, and shall call on the parties to argue any point before them, only one speech be allowed on each side, although there may be on one side several parties interested.

9. That in all cases in which, either from ordinary reports of the Examiners or from the decision of the Committee upon Special Reports, the question arises whether the Standing Orders ought or ought not to be dispensed with, the party praying for such dispensation shall set forth, in a written or printed statement, the grounds on which he rests his prayer; and the opposing party shall also set forth, in a written or printed statement, the grounds on which he rests his opposition, both parties confining themselves strictly to the points reported on by the Examiners of petitions, or determined by the committee on their consideration of any special report of such Examiners.

10. That when the committee think fit, they shall hear the parties in explanation of their statements, but that no party shall be allowed to travel into any matter that is not referred to in his statement.

11. That when any petition praying that any of the Sessional or Standing Orders of the House relating to private bills may be dispensed with, or any petition opposing the same, shall have been referred to the committee, no statement in addition to the case set forth in any such petition shall be received, and Parliamentary agents are required to leave copies of the petitions with each member of the committee not later than three o'clock, and at the Committee Office not later than one o'clock, in the afternoon of the day before the day on which the committee is appointed to meet.

12. In all cases where an agent applies for the postponement of the consideration of a report referred to the committee, such agent shall attend and state the grounds on which he rests his application.

13. That the decision of the committee with respect to any petition or bill be communicated by the clerk of the committee to the chairman of the committee on the bill affected by such decision, on or before the commencement of the case.

Y

PRIVATE BILLS.

RULES FOR THE PRACTICE AND PROCEDURE OF THE REFEREES ON PRIVATE BILLS (IN PURSUANCE OF STANDING ORDER 88).

Locus Standi.

1. The promoters of any private bill, who intend to object to the right of petitioners to be heard against the same, shall give notice of such intention, and of the grounds of their objection, to the clerks to the referees and to the agents for the petitioners, not later than the eighth day after the day on which the petition has been deposited in the Private Bill Office ; but it shall be competent to the referees to allow such notices to be given, under special circumstances, although the time above limited may have expired. All notices shall be indorsed with the names of the petitioners' agents.

2. Copies of all petitions against private bills, to which notices of objection have been given, shall be deposited at the Referees' Office one clear day before the hearing of the case by the Court.

3. Parties who have given such notice as above, may at any time withdraw the same by giving notice in writing of withdrawal to the clerks to the referees, and to the agents for the petitioners.

4. The cases shall be heard in such order as the Chairman of Ways and Means shall appoint, and according to a list prepared under his direction, and kept in the Referees' Office.

5. When a bill is called on for consideration, the agents for the petitioners against the same shall be required to produce a certificate of appearance from the Private Bill Office, in which shall be stated the names of the petitioners, their counsel and agents.

6. Not less than one clear day's notice shall be given by the clerks to the referees to the clerks in the Private Bill Office, of the days on which the objections to the right of petitioners to be heard will be severally taken into consideration by the referees.

7. All notices required to be given, or deposits to be made in the Referees' Office, shall be delivered in the said office before five of the clock in the evening of any day on which the House shall sit, and before one of the clock on any day on which the House shall not sit.

8. Notices and grounds of objections will be deemed to have been sufficiently served upon agents, if left at the Agent's Office before six of the clock in the evening of any day, Sundays excepted.

Committees.

9. Two clear days at least before the day appointed for the consideration of any private bill by a committee of which a referee has been appointed a member, a filled-up copy of the bill, as proposed to be submitted to the committee, shall be deposited by the agent at the Referees' Office, for the use of such referee.

10. Two clear days before the day appointed for the consideration of the bill, copies of all petitions upon which opponents intend to appear before such committee shall be deposited at the Referees' Office.

(Signed) JAMES W. LOWTHER,
Chairman of Ways and Means.

House of Commons,
February 1896.

PARLIAMENTARY AGENTS.

RULES TO BE OBSERVED BY THE OFFICERS OF THE HOUSE, AND BY ALL PARLIAMENTARY AGENTS AND SOLICITORS ENGAGED IN PROSECUTING PROCEEDINGS IN THE HOUSE OF COMMONS UPON ANY PETITION OR BILL.

Declaration and recognizance.

1. No person shall be allowed to act as a Parliamentary agent until he shall have subscribed a declaration before one of the clerks in the Private Bill Office, engaging to observe and obey the rules, regulations, orders, and practices of the House of Commons, and also to pay and discharge from time to time, when the same shall be demanded, all fees and charges due and payable upon any petition or bill upon which such agent may appear; and after having subscribed such declaration, and entered into a recognizance or bond (if hereafter required), in the penal sum of 500*l.*, with two sureties of 250*l.* each, to observe the said declaration, such person, if in other respects qualified to act as hereinafter provided, shall be registered in a book to be kept in the Private Bill Office, and shall then be entitled to act as a Parliamentary agent : provided that upon the said declaration, recognizance or bond and registry, no fee shall be payable.

Form.

2. The declaration before mentioned, and the recognizance and bond, if hereafter required, shall be in such form as the Speaker may, from time to time, direct.

3. One member of a firm of Parliamentary agents may subscribe the required declaration, or enter into the required recognizance or bond, on behalf of his firm ; but the names of all the partners of such firm shall be registered with such declaration ; and notice shall be given, from time to time, to the clerks of the Private Bill Office, of any addition thereto, or change therein.

4. No person shall be allowed to be registered as a Parliamentary agent unless he is actually employed in promoting or opposing some private bill or petition pending in Parliament.

5. When any person (not being an attorney, or solicitor, or writer to the signet) applies to qualify himself, for the first time, to act as a Parliamentary agent, such application shall be made in writing, and he shall produce to one of the clerks of the Private Bill Office a certificate of his respectability from a member of

Parliament, or a justice of the peace, or a barrister-at-law, or an attorney, or solicitor.

6. No person's name, other than that of an attorney, or solicitor, or writer to the signet, shall be printed on any private bill, as Parliamentary agent to such bill, unless and until his name has been duly inscribed upon the register of Parliamentary agents.

7. No notice shall be received in the Private Bill Office for any proceeding upon a petition, or bill, until an appearance to act as the Parliamentary agent upon the same shall have been entered in the Private Bill Office; in which appearance shall also be specified the name of the solicitor (if any) for such petition or bill. *Appearance to be entered upon bills.*

8. Before any person desiring to appear by a Parliamentary agent shall be allowed to appear, or be heard, upon any petition against a bill, an appearance to act as the Parliamentary agent upon the same shall be entered in the Private Bill Office; in which appearance shall also be specified the name of the solicitor and of the counsel who appear in support of any such petition (if any counsel or solicitor are then engaged), and a certificate of such appearance shall be delivered to the Parliamentary Agent, to be produced to the committee clerk. *Appearance to be entered on petitions against bills.*

9. In case the Parliamentary agent for any petition or bill shall be displaced by the solicitor thereof, or such Parliamentary agent shall decline to act, the responsibility of such agent shall cease upon a notice being given in the Private Bill Office and a fresh appearance shall be entered upon such petition or bill. *A fresh appearance on change of parliamentary agent.*

10. Every Parliamentary agent and solicitor conducting proceedings in Parliament before the House of Commons shall be personally responsible to the House, and to the Speaker, for the observance of the rules, orders, and practice of Parliament, as well as of any rules which may from to time be prescribed by the Speaker, and also for the payment of the fees and charges due and payable under the Standing Orders. *Agents personally responsible.*

11. Any Parliamentary agent who shall wilfully act in violation of the rules and practices of Parliament, or of any rules to be prescribed by the Speaker, or who shall wilfully misconduct himself in prosecuting any proceedings before Parliament, shall be liable to an absolute or temporary prohibition to practise as a Parliamentary agent, at the pleasure of the Speaker: provided that upon the application of such Parliamentary agent the Speaker shall state, in writing, the grounds for such prohibition. *Speaker may, on misconduct, prohibit agent from practising.*

12. No person who has been suspended, or prohibited from practising as a Parliamentary agent, or struck off the roll of attorneys or solicitors, or disbarred by any of the Inns of Court, shall be allowed to be registered as a Parliamentary agent without the express authority of the Speaker.

13. No written or printed statement relating to any private bill shall be circulated within the precincts of the House of Commons without the name of a Parliamentary agent attached to it, who will be held responsible for its accuracy.

14. The sanction of the Chairman of Ways and Means, is writing, is required to every notice of a motion prepared by a Parliamentary Agent, for dispensing with any sessional or Standing Order of the House.

FORM OF DECLARATION.

We the undersigned do hereby declare, that we respectively intend during the present session of Parliament to practise as Parliamentary agents in the prosecuting, promoting, and opposing private bills in the House of Commons, and we severally and respectively do hereby engage to observe, submit to, perform, and abide by all and every the orders, rules, regulations, and practice of the said House, now in force or hereafter from time to time to be made in relation thereto, and also to pay and discharge from time to time when the same shall be demanded, all fees, charges, and sums of money due and payable in respect of any petition, bill, or other proceeding or matter, in or upon which we shall severally and respectively appear as such agents as aforesaid.

Date.	Name.	Residence and House of Business.	Witness.

[The rules published by the House of Lords are similar.]

TIME-TABLE.

* When the second or third reading of a private bill, or the consideration of the bill as amended by the committee, or any proposed clause or amendment, is opposed, the same shall be postponed until the day on which the House shall next sit.—S. O. 207.

No private bill shall pass through two stages on one and the same day without the special leave of the House; and, except in cases of urgent and pressing necessity, no motion shall be made to dispense with any Sessional or Standing Order of the House without due notice thereof.—S. O. 223, 224.

NOTE. If, upon the reading, by the clerk at the table, of the title of each bill from the daily private business list, no motion shall be made with respect to any such bill, the further proceeding thereon shall be adjourned until the next sitting of the House.—S. O. 225.

All bills for confirming provisional orders or certificates shall be set down for consideration each day, in a separate list, after the private business, and arranged in the same order as that prescribed by the Standing Orders for private bills.—S. O. 225a.

All notices must be given, or deposits made, at the Private Bill Office before six o'clock in the evening of any day on which the House shall sit, and between eleven and one o'clock on any day on which the House shall NOT sit; and after any day on which the House shall have adjourned beyond the following day, no notice can be given for the first day on which it shall again sit.—S. O. 217.

Private Bill Office, House of Commons, December 1885.

Petition for Bill.	First Reading.	Second Reading.	Petitions Against, or in Favour of, or Relating to, Private Bills, &c.	Petitions Relating to Sessional or Standing Orders, &c.	Petitions for Additional Provision, Estate Bills, &c.
To be deposited in the Private Bill Office on or before 21 December, and printed copies of the proposed bill to be delivered therewith for the use of any member, or agent, who may apply for the same.—S. O. 32. To be presented to the House not later than three clear days after it shall have been indorsed by the examiner; but if the House shall not be sitting, then not later than three clear days after the first sitting thereof subsequent to such indorsement.—S. O. 195.	Bill to be presented for first reading, by being deposited in the Private Bill Office, not later than one clear day after the presentation of the petition; or if the petition shall have been referred to the Standing Orders Committee, then not later than one clear day after leave has been given by the House to proceed with the bill.—S. O. 196, 197. Printed copies for members to be delivered to the Vote Office before the first reading.—S. O. 203.	Not less than three clear days, nor more than seven, to intervene between the first and second reading, unless the bill shall have been referred to the examiners, in which case not more than seven clear days to intervene between the report of the examiner, or of the Standing Orders Committee, and the second reading.—S. O. 204. Three clear days' notice of second reading to be given at the Private Bill Office; such notice not to be given until the day after that on which the bill has been ordered to be read a second time.—S. O. 205.	Petitions against private bills to be presented to the House, by being deposited in the Private Bill Office, not later than ten clear days after the first reading.—S. O. 128, 205, 210. Petitions against bills to confirm Provisional Orders or certificates to be presented to the House, by being deposited in the Private Bill Office, not later than seven clear days after of the day on which the bills will be examined.—S. O. 128, 205, 210. Other petitions, either in favour of or relating to private bills, or bills to confirm provisional orders or certificates (not being petitions for additional provision), to be presented to the House, by being deposited in the Private Bill Office, but no time limited.—S. O. 205.	Petitions for or against dispensing with Sessional or Standing Orders, and also petitions for re-insertion in the "General List of Petitions," or for leave to deposit a petition for bill, to be presented to the House, by being deposited in the Private Bill Office; all which petitions are referred to the Standing Orders Committee.—S. O. 200.	Petitions for additional provision to be presented to the House, with a printed copy of the proposed clauses annexed and referred to the Examiners of Petitions.—Private bills brought from the House of Lords, and bills introduced in lieu of other bills withdrawn, and bills for confirming provisional orders or certificates, are also referred to the Examiners of Petitions after having been read a first time.—S. O. 72, 198. The Examiners to give two clear days' notice at the Private Bill Office of the day appointed for the examination of such petitions and bills.—S. O. 73.

TIME-TABLE.

(See Note on previous page.)

Committees on Bills.	Report.	Consideration of Bills ordered to Lie upon the Table.	Third Reading.	Clauses or Amendments to be proposed on the Consideration or Third Reading.	Lords' Amendments, or Proposed Amendments thereto.
Six clear days to intervene between the second reading and the sitting of the committee, for all private bills, bills to confirm provisional orders or provisional certificates, divorce bills, and estate bills relating to Crown, Church, or Corporation property, or property held in trust for public or charitable purposes; and three clear days for other estate bills, naturalization bills, and name bills. S. O. 211. Four clear days' notice of the meeting of committees on all opposed private bills, and one clear day's notice in the case of unopposed and re-committed bills, to be given at the private bill office. S. O. 236. *[The notices for bills referred to the Committee of Selection, or to the general committee on railway and canal bills, are given by the clerks to those committees respectively; and the notices for all bills not referred to either of those committees are given by the clerk to the committee to which any such bill is either referred or re-committed.]* A filled-up bill, signed by the agent, as proposed to be submitted to the committee, to be deposited in the Private Bill Office two clear days before the meeting of the committee on the bill. S. O. 257. Notice of postponement of committees on private bills referred either to the Committee of Selection, or to the general committee on railway and canal bills, to be given at the Private Bill Office by the clerks to those committees respectively, on the day on which such postponement is made; and in the case of bills not referred to either of those committees, a like notice of postponement to be given by the clerk to the committee to which any such bill has been referred.— S. O. 256.	Reports upon all private bills to lie upon the table; and the bill, if amended in committee, or a railway or a tramway bill, to be also ordered to lie upon the table; but if not amended, and not a railway or a tramway bill, when reported, to be ordered a third time. — S. O. 213.	Three clear days to intervene between the report of the committee and the consideration of bill ordered to lie upon the table, and if the bill has been amended in committee, amended prints to be delivered to the vote office for the use of members three clear days before such consideration. — S. O. 214, 215. One clear day's notice of consideration to be given at the Private Bill Office. S. O. 239.*	One clear day's notice of third reading to be given at the Private Bill Office; such notice not to be given until the day after that on which the bill shall have been ordered to be read a third time. — S. O. 243.*	One clear days' notice to be given at the Private Bill Office of any clause or amendments to be proposed on the consideration, or of any verbal amendment on the third reading; and such clause or amendments to be printed—S.O. 217, 242.* No amendments, not being merely verbal, shall be made to any private bill on the third reading.—S. O. 219.	One clear day's notice on consideration to be given at the Private Bill Office; such notice not to be given until the day after that on which the Bill shall have been returned from the House of Lords; and the amendments to be printed and circulated with the votes previously to their being taken into consideration. — S.O. 220, 246.*

LIST OF MODEL BILLS AND CLAUSES.

[To be obtained at the Queen's Printers.]

Railway Bill (Form A).

Special Clauses:

1. Capital and Borrowing Powers.

2. Taking of Lands, Plans, Construction of Works.

3. Penalty if Line not opened within Period fixed.

4. Abandonment of Railway, and Compensation to Land-owners.

5. Agreement with other Companies.

6. Priority of Mortgages over other Debts.

7. Payment of Interest out of Capital during Construction.

8. Clauses in Tramway Bills.

9. Clauses to be inserted in all Tramway Bills authorizing the use of Mechanical Power.

10. Clauses in Hydraulic Bills.

11. Confirmation of Terms of Agreement.

12. Loans by Public Works Loan Commissioners.

13. As to Labouring Class Houses.

Gas Bill (Form B).

Auction Clauses.

Model Clauses for Corporation Stock.

Improvement Bill Clauses.

10 & 11 VICT. c. 69.

An Act for the more effectual Taxation of Costs on Private Bills in the House of Commons.   [22nd July 1847.]

Parliamentary agent, or solicitor not to sue for costs until one month after delivery of his bill.

II. No Parliamentary agent, or solicitor, nor any executor, administrator, or assignee of any Parliamentary agent, or solicitor, shall commence or maintain any action or suit for the recovery of any costs, charges, or expenses in respect of any proceedings in the House of Commons in any future session of Parliament relating to any petition for a private bill, or private bill, or in respect of complying with the Standing Orders of the said House relative thereto, or in preparing, bringing in, and carrying the same through, or opposing the same in, the House of Commons, until the expiration of one month after such Parliamentary agent, or solicitor, or executor, administrator, or assignee of such Parliamentary agent, or solicitor, has delivered unto the party to be charged therewith, or sent by post to or left for him at his counting-house, office of business, dwelling-house, or last known place of abode, a bill of such costs, charges, and expenses, and which bill shall either be subscribed with the proper hand of such Parliamentary agent, or solicitor, or in the case of a partnership by any of the partners, either with his own name or with the name of such partnership, or of the executor, administrator, or assignee of such Parliamentary agent, or solicitor, or be enclosed in or accompanied by a letter

Evidence of delivery of bill.

subscribed in like manner referring to such bill: Provided always, that it shall not in any case be necessary, in the first instance, for such Parliamentary agent, or solicitor, or the executor, administrator, or assignee of such Parliamentary agent, or solicitor, in proving a compliance with this Act to prove the contents of the bill delivered, sent, or left by him, but it shall be sufficient to prove that a bill of costs, charges, and expenses subscribed in manner aforesaid, or inclosed in or accompanied by such letter as aforesaid, was delivered, sent, or left in manner aforesaid; but nevertheless it shall be competent for the other party to show that the bill so

Power to judge to authorize action before expiration of one month.

delivered, sent, or left was not such a bill as constituted a *bonâ fide* compliance with this Act: Provided also, that it shall be lawful for any Judge of the Superior Courts of Law or Equity in England or Ireland, or of the Court of Session in Scotland, to authorize a Parliamentary agent or solicitor to commence an action or suit for the recovery of his costs, charges, and expenses against the party chargeable therewith, although one month has not expired from the delivery of a bill as aforesaid, on proof to the satisfaction of the said judge that there is probable cause for believing that such party is about to quit that part of the United Kingdom in which such judge hath jurisdiction.

III. The Speaker of the House of Commons shall appoint a fit person to be the Taxing Officer of the House of Commons, and every person so appointed shall hold his office during the pleasure of the Speaker, and shall execute the duties of his office conformably to such directions as he may from time to time receive from the Speaker.

Taxing Officer to be appointed by the Speaker.

IV. The Speaker may from time to time prepare a list of such charges as it shall appear to him that, after the present Session of Parliament, Parliamentary agents, solicitors, and others may justly make with reference to the several matters comprised in such list; and the several charges therein specified shall be the utmost charges thenceforth to be allowed upon the taxation of any such bill of costs, charges, and expenses in respect of the several matters therein specified: Provided always, that the said Taxing Officer may allow all fair and reasonable costs, charges, and expenses in respect of any matters not included in such list.

The Speaker to prepare list of charges thenceforth to be allowed.

V. For the purpose of any such taxation, the said Taxing Officer may examine upon oath any party to such taxation, and any witnesses who may be examined in relation thereto, and may receive affidavits, sworn before him or before any Master or Master Extraordinary of the High Court of Chancery, relative to such costs, charges, or expenses; and any person who, on such examination on oath, or in any such affidavit, shall wilfully or corruptly give false evidence, shall be liable to the penalties of wilful and corrupt perjury.

Taxing Officer empowered to examine parties and witnesses on oath.

VI. The said Taxing Officer shall be empowered to call for the production of any books or writings in the hands of any party to such taxation relating to the matters of such taxation: Provided always, that nothing herein contained shall be construed to authorize such Taxing Officer to determine the amount of fees which may have been payable to the House of Commons in respect of the proceedings upon any private bill.

Taxing Officer empowered to call for books and papers.

VII. It shall be lawful for the said Taxing Officer to demand and receive for any such taxation such fees as the House of Commons may from time to time by any Standing Order authorize and

Taxing Officer to take such fees as may be allowed by House of Commons.

direct, and to charge the said fees, and also to award costs of such taxation against either party to such taxation, or in such proportion against each party as he may think fit, and he shall pay and apply the fees so received by him in such manner as shall be directed by any such Standing Order as aforesaid.

VIII. If any person upon whom any demand shall be made by any Parliamentary agent, solicitor, or executor, administrator, or assignee of such Parliamentary agent, or solicitor, or other person, for any costs, charges, or expenses in respect of any proceedings in the House of Commons in any future session of Parliament relating to any petition for a private bill, or private bill, or in respect of complying with the Standing Orders of the said House relative thereto, or in preparing, bringing in, or carrying the same through, or in opposing the same in the House of Commons, or if any Parliamentary agent, or solicitor, or the executor, administrator, or assignee of such Parliamentary agent, or solicitor, or other person, who shall be aggrieved by the non-payment of any costs, charges, and expenses incurred or charged by him in respect of any such proceedings as aforesaid, shall make application to the said Taxing Officer at his office for the taxation of such costs, charges, and expenses, the said Taxing Officer, on receiving a true copy of the bill of such costs, charges, and expenses which shall have been duly delivered as aforesaid to the party charged therewith, shall in due course proceed to tax and settle the same; and upon every such taxation, if either the Parliamentary agent, or solicitor, or the executor, administrator, or assignee of such Parliamentary agent, or solicitor, or other person, by whom such demand shall be made as aforesaid, or the party charged with such bill of costs, charges, and expenses, having due notice, shall refuse or neglect to attend such taxation, the said Taxing Officer may proceed to tax and settle such bill and demand *ex parte:* and if pending such taxation any action or other proceeding shall be commenced for the recovery of such bill of costs, charges, and expenses, the court or judge before whom the same shall be brought shall stay all proceedings thereon until the amount of such bill shall have been duly certified by the Speaker as hereinafter provided: Provided always, that no such application shall be entertained by the said Taxing Officer if made by the party charged with such bill after a verdict shall have been obtained or a writ of inquiry executed in any action for the recovery of the demand of any such Parliamentary agent, or solicitor, or the executor, administrator, or assignee of such

Parliamentary agent, or solicitor, or other person, or after the expiration of six months after such bill shall have been delivered, sent, or left as aforesaid: Provided also, that if any such application shall be made after the expiration of six months as aforesaid, it shall be lawful for the Speaker, if he shall so think fit, on receiving a report of special circumstances from the said Taxing Officer, to direct such bill to be taxed.

IX. The said Taxing Officer shall, if required by either party, report his taxation to the Speaker, and in such report shall state the amount fairly chargeable in respect of such costs, charges, and expenses, together with the amount of costs and fees payable in respect of such taxation as aforesaid; and within twenty-one clear days after any such report shall have been made either party may deposit in the office of the said Taxing Officer a memorial, addressed to the Speaker, complaining of such report or any part thereof, and the Speaker may, if he shall so think fit, refer the same, together with such report, to the said Taxing Officer, and may require a further report in relation thereto, and on receiving such further report may direct the said Taxing Officer, if necessary, to amend his report; and if no such memorial be deposited as aforesaid, or so soon as the matters complained of in any such memorial shall have been finally disposed of, the Speaker shall, upon application made to him, deliver to the party concerned therein, and requiring the same, a certificate of the amount so ascertained, which certificate shall be binding and conclusive on the parties as to the matters comprised in such taxation, and as to the amount of such costs, charges, and expenses, and of the costs and fees payable in respect of such taxation, in all proceedings at law or in equity or otherwise; and in any action or other proceeding brought for the recovery of the amount so certified such certificate shall have the effect of a warrant of attorney to confess judgment; and the court in which such action shall be commenced, or any judge thereof, shall, on production of such certificate, order judgment to be entered up for the sum specified in such certificate in like manner as if the defendant in any such action had signed a warrant to confess judgment in such action to that amount: Provided always, that if such defendant shall have pleaded that he is not liable to the payment of such costs, charges, and expenses, such certificate shall be conclusive only as to the amount thereof which shall be payable by such defendant in case the plaintiff shall in such action recover the same.

Taxing Officer report to the Speaker.

If either party complain of report, they may deposit a memorial, and the Speaker may require a further report.

If no memorial deposited, Speaker may issue certificate of the amount found due.

Certificate to have the effect of a warrant to confess judgment.

Construction of certain words in this Act.

X. In the construction of this Act the word "month" shall be taken to mean a calendar month; and every word importing the singular number only shall extend and be applied to several persons, matters, or things as well as one person, matter, or thing; and every word importing the plural number shall extend and be applied to one person, matter, or thing as well as several persons, matters, or things; and every word importing the masculine gender only shall extend and be applied to a female as well as a male; and the word "person" shall extend to any body politic, corporate, or collegiate, municipal, civil, or ecclesiastical, aggregate or sole, as well as an individual; and the word "oath" shall include affirmation in the case of Quakers, and any declaration lawfully substituted for an oath in the case of any other person allowed by law to make a declaration instead of taking an oath; unless in any of the cases aforesaid it be otherwise specially provided, or there be something in the subject or context repugnant to such construction.

Form of citing the Act.

XI. In citing this Act in other Acts of Parliament, and in legal and other instruments, it shall be sufficient to use the expression "The House of Commons Costs Taxation Act, 1847."

12 & 13 VICT. c. 78.

An Act for the more effectual taxation of costs on private bills in the House of Lords, and to facilitate the taxation of other costs on private bills in certain cases. [28th July 1849.]

Parliamentary agent or solicitor not to sue for costs until one month after delivery of his bill.

II. No Parliamentary agent, or solicitor, nor any executor, administrator, or assignee of any Parliamentary agent or solicitor, shall commence or maintain any action or suit for the recovery of any costs, charges, or expenses in respect of any proceedings in the House of Lords in any future sessions of Parliament relating to any petition for a private bill, or private bill, or in respect of complying with the Standing Orders of the said House relative thereto, or in preparing, bringing in, and carrying the same through, or opposing the same in, the House of Lords, until the expiration of one month after such Parliamentary agent, or solicitor, or executor, administrator, or assignee of such Parliamentary agent, or solicitor, has delivered unto the party to be charged therewith, or sent by post to or left for him at his counting-house, office of business, dwelling-house, or last known place of abode, a bill of such costs, charges, and expenses, and which bill shall either be subscribed with the proper hand of such Parliamentary agent, or solicitor, or in the case of a partnership by any of the partners, either with his own name or with the name of such partnership, or of the executor, administrator, or assignee of such Parliamentary agent, or solicitor, or be enclosed in or accompanied by a letter subscribed in like manner referring to such bill : Provided always, that it shall not in any case be necessary, in the first instance, for such Parliamentary agent, or solicitor, or the executor, or administrator, or assignee of such Parliamentary agent, or solicitor, in proving a compliance with this Act, to prove the contents of the bill delivered, sent, or left by him, but it shall be sufficient to prove that a bill of costs, charges and expenses, subscribed in manner aforesaid, or enclosed in or accompanied by such letter as aforesaid, was delivered, sent, or left in manner aforesaid ; but nevertheless it shall be competent for the other party to show that the bill so delivered, sent, or left was not such a bill as constituted a *bonâ fide* compliance with this Act : Provided also that it shall be lawful for any judge of the Superior Courts of Law or Equity in England or Ireland, or of the Court of Sessions in Scotland, to authorize a Parliamentary agent, or solicitor, to commence an action or suit for the recovery of his costs, charges, and expenses against the party chargeable therewith, although one month has not expired from the delivery of a bill as aforesaid, on proof to the satisfaction of the said judge that there is probable cause for believing that such party is about to quit that part of the United Kingdom in which such judge hath jurisdiction.

Evidence of delivery of bill.

Power to judge to authorize action before expiration of one month.

III. The Clerk of the Parliaments, when discharging the duties of his office in person, or in his absence the clerk assistant, shall appoint a fit person to be the Taxing Officer of the House of Lords ; and every person so appointed shall hold his office during the pleasure of the Clerk of the Parliaments or clerk assistant, and shall execute the duties of his office conformably to such directions as he may from time to time receive from the Clerk of the Parliaments or clerk assistant.

Taxing Officer to be appointed by the Clerk of Parliaments or clerk assistant.

IV. The Clerk of the Parliaments, when discharging the duties of his office in person, or in his absence the clerk assistant, may from time to time prepare a list of such charges as it shall appear to him that Parliamentary agents, solicitors, and others may justly make with reference to the several matters comprised in such list ; and the several charges therein specified shall be the utmost charges thenceforth to be allowed upon the taxation of any such bill of costs, charges, and expenses in respect of the several matters

The Clerk of Parliaments or clerk assistant to prepare list of charges thenceforth to be allowed.

therein specified : Provided always, that the said Taxing Officer may allow all fair and reasonable costs, charges, and expenses in respect of any matters not included in such list.

Taxing Officer empowered to examine parties and witnesses on oath.

V. For the purpose of any such taxation the said Taxing Officer may examine upon oath any party to such taxation, and any witnesses who may be examined in relation thereto, and may receive affidavits, sworn before him or before any master or master extraordinary of the High Court of Chancery, relative to such costs, charges, or expenses : and any person who on such examination on oath or in any such affidavit shall wilfully or corruptly give false evidence shall be liable to the penalties of wilful and corrupt perjury.

Taxing Officer empowered to call for books and papers.

VI. The said Taxing Officer shall be empowered to call for the production of any books or writings in the hands of any party to such taxation relating to the matters of such taxation.

Taxing Officer to take such fees as may be allowed by House of Lords.

VII. It shall be lawful for the said Taxing Officer to demand and receive for any such taxation such fees as the House of Lords may from time to time by any order authorize and direct, and to charge the said fees, and also to award costs of such taxation against either party to such taxation, or in such proportion against each party as he may think fit, and he shall pay and apply the fees so received by him in such manner as shall be directed by any such order as aforesaid.

Application of fees.

On application of party chargeable, or on application of Parliamentary agent or solicitor, the Taxing Officer to tax the bill.

VIII. If any person upon whom any demand shall be made by any Parliamentary agent, or solicitor, or executor, administrator, or assignee of such Parliamentary agent or solicitor, or other person, for any costs, charges, or expenses in respect of any proceedings in the House of Lords in any future session of Parliament relating to any petition for a private bill, or private bill, or in respect of complying with the Standing Orders of the said House relative thereto or in preparing, bringing in, or carrying the same through, or in opposing the same in the House of Lords, or of any Parliamentary agent, or solicitor, or the executor, administrator, or assignee of such Parliamentary agent, or solicitor, or other person, who shall be aggrieved by the nonpayment of any costs, charges, and expenses incurred or charged by him in respect of any such proceedings as aforesaid, shall make application to the said Taxing Officer at his office for the taxation of such costs, charges, and expenses, the said Taxing Officer, on receiving a true copy of the bill of such costs, charges, and expenses which shall have been duly delivered as aforesaid to the party charged therewith, shall in due course proceed to tax and settle the same ; and upon every such taxation, if either the Parliamentary agent, or solicitor, or the executor, administrator, or assignee of such Parliamentary agent, or solicitor, or other person, by whom such demand shall be made as aforesaid, or the party charged with such bill of costs, charges, and expenses, having due notice, shall refuse or neglect to attend such taxation, the said Taxing Officer may proceed to tax and settle such bill and demand *ex parte ;* and if pending such taxation any action or other proceeding shall be commenced for the recovery of such bill of costs, charges, and expenses, the court or judge before whom the same shall be brought shall stay all proceedings thereon until the amount of such bill shall have been duly certified by the Clerk of the Parliaments or clerk assistant as hereinafter provided : Provided always, that no such application shall be entertained by the said taxing officer if made by the party charged with such bill after a verdict shall have been obtained or a writ of inquiry executed in any action for the recovery of the demand of any such Parliamentary agent, or solicitor, or the executor, administrator, or assignee of such Parliamentary agent, or solicitor, or other person, or after the expiration of six months after such bill shall have been delivered, sent, or left as aforesaid : Provided also, that if any such application shall be made after the expiration of six months as aforesaid it shall be lawful for the Clerk of the Parliaments or clerk assistant aforesaid, if he shall so think fit, on receiving a report of special circumstances from the said Taxing Officer, to direct such bill to be taxed.

No application to be entertained by Taxing Officer after verdict obtained.

IX. The said Taxing Officer shall report his taxation to the Clerk of the Parliaments or clerk assistant as aforesaid, and in such report shall state the amount fairly chargeable in respect of such costs, charges, and expenses, together with the amount of costs and fees payable in respect of such taxation as aforesaid, and shall also state in such report the amount due in respect of the said costs, charges, and expenses ; and within twenty-one clear days after any such report shall have been made either party may deposit in the office of the Clerk of the Parliaments a memorial, addressed to the Clerk of the Parliaments or clerk assistant as aforesaid, complaining of such report or any part thereof, and such Clerk of the Parliaments or clerk assistant as aforesaid may, if he shall so think fit, refer the same, together with such report, to the said Taxing Officer, and may require a further report in relation thereto, and on receiving such further report may direct the said Taxing Officer, if necessary, to amend his report ; and if no such memorial be deposited as aforesaid, or so soon as the matters complained of in any such memorial shall have been finally disposed of, such Clerk of the

Taxing Officer to report to the Clerk of the Parliaments.

If either party complain of report, they may deposit a memorial, and the Clerk of the Parliaments may require a further report.

If no memorial deposited, Clerk of the Parliaments may issue certificate of the amount found due.

z

Parliaments or clerk assistant as aforesaid shall, upon application made to him, deliver to the party concerned therein, and requiring the same, a certificate of the amount so ascertained, which certificate shall be binding and conclusive on the parties as to the matters comprised in such taxation, and as to the amount of such costs, charges, and expenses, and the amount due in respect of the same, and of the costs and fees payable in respect of such taxation, in all proceedings at law or in equity or otherwise ; and in any action or other proceeding brought for the recovery of the amount so certified to be due such certificate shall have the effect of a warrant of attorney to confess judgment ; and the court in which such action shall be commenced, or any judge thereof, shall, on production of such certificate, order judgment to be entered up for the sum specified in such certificate, in like manner as if the defendant in any such action had signed a warrant to confess judgment in such action to that amount : Provided always, that if such defendant shall have pleaded that he is not liable to the payment of such costs, charges, and expenses, such certificate shall be conclusive only as to the amount thereof which shall be payable by such defendant in case the plaintiff shall in such action recover the same.

Certificate to have the effect of a warrant to confess judgment.

X. If any bill of costs taxable by virtue of this Act, or of "The House of Commons Costs Taxation Act, 1847," shall comprise any costs, charges, and expenses incurred in respect of a private bill, but not taxable by virtue of the Act in pursuance whereof such bill shall come to be taxed, it shall be lawful for the Taxing Officer of the House of Lords, or for the Taxing Officer of the House of Commons, as the case may be, either to tax and settle such last-mentioned costs, charges, and expenses, or to request the Taxing Officer of the other House of Parliament, or the proper officer of any other court having such an officer, to assist him in taxing and settling any part of such bill ; and such officer so requested shall thereupon proceed to tax and settle the same, and shall return the same, with his opinion thereupon, to the officer who shall have so requested him to tax and settle the same ; and in taxing such costs, charges, and expenses the Taxing Officer of the House of Lords and the Taxing Officer of the House of Commons respectively shall have the same powers and may receive the same fees in respect of such taxation as if such costs, charges, and expenses were taxable by virtue of this Act, or of "The House of Commons Costs Taxation Act, 1847," as the case may be ; and the proper officer of any court so requested to tax the same shall have

Taxing Officer of either House may tax costs not otherwise taxable under the Act by virtue of which any bill shall be taxed ; and may request other officers to assist him.

Such officers to have the same powers as in taxing other costs.

the same powers and may receive the same fees as upon a reference from the court of which he is such officer.

XI. The Taxing Officer of the House of Lords, or the Taxing Officer of the House of Commons, as the case may be, may include the amount of such last-mentioned costs, charges, and expenses in the report of his taxation of any such bill of costs; and in case the Clerk of the Parliaments or clerk assistant, or the Speaker of the House of Commons, as the case may be, shall deliver a certificate of the amount so ascertained and declared in such report, including such last-mentioned costs, charges, and expenses, such certificate shall have the same force and effect as if the whole of such bill of costs were taxable by virtue of the Act in pursuance whereof such certificate shall be so delivered.

Taxing Officers to include certain costs in their reports, and certificates of the amount to be delivered.

XII. In case the Taxing Officer of the House of Lords, or the Taxing Officer of the House of Commons, shall be requested by the proper officer of any other court to assist him in taxing and settling any costs, charges, and expenses incurred in respect of a private bill, being part of any bill of costs which shall have been referred to him by the court of which he is such officer, such Taxing officer so requested shall thereupon proceed to tax and settle the same, and shall return the same, with his opinion thereupon, to the officer who shall have so requested him to tax and settle the same, and shall have the same powers and may receive the same fees in respect of such taxation as if application had been made to him for the taxation thereof in pursuance of this Act, or of the " House of Commons Costs Taxation Act, 1847," as the case may be.

Officers of other courts may request theTaxing Officer of either House to tax parts of bills.

XIII. It shall be lawful for the Taxing Officer of the House of Lords and for the Taxing Officer of the House of Commons to take an account between the parties to any taxation under this Act or the " House of Commons Costs Taxation Act, 1847," of all sums of money paid or received in respect of any bill of costs which is the subject of such taxation, or any matters contained therein, and to report the amount of all such sums of money and the amount due in respect of such bills of costs.

Taxing Officer of either House may take an account between the parties.

XIV. In the construction of this Act the word " month " shall be taken to mean a calendar month; and every word importing the singular number only shall extend and be applied to several persons, matters, or things, as well as one person, matter, or thing; and every word importing the plural number shall extend and be applied to one person, matter, or thing, as well as several persons, matters, or things; and every word importing the masculine gender

Construction of certain words in this Act.

344 PRIVATE BILL PROCEDURE.

only shall extend and be applied to a female as well as a male; and the word "person" shall extend to any body politic, corporate, or collegiate, municipal, civil, or ecclesiastical, aggregate or sole, as well as an individual; and the word "oath" shall include affirmation in the case of Quakers, and any declaration lawfully substituted for an oath in the case of any other person allowed by law to make a declaration instead of taking an oath; unless in any of the cases aforesaid it be otherwise specially provided, or there be something in the subject or context repugnant to such construction.

Form of citing the Act.

XV. In citing this Act in other Acts of Parliament, and in legal and other instruments, it shall be sufficient to use the expression "The House of Lords Costs Taxation Act, 1849."

---

28 VICT. c. 27.

An Act for awarding costs in certain cases of Private Bills
[26th May 1865.]

When committee report "Preamble not proved," opponents to be entitled to recover costs.

1. When the committee on a private bill shall decide that the preamble is not proved, or shall insert in such bill any provision for the protection of any petitioner, or strike out or alter any provision of such bill for the protection of such petitioner, and further unanimously report, with respect to any or all of the petitioners against the bill, that such petitioner or petitioners has or have been unreasonably or vexatiously subjected to expense in defending his or their rights proposed to be interfered with by the bill, such petitioner or petitioners shall be entitled to recover from the promoters of such bill his or their costs in relation thereto, or such portion thereof as the committee may think fit, such costs to be taxed by the Taxing Officer of the House, as herein-aftermentioned, or the committee may award such a sum for costs as they shall think fit, with the consent of the parties affected.

When committee report unanimously "Opposition unfounded," promoters to be entitled to recover costs.

2. When the committee on a private bill shall decide that the preamble is proved, and further unanimously report that the promoters of the bill have been vexatiously subjected to expense in the promotion of the said bill by the opposition of any petitioner or petitioners against the same, then the promoters shall be entitled to recover from the petitioners, or such of them as the committee shall think fit, such portion of their costs of the promotion of the bill as the committee may think fit, such costs to be taxed by the Taxing Officer of the House as herein-after mentioned, or such a sum for costs as the committee shall name, with

the consent of the parties affected; and in their report to the House the committee shall state what portion of the costs, or what sum for costs, they shall so think fit to award, together with the names of the parties liable to pay the same, and the names of the parties entitled to receive the same: Provided always that no landowner, who *bonâ fide* at his own sole risk and charge opposes a bill which proposes to take any portion of the said petitioners property for the purposes of the bill, shall be liable to any costs in respect of his opposition to such bill.

Proviso.

3. On application made to the Taxing Officer of the House by such promoters or petitioners, or by their solicitors or parliamentary agents, not later than six calendar months after the report of such committee, and in cases where no sum shall have been named by the committee, with the consent of the parties affected, not until one month after a bill of such costs shall have been delivered to the party chargeable therewith, which bill shall be sealed with a seal or subscribed with the proper hand of the parties claiming such costs, or of their solicitor or parliamentary agent, the Taxing Officer shall examine and tax such costs, and shall deliver to the parties affected, or either or any of them on application, a certificate signed by himself expressing the amount of such costs, or in cases where a sum for costs shall have been named by the committee with the consent as aforesaid, such sum as shall have been so named, with the name of the party liable to pay the same, and the name of the party entitled to receive the same; and such certificate shall be conclusive evidence as well of the amount of the demand as of the title of the party therein named to recover the same from the party therein stated to be liable to the payment thereof; and the party claiming under the same, shall upon payment thereof, give a receipt at the foot of such certificate, which shall be a sufficient discharge for the same.

Costs to be taxed.

4. All powers given to the Taxing Officer by the Acts 10 & 11 Vict. c. 69., and 12 & 13 Vict. c. 78. with reference to the examination of parties and witnesses on oath, and with reference to the production of documents, and with reference to the fees payable in respect of any taxation, shall be vested in the Taxing Officer for the purposes of this Act.

Powers of Taxing Officers.

5. The party entitled to such taxed costs, or such sum named by the committee, with such consent as aforesaid, or his executors or administrators, may demand the whole amount thereof so certified as above, from any one or more of the persons liable to

Recovery of costs when taxed.

the payment thereof, and in case of nonpayment thereof on demand, may recover the same by action of debt in any of Her Majesty's Courts of Record at Westminster or Dublin, or by action in the Court of Session in Scotland. In such action it shall be sufficient, in England or Ireland, for the plaintiff to declare that the defendant is indebted to him in the sum mentioned in the said certificate; and the said plaintiff shall, upon filing the said declaration, together with the said certificate and an affidavit of such demand as aforesaid, be at liberty to sign judgment as for want of plea by *nil dicit*, and take out execution for the said sum so mentioned in the said certificate, together with the costs of the said action, according to due course of law: Provided always that the validity of such certificate shall not be called in question in any court.

Form of action in Scotland.

6. In such action it shall be sufficient, in Scotland, for the pursuer to allege that the defender is indebted to him in the sum mentioned in the said certificate, under the like proviso in regard to the validity of the certificate.

Persons paying costs may recover a proportion from other persons liable thereto.

7. In every case it shall be lawful for any person from whom the amount of such costs or sum named by the committee, with consent as aforesaid, has been so recovered, to recover from the other persons, or any of them, who are liable to the payment of such costs or sum named by the committee, with consent as aforesaid, a proportionate share thereof, according to the number of persons so liable, and according to the extent of the liability of each person.

When committee report "Preamble not proved," promoters to pay costs out of deposits.

8. In any case in which the committee shall have reported that the preamble is not proved, and where, in accordance with the Standing Orders of either House of Parliament, and of an Act of the ninth year of Her present Majesty, chapter 20, a deposit of money or stock is made with respect to the application to Parliament for an Act, the money or stock so deposited shall be a security for the payment by the promoters of the bill for the Act of all costs or sums in respect of costs, if any, payable by them under this Act; and every party entitled to receive any costs or sum so payable shall accordingly have a lien available in equity for the same on the money or stock so deposited, and the lien shall attach thereon at the time when the bill is first referred to a committee of either House of Parliament; Provided that where several parties have the lien for an amount exceeding in the aggregate the net value of the money or stock, their respective claims shall proportionately abate.

9. When a bill is not promoted by a company already formed Definition of all persons whose names shall appear in such bill as promoting the promoters. same, and in the event of the bill passing, the company thereby incorporated shall be deemed to be promoters of such bill for all the purposes of this Act.

10. For the purposes of this Act, the expression "private bill" Meaning of shall extend to and include any bill for a local and personal Act. private bill.

11. That this Act shall not take effect before November 1st Commencement 1865. of Act.

[As to the construction of this Act, see *ante*, p. 77.]

— — — ———————

REGULATIONS FOR POSTING PARLIAMENTARY NOTICES.

[See S. O. 19, *ante*, p. 93; S. O. 19, H. L.]

1. Parliamentary notices may be posted at any Money Order office in the United Kingdom.

2. On the address side of the cover of each notice must be printed or legibly written the words "Parliamentary Notice," and the name and address of the solicitor or agent issuing the notice.

3. Notices, which by the Standing Orders of either House of Parliament, must be served on, or before, the 15th December, must be posted not later than the 12th December, and those notices which, by the same orders, may be served after the 15th, must be posted not later than the 18th of December.

4. The postage—at the letter rate—chargeable on these notices and the registration fee of 2*d.* on each must be prepaid by stamps. For re-direction they are liable to the same regulations as letters.

5. The notices must be presented at the Post Office counter, accompanied by duplicate lists of the names and addresses of the addressees, and arranged for the convenience of comparison in the order of the lists. These lists will be examined by the officer in attendance at the counter, and if they correspond with the names and addresses on the notices he will sign or stamp every sheet of each list. One of the duplicate lists will then be returned to the person who brought the notices, and the other forwarded to the secretary, General Post Office, London.

6. Any person presenting more than one notice addressed to the same person at the same address must number such notices consecutively, and enter the same on the duplicate lists in numerical order.

7. The hours for receiving such notices are the same as those for the registration of ordinary letters, unless they be presented at such a time as to interfere with the other duties of the office, in which case the postmaster may appoint any other time within the next twenty-four hours for receiving the same, provided that, when the notices are to be served on or before the 15th December, such arrangement do not delay the posting beyond the 12th.

8. The senders of Parliamentary notices should, if possible, arrange on the previous day with the postmaster as to the most convenient time for posting them, and should state the probable number.

GENERAL INDEX.

[See for Index of the Standing Orders *of the* House of Commons, *ante,* pp. 174–223. *For Contents of the* Standing Orders *of the* House of Lords *see* STANDING ORDERS, *post* 359.

A A

Eyre & Spottiswoode, Her Majesty's Printers, Downs Park Road, Hackney, N.E.

www.ingramcontent.com/pod-product-compliance
Lightning Source LLC
Chambersburg PA
CBHW030911270326
41929CB00008B/647